Unbridled

Books by Michael Engelhard

Hell's Half Mile:
River Runners' Tales of Hilarity and Misadventure

Where the Rain Children Sleep:
A Sacred Geography of the Colorado Plateau

Unbridled

THE WESTERN HORSE
IN FICTION AND NONFICTION

Edited by
Michael
Engelhard

THE LYONS PRESS
Guilford, Connecticut
An imprint of The Globe Pequot Press

10 9 8 7 6 5 4 3 2 1

Printed in the United States of America

Designed by Kirsten Livingston

ISBN 1-59228-670-4

Library of Congress Cataloging-in-Publication Data is available on file.

Acknowledgments

After finishing a compilation of humorous river running stories, I swore to stay away from anthologies. But how could I possibly resist gathering my favorite tales on a favorite topic in one handy volume? For the completion of this book, I am grateful to all agents, publishers, authors, and their heirs, who allowed me to use material for very moderate or no compensation at all—simply out of their love for western horses and good writing.

The following people in particular have been extremely helpful in rounding up and grooming this incredible bunch: Robert Andrus, Gail Blackhall, Javier Castano, Ron Chrisman, Cristina Concepcion, Belle Edwards Fenley, Kim Engelstad, Nancy Freely, Scott Gipson, Kristen Hagenbuckle, Teresa Jordan, Sandi Keeton, Elaine Maruhn, Jim Murphy, Slim Randles, Michael Rosen, Mimi Ross, Nancy Stauffer Cahoon, Carrie Valdez, Ann Welshko, and Clark Whitehorn.

Special thanks go to Garth Battista of Breakaway Books for initial publishing contacts, and to Lilly Golden, seasoned horsewoman and editor at The Lyons Press, who applied gentle pressure and had me switch leads, but also reined in when necessary. The staff of the University of Utah Marriott Library's special collections in Salt Lake City was forthcoming and generous in photocopying and handling special requests. Howard Trenholme in Moab provided caffeine infusions and computer time. I am forever indebted to Sharon Miller, for use of her laptop when I was cleaning horse stalls, living in a trailer, and only dreamt of being a writer. (Still sorry I broke the damn thing, Sharon.)

More than anybody, my companion Melissa Guy has been a source of inspiration and support throughout this daunting project, contributing a fine book jacket as well.

Contents

Casualties & Survivors

Preface

became a fool for horses rather late in life. In my early thirties I took a job as a counselor in a horseback program for juvenile delinquents. Except for a few pony rides as a kid, I had no experience with horses and learned along with my charges. The majority of the teenagers I worked with were African Americans, and the program was based on the Buffalo Soldiers. (The Buffalo Soldiers—9th and 10th Cavalry and 24th and 25th Infantry Regiments—were the first all-black units established in the U.S. military and instrumental in campaigns against the Comanche and Apache.) We went through all the original mounted drills, countless injuries and embarrassments, and about once a month, to a re-enactment. Our "battlefields" were eastern, the McClellan saddles and tack English-inspired, but our horses had been bred on desert and prairie soils: hardy west Texas and Arizona ponies, some of them bearing white freeze brands on their necks that marked them as mustangs auctioned off by the Bureau of Land Management.

My first horse was Madman, and he was true to his name. A barrel-chested, short-legged sorrel gelding standing little over fourteen hands, and with a blaze running from his ears to his nostrils, he tended to chomp at the bit, quickly wearing himself out during our mock charges. Fellow galloping horses electrified him; he was not one to be left behind. On the other hand, he was so stolid that I could run up from behind and jump into the saddle, taking off at a canter. Unfazed by the flashing and waving of blank sabers or fluttering standards, by yelling or the booming of canons, he was bombproof. I could fire my pistol next to his head without spooking him and ride into a melee to double up with an unhorsed or a "wounded" trooper. On the down side, he was foam-flecked and winded within an hour if I did not check him. A bit hard-mouthed, you could say. Nevertheless, I was hooked for good.

For the next five years or so, western horses determined my life. I hired on with outfits in Texas, Arizona, New Mexico, Wyoming, and western Canada, getting dusty and dirty and wet (and occasionally bitten and kicked) as a trail guide and wrangler. Many of the horses I encountered left deeper impressions than most people I met. There came a string of personal mounts, and as I got to know them, I discovered personalities as multifaceted and colorful as Mark Twain characters. Cinnabar, a blood bay stallion, had a disposition that allowed me to lean out of the saddle and pick up hats or sunglasses the "dudes" had dropped while at a trot. Buster, a green-broke dappled gray with a neck sore from distemper—and not too smart—threw me one day. It happened the very instant he saw his first cow; he streaked back to the ranch house, riderless and wide-eyed, saddle flopping under his belly. (Did I mention he had practically no withers?) Then there was Nevada, the skittish white Arabian mare deadly afraid of crossing running water, even on bridges. She routinely spooked at her own shadow and almost cost me my thumb, when I tied her up to the rail one blustery day.

Some of my most precious memories come from gathering the *remuda* of a guest ranch near the Continental Divide every morning before breakfast. We would ride out before sunrise, climbing to the stretch of National Forest into which stock had been turned out to graze overnight. As the sun rose, golden fog would drift between the trees. Pine needles glistened. Moisture beaded leaves and blades of grass, slicking saddles and shaggy coats. Over my horse's snorting, the creaking of leather, and awakening birds, I'd strain my ears for the muted clanging of bells we had put onto the leaders. Almost all horses hung out in small clusters, and a few rogues always tried to get out of work for a day by dodging into thick underbrush. Once their gray forms took shape in the mist, however, most were only too willing. All it took was to push them toward the main trail, where they'd start back to the ranch on their own. After unsaddling them in the evenings, and flinging the corral gates open, we watched in awe from the fence rails as they stampeded back into the forest, kicking and snorting, bucking and running, charging through clouds of dust.

As I immersed myself more and more in the world of horses, I realized that this new infatuation affected more than just teenage girls and myself. Hardened cowboys described the character and physique of their favorite horses like those of a lover. Grown men would choke up over the loss of a pony. Boarders at our stables admitted to being "out of it" if they did not get to ride regularly. Soon I was no longer surprised that many people used personal pronouns when referring to their equine companions.

This blending of interdependency and adoration has a long tradition out West. On the frontier, a man on foot was often as good as dead. Horse stealing was therefore a capital crime punished with hanging. (Or else a feat of courage and cunning immortalized in story and song.) Plains Indian culture flourished briefly, and Native Americans valued their buffalo runners and war ponies above everything else. They expressed their awe of the "big dog" in taboos, rituals, and myths that fostered a bonding of species. The size of his horse herd determined a man's wealth and standing, and even his marriage prospects. Stagecoaches, Pony Express riders, the Law and those running from it, traders and trappers, prospectors, farmers, buckaroos, and the Cavalry—they all relied heavily on horses for transportation. To a degree, the western horse was the great equalizer, evening out the odds for swiftness and mobility. Horses shaped our ideas of speed, grace, and strength (we still measure engine output in "horse powers"), and—through grazing—even the physical nature of the range. Perhaps, as a mongrel-breed of runaways, the western horse also reminded the New Americans of their own mixed and frequently haunted heritage. The most fickle of all domesticated species became an icon, even more so than Texas Longhorns, wolves, bison, or grizzly bears, linking diverse cultural groups across space and time. It is hard to imagine how completely and quickly the horse transformed frontier society during the golden age of horse culture in little more than two hundred years. An aura of nostalgia still surrounds horses. The smells. The sounds. The tack. The terminology. Before the advent of automobiles, from the back of a cayuse, the West seemed endless indeed. To many, life nowadays feels fenced-in by comparison. Only the open-range mustang is left as a symbol of unfettered freedom.

Sadly enough, there exists a parallel history, a history of carelessness, neglect, and abuse. Horses were frequently sacrificed in military engagements, or killed and eaten under duress. Mustanging practices were inhumane in the extreme. During the Depression, the U.S. government killed thousands of horses (and sheep) on the Navajo reservation to reduce overgrazing. And just recently, the same government passed legislation that dooms wild horse herds to be sent to the slaughterhouses.

Our complex relations with equines—ranging from brutal submission and exploitation to partnership, protection, and respect—perfectly mirror attitudes about the natural world at large, and as such are worthy of documentation. Although violations of the age-old pact between the two species still occur, the selections in this book reflect a succession of sensibilities: from "bronc busting" and "horse breaking" to more enlightened training approaches like "horse gentling" or "dancing at a distance." They have been chosen with a focus on individuality. Rather than gather general accounts of this breed, I wanted to show the full spectrum, to offer intimate views of a cast of characters and their human counterparts, who are often changed by mutual contact. To avoid narrowing my choices to strictly western, registered breeds like Paints, Appaloosas, or Quarter Horses, I employed the term "western horse" loosely. For the purpose of this book, I considered any horse that was born, lived, died, or worked in the still wide, if not open, spaces between Sonora and Alberta, between the Dakotas and the coast of California. This definition is grounded in the transplant's hope that the land and its creatures shape us as much as we shape them.

I firmly believe that the next best thing to riding or watching these spirited, tough, big-hearted animals is reading about them. As their outsides are good for the inside of a woman or man, so are their stories. By keeping this lore alive, we not only honor past contributions, but also ensure western horses a place in our increasingly mechanized future.

Broncs
&
Rogues

A Genuine Mexican Plug

MARK TWAIN

I resolved to have a horse to ride. I had never seen such wild, free, magnificent horsemanship outside of a circus as these picturesquely clad Mexicans, Californians, and Mexicanized Americans displayed in Carson streets every day. How they rode! Leaning just gently forward out of the perpendicular, easy and nonchalant, with broad slouch-hat brim blown square up in front, and long *riata* swinging above the head, they swept through the town like the wind! The next minute they were only a sailing puff of dust on the far desert. If they trotted, they sat up gallantly and gracefully, and seemed part of the horse; did not go jiggering up and down after the silly Miss-Nancy fashion of the riding-schools. I had quickly learned to tell a horse from a cow, and was full of anxiety to learn more. I was resolved to buy a horse.

While the thought was rankling in my mind, the auctioneer came scurrying through the plaza on a black beast that had as many humps and corners on him as a dromedary, and was necessarily uncomely; but he was "going, going, at twenty-two!—horse, saddle, and bridle at twenty-two dollars, gentlemen!" and I could hardly resist.

A man whom I did not know (he turned out to be the auctioneer's brother) noticed the wistful look in my eye, and observed that that was a very remarkable horse to be going at such a price; and added that the saddle alone was worth the money. It was a Spanish saddle, with ponderous *tapidaros*, and furnished with the ungainly sole-leather covering with the unspellable name.

I said I had half a notion to bid. Then this keen-eyed person appeared to me to be "taking my measure"; but I dismissed the suspicion when he spoke, for his manner was full of guileless candor and truthfulness. Said he:

"I know that horse—know him well. You are a stranger, I take it, and so you might think he was an American horse, maybe, but I assure you he is not. He is nothing of the kind; but—excuse my speaking in a low voice, other people being near—he is, without the shadow of a doubt, a Genuine Mexican Plug!"

I did not know what a Genuine Mexican Plug was, but there was something about this man's way of saying it, that made me swear inwardly that I would own a Genuine Mexican Plug, or die.

"Has he any other—er—advantages?" I inquired, suppressing what eagerness I could.

He hooked his forefinger in the pocket of my army shirt, led me to one side, and breathed in my ear impressively these words:

"He can out-buck anything in America!"

"Going, going, going—at *twent-ty*-four dollars and a half, gen—"

"Twenty-seven!" I shouted, in a frenzy.

"And sold!" said the auctioneer, and passed over the Genuine Mexican Plug to me.

I could scarcely contain my exultation. I paid the money, and put the animal in a neighboring livery stable to dine and rest himself.

In the afternoon I brought the creature into the plaza, and certain citizens held him by the head, and others by the tail, while I mounted him. As soon as they let go, he placed all his feet in a bunch together, lowered his back, and then suddenly arched it upward, and shot me straight into the air a matter of three or four feet! I came as straight down again, lit in the saddle, went instantly up again, came down almost on the high pommel, shot up again, and came down on the horse's neck—all in the space of three or four seconds. Then he rose and stood almost straight up on his hind feet, and I, clasping his lean neck desperately, slid back into the saddle, and held on. He came down, and immediately hoisted his heels into the air, delivering a vicious kick at the sky, and stood on his fore feet. And then down he came once more, and began the original exercise of shooting me straight up again.

The third time I went up I heard a stranger say: "Oh, *don't* he buck, though!"

While I was up, somebody struck the horse a sounding thwack with a leathern strap, and when I arrived again the Genuine Mexican Plug was not there. A Californian youth chased him up and caught him, and asked if he might have a ride. I granted him that luxury. He mounted the Genuine, got lifted into the air once, but sent his spurs home as he descended, and the horse darted away like a telegram. He soared over three fences like a bird, and disappeared down the road toward the Washoe Valley.

I sat down on a stone with a sigh, and by a natural impulse one of my hands sought my forehead, and the other the base of my stomach. I believe I never appreciated, till then, the poverty of the human machinery—for I still needed a hand or two to place elsewhere. Pen cannot describe how I was jolted up. Imagination cannot conceive how disjointed I was—how internally, externally, and universally I was unsettled, mixed up, and ruptured. There was a sympathetic crowd around me, though.

One elderly-looking comforter said:

"Stranger, you've been taken in. Everybody in this camp knows that horse. Any child, any Injun, could have told you that he'd buck; he is the very worst devil to buck on the continent of America. You hear *me*. I'm Curry. *Old* Curry. Old *Abe* Curry. And moreover, he is a simon-pure, out-and-out, genuine d—d Mexican plug, and an uncommon mean one at that, too. Why, you turnip, if you had laid low and kept dark, there's chances to buy an *American* horse for mighty little more than you paid for that bloody old foreign relic."

I gave no sign; but I made up my mind that if the auctioneer's brother's funeral took place while I was in the territory I would postpone all other recreations and attend it.

After a gallop of sixteen miles the Californian youth and the Genuine Mexican Plug came tearing into town again, shedding foam-flakes like the spume-spray that drives before a typhoon, and, with one final skip over a wheelbarrow and a Chinaman, cast anchor in front of the "ranch."

Such panting and blowing! Such spreading and contracting of the red equine nostrils, and glaring of the wild equine eye! But was the imperial beast subjugated? Indeed, he was not. His lordship the Speaker of the House thought he was, and mounted him to go down to the Capitol; but the first dash the creature made was over a pile of telegraph-poles half as high as a church; and his time to the Capitol—one mile and three-quarters—remains unbeaten to this day. But then he took an advantage—he left out the mile, and only did the three-quarters. That is to say, he made a straight cut across lots, preferring fences and ditches to a crooked road; and when the Speaker

got to the Capitol he said he had been in the air so much he felt as if he had
made the trip on a comet.

In the evening the Speaker came home afoot for exercise, and got the
Genuine towed back behind a quartz-wagon. The next day I loaned the animal to the Clerk of the House to go down to the Dana silver-mine, six miles,
and *he* walked back for exercise, and got the horse towed. Everybody I loaned
him to always walked back; they never could get enough exercise any other
way. Still, I continued to loan him to anybody who was willing to borrow him,
my idea being to get him crippled, and throw him on the borrower's hands,
or killed, and make the borrower pay for him. But somehow nothing ever happened to him. He took chances that no other horse ever took and survived,
but he always came out safe. It was his daily habit to try experiments that had
always before been considered impossible, but he always got through. Sometimes he miscalculated a little, and did not get his rider through intact, but *he*
always got through himself. Of course I had tried to sell him; but that was a
stretch of simplicity which met with little sympathy. The auctioneer stormed
up and down the streets on him for four days, dispersing the populace, inter-
rupting business, and destroying children, and never got a bid—at least never
any but the eighteen-dollar one he hired a notoriously substanceless bummer
to make. The people only smiled pleasantly, and restrained their desire to buy,
if they had any. Then the auctioneer brought in his bill, and I withdrew the
horse from the market. We tried to trade him off at private vendue next, offer-
ing him at a sacrifice for second-hand tombstones, old iron, temperance
tracts—any kind of property. But holders were stiff, and we retired from the
market again. I never tried to ride the horse any more. Walking was good
enough exercise for a man like me, that had nothing the matter with him except ruptures, internal injuries, and such things. Finally I tried to *give* him
away. But it was a failure. Parties said earthquakes were handy enough on the
Pacific coast—they did not wish to own one. As a last resort I offered him to
the Governor for the use of the "Brigade." His face lit up eagerly at first, but
toned down again, and he said the thing would be too palpable.

Just then the livery-stable man brought in his bill for six weeks' keeping—stall-room for the horse, fifteen dollars; hay for the horse, two hundred
and fifty! The Genuine Mexican Plug had eaten a ton of the article, and the
man said he would have eaten a hundred if he had let him.

I will remark here, in all seriousness, that the regular price of hay during
that year and a part of the next was really two hundred and fifty dollars a ton.

During a part of the previous year it had sold at five hundred a ton, in gold, and during the winter before that there was such scarcity of the article that in several instances small quantities had brought eight hundred dollars a ton in coin! The consequence might be guessed without my telling it: people turned their stock loose to starve, and before the spring arrived Carson and Eagle Valleys were almost literally carpeted with their carcasses! Any old settler there will verify these statements.

I managed to pay the livery bill, and that same day I gave the Genuine Mexican Plug to a passing Arkansas emigrant whom fortune delivered into my hand. If this ever meets his eye, he will doubtless remember the donation.

Now whoever has had the luck to ride a real Mexican plug will recognize the animal depicted in this chapter, and hardly consider him exaggerated—but the uninitiated will feel justified in regarding his portrait as a fancy sketch, perhaps.

Roanie

THOMAS MCGUANE

There is a notion that you get only one great horse in a lifetime, a persistent notion that I hope isn't true; because, if that is the case, I've already had mine, in fact still have him though he is an arthritic old man twenty-six years old. His name is Lucky Bottom 79 and he was already a terrific horse when I acquired him over twenty years ago, though for some reason, he wasn't doing much and had a reputation for being a bronc that had probably kept someone else from buying him. He is called Roanie for his red roan coat, a coat that turns almost purple in the summer, and he is not a very pretty horse. In fact, he won an informal contest one year in Hamilton for being the ugliest horse in Montana. He has a slight Roman nose, actually called the "Burt bump" for a trait inherited from his grandsire Burt. As to the length of his head, it's been remarked that he can drink from a fifty-gallon drum and still keep an eye on you. His sire was a good horse called Lucky Star Mac, an Oklahoma Star–bred horse; and his mother was a racehorse named Miss Glimpse. Roanie is one of those hotheaded horses about which people say, "The only safe place is on his back." He can kick in any direction, has actually stripped the buttons off the front of a man's shirt, and the extreme suspicion that is continuously in his eye doesn't come from nowhere. Roanie was not the sort of horse Buster prefers but he once said to me, "Boy, when he was on, that roan horse was unbelievable!"

Lucky Bottom 79 was trained by a part-Cherokee cowboy named Ed Bottom, who is, any way you look at it, an outstanding horseman who has made an everlasting mark training calf-roping and cutting horses for nearly half a century. Like Buster Welch, Ed is a member of the Cutting Horse Hall of Fame. Yesterday, I tried to catch swaybacked old Roanie in a twenty-foot loafing shed. He went by me like mercury, low, quick, and throwing me such an elegant head fake I'm lucky I didn't fall down.

Ed Bottom lives in Asher, Oklahoma, next door to the Barrow farm, former home of Clyde Barrow. One of Ed's childhood heroes was a family friend, Pretty Boy Floyd, and Ed remembers Pretty Boy coming home from robberies, hiding his shot-up Hudson in a sheep shed, giving all the kids silver dollars, and pitching horseshoes with the grown-ups.

I traveled to Oklahoma to try Roanie and I remember two things distinctly. When I went out to the corral to saddle and work a cow on him, Mrs. Bottom said, "Don't fall off."

Responding to this nicety, I said, "I won't."

Mrs. Bottom said, "You won't?"

I had some time to think about this as we got Roanie ready. Roanie hadn't seen me before and I have never been around a horse that exuded such all-consuming distrust of strangers. However, once I was on his back and loping in a circle all was well, with the exception of one small thing: the horse kept his head turned so that he could look back and watch me the whole while.

I cut the first cow on him. The cow stopped, looked, prepared for sudden motion, and Roanie began to sink. I guess you would call it a crouch. But it was level all around and I simply sensed the ground coming up: this horse had a working altitude of about a man's waist and I soon found that he had real speed and the ability to turn right through himself like a dishrag. And he understood cattle. He could mesmerize them or stop them with sheer speed, all at hot-rod roadster height. And as I would learn over the years, either his sense of play or his sense of rightness in the world made him purely at home only when he was working cattle. At such a time, you couldn't spur him or misride him to the wrong spot with the strength of Superman. He knew with certainty where he wanted to be and the door to the suggestion box was nailed shut. Over the years, several outstanding cutting-horse riders have competed on him without success. Evidently, he disliked all their opinions and convictions. I was too ignorant and perhaps intimidated by him to let him do anything but what he wanted to do. That proved to be the right approach. For a few years, I made more money on his back than I did at my actual job. It was a great feeling to know you were probably going to win a cutting before you even unloaded the horse from the trailer.

I bought Roanie on the condition he pass a veterinary exam. We took him to the local vet and after Roanie kicked the X-ray plates all over the building and took a couple of shots at the X-ray machine itself, we decided to forgo the exam and accept instead Ed's statement, "You can't hurt him with an axe handle." The demoralized veterinarian was reduced to inquiring rhetorically, "Why do you people always want to X-ray everything?" Ed gave me two bits made by another Cherokee, John Israel, identical except for the length of the shanks and beautifully fashioned from salvaged old hay rakes. "Tune him in the long shanks and show him in the short ones." That was the end of the operating instructions. We headed home.

It was early spring on the ranch, snowy and muddy. A friend of mine stopped by to see Roanie and the muck sucked his overshoe off in the corral. He looked at the slush filling the boot as he stood in his stocking foot. "There it is," he said, "ag world." I led Roanie around, then put him in a box stall to protect him from the change of Montana weather and settled in to start building a relationship with him.

Roanie had not always done well in box stalls. At the national futurity for three-year-olds, he had a record-setting run that brought the audience to its feet. Afterward, Ed put him in one of the assigned box stalls. Someone had placed a blanket in the stall that Roanie had never seen before. By the time Roanie spotted it, his friend Ed was back in the bleachers and Roanie felt he had little choice but to kick the door, its latch and hinges, off the box stall and race out in equine hysteria to scatter spectators. Ed was summoned on the loudspeaker and things were soon put right. If there was a big problem, it was lost on Ed, who is the last word in coolheaded. His comment on Roanie's escapade: "I guess he didn't want to be in there."

I didn't know that story at the time I got Roanie home. All I know is that when I went into the box stall with him, he flattened himself against the wall in terror and when I moved, he began to whirl. It was like the end of *Little Black Sambo*, where all the tigers turn into a pool of butter, only I didn't want to be in that pool. Sharing a tiny room with an eleven-hundred-and-fifty-pound whirling panicked animal is a situation that impresses one with its gravity. I had to do something. The check hadn't cleared yet and I could hardly confine our relationship to watching him through the window. This was not a public aquarium.

The next day, I moved a small school desk into Roanie's stall. Then I went in and sat down and did my work. For the first hour, Roanie seemed to be trying to smear himself into the plank walls. He trembled from head to toe. At the end of the hour, I was still writing and he was getting tired of his exertions. He was standing with his weight equally distributed on all four feet. When I got up to pet him, he flattened himself once more. I found myself, pen in hand, seated at my desk, hunched over a legal pad, making such plaintive cries as, "Roanie, I gotta take a leak!" In three days, he was tired of my writing life, trying to figure out how to get around the desk to the hay. We'd made a start.

We began riding out on the ranch. This he adored: new country. It was always a special pleasure to simply use him as a saddle horse because he was the sort of horse that always seemed to pull you through the country, head stretched forward, ears pricked, drinking up the new space. There is nothing quite like looking over wild land from horseback.

I don't know how Roanie would have done in battle though I think once he'd gotten the idea of what the job was, he would have excelled. His panic attacks, however, would have been dangerous to friend and foe alike. Early in my ownership of him, his feet, accustomed to red Oklahoma dirt, got sore on the rocks where I live. Finally, he went quite lame. It turned out to be merely a stone bruise but a shadow on his X-rays suggested a fractured coffin bone. I sent him immediately to Colorado State University's outstanding equine veterinary center in Fort Collins and called the excellent lameness specialist there. I explained to this specialist that Roanie could be quite unpredictable; to avoid having people getting hurt, I urged caution.

"Mr. McGuane, we are well accustomed to handling horses of all kinds. Owners often give us these sorts of warnings and, while we think it is considerate, we don't worry about it too much." The doctor, a cultivated Australian, took me for a nervous sort.

Within a few days, he called me. His voice was elevated in both pitch and intensity. "Your horse is going to get this university sued back to the stone age! I have had to rescue several of my graduate students from him and I have hung a skull and crossbones on his stall!" They had tranquilized my horse from the sort of range usually considered appropriate for the rhinoceros and managed to examine him enough to conclude that his hoof injury wasn't serious. When his health papers came back with him, a notation read, "Lucky Bottom 79's rectal temperature not taken as he continually endangered human life."

"I'd like a photograph of someone riding this horse," were the doctor's last words to me.

"The only safe place is on his back," I said but I think it fell on deaf ears.

In any case, he was soon sound once again and in glistening physical condition. We worked cattle at home and he was quick and smooth. I decided to take him to a cutting-horse contest in Blackfoot, Idaho, on the weekend. I knew I had a special horse.

The cutting was held in a city park right in the middle of town. It seemed kind of odd not to have a lot of open country around us but the cattle had been, in the words of Chuck Tyson, a great old cow man, "surrounded by cleverness" and things were rather orderly. Roanie had not been to a cutting in a good while and, as I was to learn, he knew the difference between a cow in a contest and a cow anywhere else. As soon as I unloaded him and he heard the bawling cattle and saw the spectators, his blood began to boil. I tried to gallop him down but he just got crazier. I decided to walk him and keep him calm. He gaped around at everything, froze, and shied from paper cups, cigarette wrappers, the light off windshields; children who'd never seen a horse flare its nostrils, snort, and run backward from a gum wrapper gathered around and made my composure worse with their astonished questions. "Hey, mister, what's the matter with your horse?" Or, "He's loco, ain't he?" I consoled myself by knowing that as soon as I rode him into the herd, everything would settle down and the eternal cow-horse logic would take over. Boldly, I entered both the open and the non-professional classes.

I had an excellent draw in the open. I hired my herd holders and turn-back man and rode confidently toward the herd. I thought Roanie's walk was uncustomarily jerky but gave it little thought as we turned through the cattle and began to drive out. A pretty baldface heifer slipped up onto the point of the herd and I eased forward, cut her, and put my rein hand down on Roanie's neck. Roanie stood bolt upright, the perfect position, I thought, for him to jump out of his skin. He looked bug-eyed at the cow until she moved and then he reared up on his hind legs, pawing the air like Roy Rogers's Trigger on LSD, and with several huge kangaroo leaps shot past the turn-back horses, blowing snot in two directions, and bolted into the Blackfoot city park, scattering strollers and people of all ages. When I got him stopped, I turned to look back at the cutting-horse contest. All I could see was a wall of blank faces. The judge gave me a zero because he was unaware of a lower number.

I decided that the only way around this was through it and so I did not scratch from the next class; and I was only mildly unnerved by the voices I heard as I rode toward the cattle: "He's not going in there *again*, is he?" In the crowd were some unmitigated gawkers of the kind that swarm to accident scenes. I cut two cows in the course of my run and Roanie laid down a performance that was absolutely faultless. We won the cutting by a serious margin. It seemed to be that we had gotten through something together because I became abruptly more sensitive to the world as he saw it. I used to think that when I led him out of his box stall at a cutting I could tell by the look in his eye if he was going to win it that day. If he seemed to gaze upon the world with easy vigilance, I knew that we would be deep in the money. If the look of incomplete understanding was there, if he fixated on a bucket or a snakelike curve of garden hose, I knew we would have to find some way to cool out before we began, often by a ride around the neighborhood or, if we were at a local Montana cutting, a visit to one of his horse friends at another trailer. In any case, from then on the pressure was on me to cut my cows correctly and to ride him well; in doing such a tremendous job of holding up his end, he gave me much room for error. I tried not to abuse it.

I felt so competitive when I was riding this horse that I went to every last little cutting in the region and got a wonderful education in the geography of the Northern Rockies, so many little towns in which the fairgrounds were the only public gathering place. It's been more than a decade since I rode him in a contest but people still inquire about him everywhere I go. "How's the old roan horse?" they ask, shaking their heads in awe. It's so nice to tell them he's fine, and free, in a big grassy place. Not that I don't sometimes wish it were long ago and I were throwing a saddle up on his powerful withers with the feeling that I could hardly wait for my draw.

The Moon-Eyed Horse

EDWARD ABBEY

When we reached Salt Creek we stopped to water the horses. I needed a drink myself but the water here would make a man sick. We'd find good water farther up the canyon at Cigarette Spring.

While Mackie indulged himself in a smoke I looked at the scenery, staring out from under the shelter of my hat brim. The glare was hard on the eyes and for relief I looked down, past the mane and ears of my drinking horse, to something near at hand. There was the clear shallow stream, the green wiregrass standing stiff as bristles out of the alkali-encrusted mud, the usual deerflies and gnats swarming above the cattle tracks and dung.

I noticed something I thought a little odd. Cutting directly across the cattle paths were the hoofprints of an unshod horse. They led straight to the water and back again, following a vague little trail that led into the nearest side canyon, winding around blackbrush and cactus, short-cutting the meanders of the wash.

I studied the evidence for a while, trying to figure everything out for myself before mentioning it to Mackie, who knew this country far better than I ever would. He was a local man, a Moabite, temporarily filling in for Viviano Jacquez, who'd had another quarrel with old Roy Scobie and disappeared for a few days.

"There's a horse living up that canyon," I announced; "a wild horse. And a big one—feet like frying pans."

14

Slowly Mackie turned his head and looked where I pointed. "Wrong again," he said, after a moment's consideration.

"What do you mean, wrong again? If it's not a horse it must be a unicorn. Or a centaur? Look at those tracks—unshod. And from the wear and tear on that trail it's been living out here for a long time. Who runs horses out here?" We were about twenty miles from the nearest ranch.

"Nobody," Mackie agreed.

"You agree it's a horse."

"Of course it's a horse."

"Of course it's a horse. Well thank you very much. And no shoes, living out here in the middle of nothing, it must be a *wild* horse."

"Sorry," Mackie said. "Wrong again."

"Then what the hell is it?"

"Old Moon-Eye is what you might call an independent horse. He don't belong to anybody. But he ain't wild. He's a gelding and he's got Roy Scobie's brand on his hide."

I stared up the side canyon to where the tracks went out of sight around the first bend. "And this Moon-Eye lives up there all by himself?"

"That's right. He's been up in that canyon for ten years."

"Have you seen him?"

"No. Moon-Eye is very shy. But I heard about him."

Our mounts had raised their heads from the water and shifting restlessly under our weight, they seemed anxious to move on. Mackie turned his horse up the main trail along the stream and I followed, thinking.

"I want that horse," I said.

"What for?"

"I don't know."

"You can have him."

We rode steadily up the canyon, now and then splashing through the water, passing under the high red walls, the hanging gardens of poison ivy and panicgrass, the flowing sky. Where the trail widened I jogged my horse beside Mackie's and after a while, with a little prodding, extracted from him the story of the independent horse.

First of all, Moon-Eye had suffered. He had problems. His name derived from an inflamed condition of one of his eyes called moonblindness, which affected him periodically and inflamed his temper. The gelding operation had not improved his disposition. On top of that he'd been dude-spoiled, for old

Roy had used him for many years—since he made a poor cow horse—in his string of horses for hire. The horse Moon-Eye seemed safe and well-behaved but his actual feelings were revealed one day on a sightseeing tour through Arches when all his angers came to a boil and he bucked off a middle-aged lady from Salt Lake City. Viviano Jacquez, leading the ride, lost his temper and gave the horse a savage beating. Moon-Eye broke away and ran off into the canyons with a good saddle on his back. He didn't come back that night. Didn't come back the next day. Never came back at all. For two weeks Viviano and Roy tracked that horse, not because they wanted the horse but because Roy wanted his saddle back. When they found the saddle, caught on the stub of a limb, the cinch straps broken, they gave up the search for the horse. The bridle they never recovered. Later on a few boys from town came out to try to catch the horse and almost got him boxed up in Salt Creek Canyon. But he got away, clattering over the slickrock wall at an angle of 45 degrees, and was seldom seen afterward. After that he stayed out of box canyons and came down to the creek only when he needed a drink. That was the story of Moon-Eye.

We came at noon to the spring, dismounted, unsaddled the horses and let them graze on the tough brown grass near the cottonwoods. We dipped our cupped hands in the water and drank, leaned back against a log in the cool of the shade and ate some lunch. Mackie lit a cigarette. I stared out past the horses at the sweet green of the willows and cottonwoods under the hot red canyon wall. Far above, a strip of blue sky, cloudless. In the silence I heard quite clearly the buzzing of individual flies down by the creek, the shake and whisper of the dry cottonwood leaves, the bright tinkling song of a canyon wren. The horses shuffled slowly through the dead leaves, ripping up the grass with their powerful, hungry jaws—a solid and pleasing sound. The canyon filled with heat and stillness.

"Look, Mackie," I said, "what do you suppose that horse does up in there?"

"What horse?"

"Moon-Eye. You say he's been up that dry canyon by himself for ten years."

"Right."

"What does he *do* up in there?"

"That is a ridiculous question."

"All right it's a ridiculous question. Try and answer it."

"How the hell should I know? Who cares? What difference does it make?"

"Answer the question."

"He eats. He sleeps. He walks down to the creek once a day for a drink. He turns around and walks back. He eats again. He sleeps again."

"The horse is a gregarious beast," I said, "a herd animal, like the cow, like the human. It's not natural for a horse to live alone."

"Moon-Eye is not a natural horse."

"He's supernatural?"

"He's crazy. How should I know? Go ask the horse."

"Okay, I'll do that."

"Only not today," Mackie said. "Let's get on up and out of here."

We'd laid around long enough. Mackie threw away the butt of his cigarette; I tanked up on more water. We mounted again, rode on to the head of the canyon where a forty-foot overhang barred the way, turned and rode back the way we'd come, clearing out the cattle from the brush and tamarisk thickets, driving them before us in a growing herd as we proceeded. By the time we reached the mouth of the canyon we had a troop of twenty head plodding before us through the dust and heat, half of them little white-faced calves who'd never seen a man or a horse before. We drove them into the catchpen and shut them up. Tomorrow the calves would be branded, castrated, earmarked, dehorned, inoculated against blackleg, and the whole herd trucked to the mountains for the summer. But that would be a job for Mackie and Roy, not for me; for me tomorrow meant a return to sentry duty at the entrance of the Monument, the juniper guard and the cloud-formation survey.

As we loaded the horses into the truck for the return to the ranch I asked Mackie how he liked this kind of work. He looked at me. His shirt and the rag around his neck were dark with sweat, his face coated with dust; there was a stripe of dried blood across his cheek where a willow branch had struck him when he plunged through the brush after some ignorant cow.

"Look at yourself," he said.

I looked; I was in the same condition. "I do this only for fun," I explained. "If I did it for pay I might not like it. Anyway you haven't answered my question. How do *you* like this kind of work?"

"I'd rather be rich."

"What would you do if you were rich?"

He grinned through the dust. "Buy some cows of my own."

I hadn't forgotten the moon-eyed horse. A month later I was back at the
spot by Salt Creek where I'd first seen the tracks, this time alone, though
again on horseback. We were deep into the desert summer now and the
stream had shrunk to a dribble of slimy water oozing along between sun-
baked flats of mud.

As before I let my pony drink what he wanted from the stream while I
pondered the view from beneath the meager shelter of my hat. The alkali,
white as lime, dazzled the eyes; the wiregrass looked sere and shriveled and
even the hosts of flies and gnats had disappeared, hiding from the sun.

There was no sound but the noise of my drinking mount, no sight anywhere of animate life. In the still air the pinkish plumes of the tamarisk, light
and delicate as lace, drooped from the tips of their branches without a
tremor. Nothing moved, nothing stirred, except the shimmer of heat waves
rising before the red canyon walls.

I could hardly have picked a more hostile day for a venture into the
canyons. If anyone had asked I'd have said that not even a mad horse would
endure a summer in such a place. Yet there were the tracks as before, coming down the pathway out of the side canyon and leading back again. Moon-
Eye was still around. Or at any rate his tracks were still here, fresh prints in
the dust that looked as if they might have been made only minutes before
my arrival.

Out of the heat and stillness came an inaudible whisper, a sort of tele-
pathic intimation that perhaps the horse did not exist at all—only his tracks.
You ought to get out of this heat, I told myself, taking a drink from the canteen. My saddle horse raised his dripping muzzle from the water and waited.
He turned his head to look at me with one drowsy eye; strings of algae hung
from the corner of his mouth.

"No," I said, "we're not going home yet." I prodded the animal with
my heels; slowly we moved up into the side canyon following the narrow
trail. As we advanced I reviewed my strategy: since Moon-Eye had learned to
fear and distrust men on horseback I would approach him on foot; I would
carry nothing in my hands but a hackamore and a short lead rope. Better yet,
I would hide these inside my shirt and go up to Moon-Eye with empty
hands. Others had attempted the violent method of pursuit and capture and
had failed. I was going to use nothing but sympathy and understanding, in
direct violation of common sense and all precedent, to bring Moon-Eye
home again.

I rounded the first bend in the canyon and stopped. Ahead was the typical scene of dry wash, saltbush and prickly pear, talus slopes at the foot of vertical canyon walls. No hint of animal life. Nothing but the silence, the stark suspension of all sound. I rode on. I was sure that Moon-Eye would not go far from water in this weather.

At the next turn in the canyon, a mile farther, I found a pile of fresh droppings on the path. I slid from the saddle and led my pony to the east side of the nearest boulder and tied him. Late in the afternoon he'd get a little shade. It was the best I could do for him; nothing else was available.

I pulled off the saddle and sat down on the ground to open a can of tomatoes. One o'clock by the sun and not a cloud in the sky: hot. I squatted under the belly of the horse and ate my lunch.

When I was finished I got up, reluctantly, stuffed hackamore and rope inside my shirt, hung the canteen over my shoulder and started off. The pony watched me go, head hanging, the familiar look of dull misery in his eyes. I know how you feel, I thought, but by God you're just going to have to stand there and suffer. If I can take it you can. The midday heat figured in my plan: I believed that in such heat the moon-eyed outlaw would be docile as a plow horse, amenable to reason. I thought I could amble close, slip the hackamore over his head and lead him home like a pet dog on a leash.

A mile farther and I had to take refuge beneath a slight overhang in the canyon wall. I took off my hat to let the evaporation of my sweaty brow cool my brains. Tilted the canteen to my mouth. Already I was having visions of iced drinks, waterfalls, shade trees, clear deep emerald pools.

Forward. I shuffled through the sand, over the rocks, around the prickly pear and the spiny hedgehog cactus. I found a yellowish pebble the size of a crab apple and put it in my mouth. Kept going, pushing through the heat.

If you were really clever, I thought, you'd go back to Moon-Eye's watering place on Salt Creek, wait for him there, catch him by starlight. But you're not clever, you're stupid, I reminded myself: stick to the plan. I stopped to swab the sweat from my face. The silence locked around me again like a sphere of glass. Even the noise I made unscrewing the cap from the canteen seemed harsh and exaggerated, a gross intrusion.

I listened:

Something breathing nearby—I was in the presence of a tree. On the slope above stood a giant old juniper with massive, twisted trunk, its boughs sprinkled with the pale-blue inedible berries. Hanging from one of the limbs was what looked at first glance like a pair of trousers that reached to the ground. Blinking the sweat out of my eyes I looked harder and saw the trousers transform themselves into the legs of a large animal, focused my attention and distinguished through the obscurity of the branches and foliage the outline of a tall horse. A very tall horse.

Gently I lowered my canteen to the ground.

I touched the rope and hackamore bunched up inside my shirt. Still there. I took the pebble from my mouth, held it in my palm, and slowly and carefully and quietly stepped toward the tree. Out of the tree a gleaming eyeball watched me coming.

I said, "That you, Moon-Eye?"

Who else? The eyeball rolled, I saw the flash of white. The eye in the tree.

I stepped closer. "What are you doing out here, you old fool?"

The horse stood not under the tree—the juniper was not big enough for that—but within it, among its branches. There'd be an awful smashing and crashing of dry wood if he tried to drive out of there.

"Eh? What do you think you're up to anyway? Damned old idiot. . . ." I showed him the yellowish stone in my hand, round as a little apple. "Why don't you answer me, Moon-Eye? Forgotten how to talk?"

Moving closer. The horse remained rigid, ears up. I could see both eyes now, the good one and the bad one—moonstruck, like a bloodshot cueball.

"I've come to take you home, old horse. What do you think of that?"

He was a giant about seventeen hands high, with a buckskin hide as faded as an old rug and a big ugly coffin-shaped head.

"You've been out here in the wilderness long enough, old man. It's time to go home."

He looked old, all right, he looked his years. He looked more than old—he looked like a spectre. Apocalyptic, a creature out of a bad dream.

"You hear me, Moon-Eye? I'm coming closer. . . ."

His nineteen ribs jutted out like the rack of a skeleton and his neck, like a camel's, seemed far too gaunt and long to carry that oversize head off the ground.

"You old brute," I murmured, "you hideous old gargoyle. You goddamned nightmare of a horse. . . . Moon-Eye, look at this. Look at this in my hand, Moon-Eye."

He watched me, watched my eyes. I was within twenty feet of him and except for the eyes he had yet to reveal a twitch of nerve or muscle; he might have been petrified. Mesmerized by sun and loneliness. He hadn't seen a man for—how many years?

"Moon-Eye," I said, approaching slowly, one short step, a pause, another step, "how long since you've stuck that ugly face of yours into a bucket of barley and bran? Remember what alfalfa tastes like, old pardner? How about grass, Moon-Eye? Green sweet fresh succulent grass, Moon-Eye, what do you think of that, eh?"

We were ten feet apart. Only the branches of the juniper tree separated us. Standing there watching the horse I could smell the odor of cedarwood, the fragrance of the tree.

Another step. "Moon-Eye. . . ."

I hesitated; to get any closer I'd have to push through the branches or stoop underneath them. "Come on, Moon-Eye, I want to take you home. It's time to go home, oldtimer."

We stared at each other, unmoving. If that animal was breathing I couldn't hear it—the silence seemed absolute. Not a fly, not a single fly crawled over his arid skin or whined around his rheumy eyeballs. If it hadn't been for the light of something like consciousness in his good eye I might have imagined I was talking to a scarecrow, a dried stuffed completely mummified horse. He didn't even smell like a horse, didn't seem to have any smell about him at all. Perhaps if I reached out and touched him he would crumble to a cloud of dust, vanish like a shadow.

My head ached from the heat and glare and for a moment I wondered if this horselike shape in front of me was anything more than hallucination.

"Moon-Eye. . . .?" Keep talking.

I couldn't stand there all afternoon. I took another step forward, pressing against a branch. Got to keep talking.

"Moon-Eye. . . ."

He lowered his head a couple of inches, the ears flattened back. Watch out. He was still alive after all. For the first time I felt a little fear. He was a big horse and that moon-glazed eye was not comforting. We watched each other intently through the branches of the tree. If I could only wait, only be patient, I might yet sweet-talk him into surrender. But it was too hot.

"Look here, old horse, have a sniff of this." I offered him the pebble with one hand and with the other unbuttoned a button of my shirt, preparing to ease out the rope when the chance came. "Go on, have a look. . . ."

I was within six feet of the monster.

"Now you just relax, Moon-Eye old boy. I'm coming in where you are now." I started to push through the boughs of the juniper. "Easy boy, easy now. . . ."

He backed violently, jarring the whole tree. Loose twigs and berries rained around us. The good eye glared at me, the bad one shone like a boiled egg—monocular vision.

"Take it easy, old buddy." Speaking softly. I had one hand on the rope. I stepped forward again, pushing under the branches. Softly—"Easy, easy, don't be scared—"

Moon-Eye tried to back again but his retreat was blocked. Snorting like a truck he came forward, right at me, bursting through the branches. Dry wood snapped and popped, dust filled the air, and as I dove for the ground I had a glimpse of a lunatic horse expanding suddenly, growing bigger than all the world and soaring over me on wings that flapped like a bat's and nearly tore the tree out of the earth.

When I opened my eyes a second later I was still alive and Moon-Eye was down in the wash fifty feet away, motionless as a statue, waiting. He stood with his ragged broomtail and his right-angled pelvic bones toward me but had that long neck and coffin head cranked around, watching me with the good eye, waiting to see what I would do next. He didn't intend to exert himself unless he was forced to.

The shade of the tree was pleasant and I made no hurry to get up. I sat against the trunk and checked for broken bones. Everything seemed all right except my hat a few feet away, crushed into the dirt by a mighty hoof. I was thirsty though and looked around for the canteen before remembering where I'd left it; I could see it down in the wash, near the horse.

Moon-Eye didn't move. He stood rigid as stone, conserving every drop of moisture in his body. But he was in the sun now and I was in the shade. Perhaps if I waited long enough he'd be forced to come back to the tree. I made myself comfortable and waited. The silence settled in again.

But that horse wouldn't come, though I waited a full hour by the sun. The horse moved only once in all that time, lowering his head for a sniff at a bush near his foreleg.

The red cliffs rippled behind the veil of heat, radiant as hot iron. Thirst was getting to me. I stirred myself, got up painfully, and stepped out of the wreckage of the juniper. The horse made no move.

"Moon-Eye," I said—he listened carefully—"let's get out of here. What do you say? Let's go home, you miserable old bucket of guts. Okay?"

I picked up my flattened hat, reformed it, put it on.

"Well, what do you say?"

I started down the slope. He raised his head, twitched one ear, watching me. "Are you crazy, old horse, standing out here in the heat? Don't you have any sense at all?"

I did not approach him directly this time but moved obliquely across the slope, hoping to head him down the canyon toward the creek and the trail to the corral. Moon-Eye saw my purpose and started up the canyon. I hurried; the horse moved faster. I slowed to a walk; he did the same. I stopped and he stopped.

"Moon-Eye, let me tell you something. I can outrun you if I have to. These Utah cowboys would laugh themselves sick if I ever mentioned it out loud but it's a fact and you ought to know it. Over the long haul, say twenty or thirty miles, it's a known fact that a healthy man can outrun a horse."

Moon-Eye listened.

"But my God, in this heat, Moon-Eye, do you think we should? Be sensible. Let's not make fools of ourselves."

He waited. I squatted on my heels and passed my forefinger, like a windshield wiper, across my forehead, brushing off the streams of sweat. My head felt hot, damp, feverish.

"What's the matter with you, Moon-Eye?"

The horse kept his good eye on me.

"Are you crazy, maybe? You don't want to die out here, do you, all alone like a hermit? In this awful place. . . ." He watched me and listened. "The turkey buzzards will get you, Moon-Eye. They'll smell you dying, they'll come flapping down on you like foul and dirty kites and roost on your neck and drink your eyeballs while you're still alive. Yes, they do that. And just before that good eye is punctured you'll see those black wings shutting off the sky, shutting out the sun, you'll see a crooked yellow beak and a red neck crawling with lice and a pair of insane eyes looking into yours. You won't like that, old horse. . . ."

I paused. Moon-Eye was listening, he seemed attentive, but I sensed that he wasn't really much interested in what I was saying. Perhaps it was all an old story to him. Maybe he didn't care.

I continued with the sermon. "And when the buzzards are through with you, Moon-Eye—and you'll be glad when *that's* over—why then a quiet little coyote will come loping down the canyon in the middle of the night under the moon, Moon-Eye, nosing out your soul. He'll come to within fifty yards of you, old comrade, and sit for a few hours, thinking, and then he'll circle around you a few times trying to smell out the hand of man. Pretty soon his belly will get the best of his caution—maybe he hasn't eaten for two weeks and hasn't had a chance at a dead horse for two years—and so he'll come nosing close to you, tongue out and eyes bright with happiness, and all at once when you're hardly expecting it he'll pounce and hook his fangs into your scrawny old haunch and tear off a steak. Are you listening to me, Moon-Eye? And when he's gorged himself sick he'll retire for a few hours of peaceful digestion. In the meantime the ants and beetles and blowflies will go to work, excavating tunnels through your lungs, kidneys, stomach, windpipe, brains and entrails and whatever else the buzzards and the coyote leave."

Moon-Eye watched me as I spoke; I watched him. "And in a couple of weeks you won't even stink anymore and after a couple of months there'll be nothing left but your mangled hide and your separated bones and—get this, Moon-Eye get the picture—way out in eternity somewhere, on the far side of the sun, they'll hang up a brass plaque with the image of your moon-eyed soul stamped on it. That's about all. Years later some tired and dirty cowboy looking for a lost horse, some weary prospector looking for potash or beryllium will stumble up this way and come across your clean white rib cage, your immaculate skull, a few other bones. . . ."

I stopped talking. I was tired. Would that sun never go down beyond the canyon wall? Wasn't there a cloud in the whole state of Utah?

The horse stood motionless as a rock. He looked like part of that burnt-out landscape. He looked like the steed of Don Quixote carved out of wood by Giacometti. I could see the blue of the sky between his ribs, through the eyesockets of his skull. Dry, odorless, still and silent, he looked like the idea—without the substance—of a horse.

My brain and eyes ached, my limbs felt hollow, I had to breathe deliberately, making a conscious effort. The thought of the long walk back to my saddle pony, the long ride back to the pickup truck, made my heart sink. I didn't want to move. So I'd wait, too, wait for sundown before starting the march home, the *anabasis* in retreat. I glanced toward the sun. About four o'clock. Another hour before that sun would reach the rim of the canyon. I crawled back to the spotted shade of the juniper and waited.

We waited then, the horse and I, enduring the endless afternoon, the heartbreaking heat, and passed the time as best we could in one-sided conversation. I'd speak a sentence and wait about ten minutes for the next thought and speak again. Moon-Eye watched me all the time and made no move.

At last the sun touched the skyline, merged with it for a moment in a final explosive blaze of light and heat and sank out of sight. The shadow of the canyon wall advanced across the canyon floor, included the horse, touched the rocks and brush on the far side. A wave of cooling relief like a breeze, like an actual movement of air, washed through the canyon. A rock wren sang, a few flies came out of hiding and droned around the juniper tree. I could almost see the leaves of the saltbush and blackbush relax a little, uncurling in the evening air.

I stood up and emerged from the shelter of the broken tree. Old Moon-Eye took a few steps away from me, stopped. Still watching. We faced each other across some fifty feet of sand and rock. No doubt for the last time. I tried to think of something suitable to say but my mouth was so dry, my tongue so stiff, my lips so dried-out and cracked, I could barely utter a word.

"You damned stupid harrr. . . ." I croaked, and gave it up.

Moon-Eye blinked his good eye once, twitched his hide and kept watching me as all around us, along the wash and on the canyon walls and in the air the desert birds and desert bugs resumed their inexplicable careers. A whiptail lizard scurried past my feet. A primrose opened its petals a few inches above the still-hot sand. Knees shaking, I stepped toward the horse, pulled the ropy hackamore out of my shirt—to Moon-Eye it must have looked as if I were pulling out my intestines—and threw the thing with all the strength I had left straight at him. It slithered over his back like a hairy snake, scaring him into a few quick steps. Again he stopped, the eye on me.

Enough. I turned my back on the horse and went to the canteen, picked it up. The water was almost too hot to drink but I drank it. Drank it all, except a few drops which I poured on my fingers and dabbed on my aching forehead. Refusing to look again at the spectre horse, I slung the canteen over my shoulder and started homeward, trudging over the clashing stones and through the sand down-canyon toward my pony and Salt Creek.

Once, twice, I thought I heard footsteps following me but when I looked back I saw nothing.

My Heroes Have Always Been Horses

VIRGINIA BENNETT

He touches a nerve. With his resolute cold-shoulder and determined trip to the furthest corner of the corral whenever I go to visit him, all of my old hurts and past rejections rise to the surface. Once again, I am that high school girl, a country bumpkin from out in the sticks. I never quite fit in back then because I drove a 1954 Dodge 1-ton truck to school each day and parked it out in the lot with the Volvos and Mustangs belonging to the teen-aged children of the city's aristocratic doctors and lawyers.

My horse turns his butt toward me, and cocks one rear leg. His rejections remind me of nights I attended community-center dances in the late 1960's, vainly hoping to be asked to gyrate with some acne-faced boy to a local band's version of "Wooly Bully" or "Ninety-Six Tears."

Shadow snakes his head in my direction, ears pinned back. There's no loving reception here, either, no warm and soft eye eager to receive my strokes and endearments. "Feed me and leave me alone," he seems to say, and I've learned to ignore his spurning of my proffered affections. Most of the time, that is. I admit there are moments when I yearn for a horse who runs to greet me and allows me to stroke his broad forehead or tussle with his ears and softly caress his inquisitive nose. But that's just not Shadow, and that's okay. Most of the time.

We've shared a lot of incredible miles, Shadow and I, and it all started ten years ago. My husband and I were managing a small ranch in Washington and needed to add a few more horses to the string. While investigating various ads for horses of all shapes and sizes, we stumbled across a small, sickly pinto horse. He stood only 14.3 hands and was quite underweight. The horse-trader explained the horse had shipping fever (a type of pneumonia) when he'd recently bought him in the Hermiston, Oregon horse sale. There was not enough horse there to be worth $2000, but with ranch funds, I paid it. After all, he did have an incredibly fast walk.

Back at the ranch, we fattened him up and as sometimes happens after a horse returns to good health, he evolved into too much horse for the average rider. He became my mount and I worked him hard because the only way to get through to Shadow is to work him hard. And often.

Since the day I purchased my first horse at the age of fifteen with wages earned working as a waitress after school at the Concord Dairy Bar, I've always owned a horse. Growing up in rural New Hampshire, horses were a luxury, and one my family could definitely not afford. Yet, that didn't stop me from being one of those completely horse-crazy kids. I read every book in the bookmobile that stopped along our tree-lined road each summer, and later on, in the imposing granite structure of a library in town. I remember absorbing Colonel Alois Podhajsky's volume on his *haute ecole* work with the famous, white Lippizzaner stallions of the Spanish Riding School. I pored over Walter Farley's Black Stallion series where, in my mind, I raced the sea wind upon a horse with no saddle or bridle, right along with the book's boy-hero, Alec Ramsey.

My father fashioned a horse from a sawhorse, painted it black and white like a pinto and nailed a string mop to the horse's crest to create a mane, and thus I rode in dreams of cowboys and galloping horses in the far west. When I wasn't riding that spotted horse made of pine, I envisioned myself the horse as I played. I leapt fences, bounding along in a canter and switching leads when necessary. At my elementary school playground, I encouraged my girl classmates to run in wild herds with me across the schoolyard and through the woods, whinnying as we went.

Like many of my generation, my imagination of things equine was fueled by the old television westerns. Each Saturday morning, this little girl with a passion for horses would drag her bouncy, spring-horse out to the living room in front of the old black and white Zenith TV, and spend time with the brave men in cowboy hats astride their silver-adorned horses.

Fury, the black stallion, became my favorite hero. I've forgotten the names of the actors and the characters and even the storyline of the program, but I'll never forget that handsome, ebony horse who performed at liberty, rearing on some rocky outcropping. I thought, "Wherever Fury and horses like him are, that is where I want to be!" And I was pretty sure there weren't any wild horses protecting their harems of mares in the deep woods of New Hampshire.

During the week, in the evenings, my Dad and I sat in the tiny living room on Bog Road and watched "Gunsmoke," "Bonanza," and "The Virginian." To me, these shows represented what life ought to be, riding from point A to point B on the back of a good horse. I studied the horses' movements and conformation as they galloped down through valleys and along boulder-strewn trails.

Eventually, after graduating from high school, I sold my horses and bummed a ride out to Arizona to begin living my dream. I started out riding barrel-racing horses in rodeos for a man in Apache Junction, and by the time Shadow entered my life, I'd worked on western ranches for over 20 years, and had trained and started colts to ride for the public for about that long, as well. I'd swung my right leg over some pretty good horseflesh and seen a lot of big, wide-open country. I'd been blessed to ride with the crew on a big outfit, where I first drew cowboy wages of $25 for a 16-hour day. I'd trained and shown hunter/jumpers in Colorado, and driven a team and wagon carrying ranch guests around the countryside in Washington. I'd ridden the best horse of my career, a tall, bay mare named Sally, who could get on the tail of a cow and never relent in her pursuit, up steep mountainsides and over downed timber. She never stumbled, she never gave up, she never quit.

Then, there's Shadow. Who is none of those things but who has stayed with me longer than any horse I've ever owned.

When he jumped out of that trailer on the ranch in the Methow Valley of Washington, he settled into his new surroundings with grace. However, he soon developed an abscess (a residual effect from his shipping fever) behind his jaw, and our vet, Dr. Betsy, came to incise it, drain the pus from the cavity and sew it back up. I was left with the job to administer his injections of antibiotics each day. I soon learned that Shadow did not like needles, syringes or the people attempting to use them.

Tied to the side of the barn inside the breezeway, he would rear and strike out at me with flashing hooves. His movements were explosive; he jumped with cat-like agility and little forewarning. Finally, I looped a large, cotton rope around his body at chest height to hold him securely to the side of the barn.

Today, he is one of the easiest horses we have to give shots to. But knowing Shadow, I am certain that he has reasoned something out which benefits him to allow injections. Otherwise, he'd simply never stand for it.

As Shadow returned to good health and increased in weight, so did his bad behavior under saddle. He refused to leave the barn while being ridden, and I worked over a year with him to correct his rearing, lunging and backing uncontrollably toward the barn. Once, the ranch owner was driving past the barn area when Shadow pulled a run-away with me and skittered out into the road in front of his car. Shadow reared and ran away, the owner stepped out of his car, and I yelled back over my shoulder, "I'll keep riding him until he's worth what we paid for him."

Do I enjoy a horse who is a challenge? In self-examination, I conclude that that is not necessarily the case with me. I think I am just hardheaded enough to believe that a person shouldn't have a horse out in the barn who isn't broke enough to ride. That probably hearkens back to my frugal, Yankee upbringing. If you're feeding the horse, you better be able to get some use out of him.

When Shadow was barely four years old, my husband Pete and I loaded him and another horse into the trailer and took them to a trailhead. We headed up the trail to Williams Lake, high in the Sawtooth Wilderness of the North Cascades. Shadow didn't seem too savvy about winding, alpine trails, and would walk right off the end of the switchbacks. A photo in one of my albums shows young Shadow that day, weary head hanging low and his body covered in sweat, by the banks of the lake, a late-season snowfield behind him. He had been tough and not given up. It was on that trip that I suspected I had the prospect of a good mountain horse under me.

The ranch where we worked, a corporate guest ranch, hosted many people from around the world who came to visit, attend seminars and take part in ranch activities including trail-riding. I needed a rock-solid horse for the task of safely transporting these guests back in time to the days of the Wild West. For, when guiding a line of inexperienced riders, the leader must be on a steady horse that is not prone to spookiness, as the horses in line are affected by the one in the front. You control, to the best of your ability, the other riders' horses by what you do with your mount.

It is amazing that Shadow became my lead horse, for he is, in every sense of the word, afraid of his own shadow. He looks askance and gives wide berth to anything out of place: a wheelbarrow left in the alleyway of the barn, not in its usual spot, or a leaf, blown and tossed by a capricious north wind. And heaven forbid we encounter a discarded, plastic bag along the trail.

It took me years to figure it out, but finally I reached the conclusion that though I often question whether this horse I spend my days with even likes me, he probably trusts me a great deal. He is fearful of everything in the world, but with me aboard, mountain lions cross his path and he handles it like a seasoned campaigner. I give him confidence, and he transmits that to all of the horses in line behind him.

Two years after I purchased him for the ranch, my employers called me to their house for a conference. I worried if I'd done something wrong and was about to be dressed down for my infraction, though I could think of nothing deserving such treatment. Standing in their kitchen and shifting nervously from foot to foot, I waited for what was to come. Instead, I heard, "He's been your horse all along, but we want to make it official and give you Shadow."

Shadow's American Pinto registration papers revealed that five people had already transferred this horse into their names in his three, short years. Evidently, he was not getting along with everyone, or they were not getting along with him. What was there about him that caused so many people to reject such a beautiful animal?

For Shadow is stout, strong and emblazoned with color. He is mostly white with a few large, reddish-brown markings, which lay like shields along his flanks and chest. This same color covers the top of his head like a war bonnet, painting his ears a dark, rusty hue.

Plains Indians, like the Sioux, Comanche and Kiowa, hold sacred horses with these peculiar markings. They call them Medicine Hats, and pull hair from their tails and manes to store in ceremonial pouches as "good medicine." Within some tribes, only the chiefs and elders ride these rare animals, also mystically referred to as "Ghost Horses."

My own relationship with this willful horse is complicated. We seem to have a sort of love/hate thing where one day, I can feel he is the best horse ever created to ride down a trail, and the next, I want to sell him, no . . . GIVE him away to the first person who might drive up the ranch road. My family knows this full well and takes it all in stride when I glowingly describe how I have finally figured out this horse of mine . . . or, contrarily, anguish over the fact that I can't sell him because no one else could possibly stand him.

Since he is colored like a circus performer, I decided to try teaching him a few tricks. Despite his cranky disposition, he learned to bow deeply and gracefully, to nod yes and shake his head no. He reaches around with his neck and gives me a hug, and takes my hat off and shakes it handily. I purse my lips and say, "Give me a kiss," and he reaches out naughtily try to nibble my face.

When visitors from Guatemala, New Zealand, Ireland and all points in between came to see him, he would perform these exercises, including yawning widely when I asked, "Are you tired?" They would often inquire how you could teach a horse to yawn on command and I'd answer with the key to training any trick into a horse: you spend a lot of time just being with him. The guests loved Shadow and they thought I was the epitome of the western cowgirl they'd read about in travel magazines.

And on my days off, Shadow became my conveyance to a wondrous world. As we explored the alpine wilderness nearby, I sensed that if Heaven were fashioned just for me, it would look like those mountains, those rocky trails, those lustrous lakes and all the hidden secrets around each corner. I carried my camera and took roll upon roll of photos of Shadow tied up to a tree by the side of a lake; Shadow hitched to a log on top of a windy, above-timberline ridge; Shadow staked out on a high pass. Some I took while on horseback, and these show handsome, dark-brown ears in the lower edges, while in front of his nose lurks a challenging trail or a treacherous snowfield.

I loved going to the mountains alone. Upon hearing where I had ridden on my last outing, women friends would say, "Next time you go and you want company, I'd love to go!" But I'd never call them. I wanted to be alone with nature, with God and with Shadow.

After six years on that ranch, we relocated to the central coast of California. We moved with two dogs and Shadow. When we would stop overnight, I'd unload Shadow in the motel parking lot and walk him around, loosening up his tired muscles from a day's travel. Motel guests would pause to marvel at the handsome horse and ask to take his picture.

A year later, I was once again invited to perform my cowboy poetry at a festival at the Melody Ranch motion picture studio north of Los Angeles. I asked if I could bring my horse to the event and have him do tricks for the children there.

Country-boy Shadow had never been to such goings-on! But he put his faith in me, and together we explored the old western streets where so many of my favorite TV shows had been filmed. I would visit with old-timers and youngsters, and then dismount to allow Shadow the opportunity to act the loveable show-off. He never refused, he never faltered, he did each trick I asked of him, time and again.

On Sunday morning, I arrived early at the grounds. Not many people were up and about yet, and I felt inspired to saddle my pinto and ride around the old studio. As I came around a corner in the street, lined with graying, false-front buildings whose rustic signs declared, "Longbranch Saloon" and "General Store," it suddenly dawned on me. There was not another human in sight, and I was looking right down the very street seen behind Marshall Dillon in *Gunsmoke*! Ahead of me on the left was the stairway climbing up to the second floor of a venerable, weathered storefront, where Matt went to see Doc. Over there was the board sidewalk where he walked with Miss Kitty. And here was I, born a New Hampshire girl with a heartache for horses, riding my own right down the dusty streets of Dodge City! I have to admit I rode back and forth several times and savored the moment, until someone came walking toward me. The magic was broken, but the memory stands untarnished.

So, is Shadow my hero? My gut reaction is no. He's tossed me repeatedly, knocking the wind out of me or damaging my back in each fall. Once, while doctoring his left leg, the wind blew the bandage wrapper past him on the other side and he exploded in fear, trampling me beneath him and breaking my right foot. He's scared me more than once on primitive trails clinging to the sides of steep hillsides, where he has stumbled or even spun completely around in an effort to head home. He's balked for hours at creek crossings, yet—once he learned to trust me—we even swam in ponds together. Only those who have ridden a horse out "over his head" have sensed that exhilarating moment of trust as this large animal beneath you is actually floating.

And then there's that question of rejection.

Do I love him? It's hard to say. Does he love me? I rather doubt it.

Yet, as I look back over the last ten years, I see where that curmudgeon of a horse has carried me. Upon his back, I have looked eagles in the eye. I have peered down into lakes and from his back snapped pictures as impressive as aerial photos.

I have seen the smiles of children and foreign visitors who have never had the chance to know a horse in such a way. Shadow has shown them what can exist between a horse and a woman, even between a headstrong pinto and a sometimes-less-than-patient cowgirl.

And I have known the enchantment of riding an incredibly beautiful horse and feeling that ground-covering walk as he traveled streets made famous in old-time westerns. Perhaps that would qualify him for hero status, after all.

Recently, I was working another horse in English tack for jumping. He unexpectedly stopped dead in his tracks in front of the fence. Sharing the fate of thousands of jump riders before me, I flew over his neck. But in this case, I landed on my head and was knocked out. As I came to, I struggled to my knees and felt electricity zing through my hands and feet. I eventually stood up and caught the horse, led him to the house and dialed 911. An ambulance ride to two hospitals and a CT-scan revealed I'd broken my C1 vertebra in four places.

Just like the horse I had been riding slid to a perfect stop in front of the jump, life, as I knew it, put on the brakes. After being released from the hospital, I spent much of the first week in bed. I had not been out to the barn in three weeks when I haltingly made my way outside, leaning on a cane for support. I rounded the corner of the house to where I could see the horse barn. The way in which I had to hold my head and neck, positioned with a brace, did not allow me to see well, and I could not make out the horses in their corrals.

But Shadow immediately noticed me, and he whinnied. I knew his call from all the others. And the sound of it shattered me emotionally. I cried tears I had held back since my injury, and weakly called out, "Shadow, I miss you!"

Told by the doctors that it will be a year before I can once more be horseback, and with my neurosurgeon even telling me he doubts I'll ever ride professionally again, I wrestle with thoughts about the future of my job and what to do with Shadow. He's the kind of horse who needs work and even when he's ridden every day, his emotions are volatile. I know in my heart that when I go back to riding, he is not the horse I should be on. But who would want this 13-year-old incorrigible fellow?

Then yesterday, I put that all behind me. I walked out to the barn, and he poked his head over the stall door and allowed me to scratch his forehead. His eye softened, and, rubbing his forehead lightly against my open palm, he even showed a bit of affection. I know he's fickle and that he's only after a treat of some kind. But I also know this old boy represents who I was, where I rode and how I rode, and who I will be again. I'll pull his shoes, let him have a year off, and in the meantime, I'll read maps and find the trails he and I will explore again one day.

Captain Kidd No. 30T8

FLORENCE FENLEY

Captain Kidd was a coal black horse with one white foot and a fleck of white in his forehead, and what you might have called a spoiled horse, or plain mean. He could have been called a bully, too, for he was ready to fight every horse on the post except one. He took their feed and bared his teeth at them, and he bared his teeth at men, too.

The Cavalry was called "the eyes and ears of the army" back in the early days and even until 1941, when this bunch of 300 horses was sent to Fort Clark, Texas. They were brought in to build up the strength and replace condemned horses in the regiment. Captain Kidd was one of them. His service record showed his serial number to be 30T8 and that he had been purchased from Dallas Hart of Del Rio, Texas.

Just ahead of the horses, recruits had arrived from Fort Bliss where they had finished basic training and were to replace the 5th Regiment of the last Cavalry Division at Fort Clark. Among the recruits was a ranch boy named Paul Brazel from New Mexico, who had worked on ranches in both New Mexico and Texas and who preferred to stay with the horses as long as there were any around.

Paul was born on the Brazel Ranch south of Carrizozo, New Mexico. He finished school in that section and had worked on the Lobo Ranch near Van Horn, Texas, before being inducted into the Cavalry in World War II.

While in training at Fort Bliss, Paul met a boy named Clinton Halsell of Seagraves, Texas, and the two became close friends. Paul called him Britt.

They were in the Special Weapons Troop, and Paul was in charge of horse-shoeing remounts when they came to Fort Clark. Ironically, the two horses later assigned to them became buddies too, to the exclusion of the other mounts. Upon arrival at Fort Clark, the new horses had gone into quarantine for sixty to ninety days, which was the Cavalry rule when a new bunch was brought in. The men usually didn't work with the horses during the quarantine. However, the whole unit of men and horses were shipped to Fort Bliss so they could start on maneuvers as soon as the quarantine was lifted, and Captain Kidd was already making himself known.

Late one evening the two men were sitting out on the barracks porch enjoying the cool desert air when the staff sergeant came to them and told them about two black horses on the line which were too mean to handle. The soldiers couldn't feed or water them, he said, and neither could they get close to them. He asked the men if they would see what they could do with them, for it was a shame for such pretty horses to be condemned and destroyed for being unmanageable.

"Next day," Brazel said, "we went out and looked them over. Britt picked out one of the blacks and I took the other, which happened to be Captain Kidd. Our picket line was right next to the railroad and there were some stock pens there. We finally got those two blacks out to the pens, off to ourselves, and Britt bridled his horse, then saddled 'im up, but I was having trouble. If you think I was about to put a bridle on Kidd, you're wrong. I got 'im out of the way and took him back to the picket line away from the other black, but Britt didn't have very much trouble with his horse. He didn't pitch much, he wanted to kick and bite mostly. We just had those little old army saddles, which I don't recommend for bronc bustin'.

"The saddle wasn't botherin' me; it was gettin' the bridle on that son-of-a-gun. I kept on tryin' and he'd let me touch his neck and ears but every time I touched his nose he slapped me up side of the head and he wasn't playing either. It took me from two o'clock till four that afternoon to get that bridle on 'im, and then it wasn't till later that I figured out what must be wrong with 'im. I kept watchin' and studyin' the way he acted till it come to me that somebody, sometime, had used a twist on his upper lip. It's a cruel thing. They take a pick handle and put a loop of a rope around their upper lip, then twist with the handle till sometimes the upper lip is nearly twisted off. You can't blame a horse for getting mean. He has to fight off such treatment the best he knows how when he is being tortured. So I tried a plan.

"I took the curb off and lifted the snaffle bit, unbuckling it on one side, then pulled the bit through his mouth with the bridle rein from the right side, and he let the bit come into his mouth that way.

"Kidd didn't like that bridle at all," Brazel said, "but I knew he would get used to it in a little while, so I picked up my saddle and started toward 'im. Man, he went to pieces. I tried and tried to get up to him with that saddle, but he wouldn't let me get near 'im. All right, I thought, I'll ride you bareback. I didn't know what he would do, but I finally got on 'im bareback, and he did-n't offer to pitch. He showed right quick that he was broke, and outside of sidesteppin' around awhile, he behaved himself a lot better than I expected.

"Britt's horse was all right after he rode 'im awhile and since the quar-antine period was over, we decided we'd take them on maneuvers between Fort Bliss and Oro Grande, New Mexico. We were due to leave next morn-ing to be gone ten days.

"Everything had to be packed and ready to leave by daylight, so I just left the bridle on Kidd. I wanted to pull out when the troops did. We had to take our forges, horseshoes, nails, water troughs and horse feed along. We had canvas water troughs about eight feet in diameter and we'd set them up, out on maneuvers, for the trucks to fill up with water for the horses. We also were ready to shoe a horse right on the field.

"Britt's black had developed ringbone and he'd go lame most any time, so Britt picked out a brown horse he called Stud and rode him the rest of the time. For some reason old Kidd liked that brown horse and they got along fine. In fact, they acted like long-lost buddies. But another horse couldn't even get near Kidd, and he wouldn't ride in the column with any other horse. Sometimes, I had to ride Kidd at the rear of the column, by special permission, or most any other place when we were on the march. They all knew what I was tryin' to do with 'im.

"Captain Kidd liked Britt well enough that he'd let Britt shoe him. Also, he had a special spite at an officer or a white coat. The officers all wanted 'im because he was so pretty, but they learned not to get near 'im. And a white coat had to stay out of his sight, or behind somebody else. When a vet came to vaccinate him, I had to put the needle in 'im myself.

"Another thing, when I was shoeing 'im, I had to cuss 'im all the time. He loved it and would stand with his head down and ears droopin' like he was asleep, but the minute I quit talkin', he'd pull his foot away. Then, when

I was workin' on his forefeet, he had the dangedest habit of reachin' around and bitin' me. He was just playin' but he sure played rough.

"The Army had a regulation that you had to slip the bits out of the horses' mouths when you took 'em to water," continued Brazel. "When I took the bit out of Kidd's mouth, of course, I couldn't get it back in when he quit drinkin'. All the old shenanigans started over.

"While we were on maneuvers in New Mexico, I learned something new about him that saved me lots of time. Sergeant Finley was our first sergeant of the Special Weapons Troop, and one day when I had watered Kidd he saw what a time I was having, so he stayed with me and let the troop go on. He was in charge of all the horses and was interested in Kidd.

"I kept tryin' to slip the bit in Kidd's mouth, but, no, sir, he wouldn't stand for it. Finally, it dawned on me that he might take the bit himself. I showed it to him and held it out to 'im with the headstall hanging down, and darned if he didn't reach out and get the bit in his mouth and stood perfectly still while I put the headstall on. The sergeant was as dumbfounded as I was, but we mounted and caught up with the column.

"As soon as he got with Stud, old Kidd was the nicest behaved horse in the whole bunch, and we got along fine the rest of the time we were on maneuvers.

"When we got back from New Mexico it wasn't long before we got orders to go to Louisiana on more maneuvers," Brazel resumed. "They shipped the horses and all equipment down there by train, and there were about three trains. I went along with the horses. We carried lumber, nails, hammers and saws along, for those horses were invariably kicking holes through the boxcar sides and we'd have to patch up the holes. Several horses broke their legs by kicking through the boxcar and then couldn't get their feet back through. When they broke their legs in the cars like that, there wasn't much we could do about it till we unloaded for feed and water. I remember that we unloaded in Houston, fed and watered 'em, and those that were in too bad a shape had to be left there.

"The Army was a great hand to try to patch up a horse, if there was a chance at all, even to patching up a broken leg if possible. You wouldn't think they'd fool with one, for it was easier to destroy 'em, but they did. The vets were right there to save any of them they could, and they even doctored me when I got a nail stuck in me.

"When we got to Louisiana we unloaded at some little jerkwater stop on the other side of Shreveport. I had a time finding old Kidd for I didn't know which car he was in, or which train either. We'd had all we could do from the time we left the post just keepin' horses and boxcars repaired.

"It was the Army against the Cavalry when we got ready for maneuvers. You know, they are sham battles and each side uses all the strategy they know. We were down on the Sabine River where the brush was thick and we had regular referees who made some of us pretend to be killed or wounded, etc.

"There was a ten-minute break about every hour and I would have to go down the column and inspect the horses for lost shoes or other trouble, and I would lead Kidd as I went. But I got to where I would let him follow me and leave the reins over his neck.

"He would graze along as I went from horse to horse and sometimes he would get 'way behind before he missed me. I might be fifty yards off by then, and when he'd look up and see me, look out! He'd run over horses, men or anything in his path till he got to me. The troopers sure learned to get out of his way for he wouldn't check till he got to me unless Britt and Stud were in his path, then he would stop and have a conversation with Stud. I've seen them scratch each other's necks and stand together for ever so long, but no other horse could get near 'em.

"Sometimes the troops split up into small patrols and if the other patrols didn't have a horseshoer along, they just had to wait till they got back to us.

"Of course, we were a part of the unit and were trained same as the other men, and we carried weapons too, but most of the time we were messengers between the units and could take any man's place that was counted dead or wounded.

"The enemy even bombed us from planes with flour. I think the flour was in little two-pound sacks and one day when they bombed the column, one boy was knocked clean off his horse! Such confusion as ever took place! Those horses were wild and threw their riders off and away they went. Practically every third man had a packhorse to lead, and they broke loose and scattered equipment and rations all over that country. It took us two whole hours to get men and horses back together.

"In all that wild stampede old Kidd never got one bit excited. Once when the enemy captured us they began rounding up the men and then the horses, but they sure didn't round up old Kidd in the bunch. He stayed by a little bush and wouldn't let any of 'em come in ten feet of 'im. I just sat there and grinned at 'em, so they finally left me with Kidd and said, 'Hell with 'em!'

"On dark nights we sure had a time trying to see how to get everything ready for a march. We didn't dare light a match or make any noise either. On moonlight nights we did better and could, at least, see our horses and where we were goin'.

"And we were on the march so much, everyone of us was dead for sleep. When we stopped to rest we would be called out most any minute, so it got to where, if no horses needed attention, I would grab every minute to rest that I could. I would slide off of Kidd and fall on the ground with my bridle reins over my arm, and when the order came to 'mount up,' Kidd would always raise his head and that would pull the reins and wake me up. He always seemed to know what it was all about. He was stout and tough and never got nervous.

"One night we called a halt and I was asleep by the time I hit the ground. After awhile I was aware that someone was callin' my name. It was real low, and I thought at first I was dreamin', but when I did wake up, Captain Kidd was standing astraddle of me watchin' the sergeant who was callin' me. As soon as I made a little move, Kidd backed off of me as easy as though he knew he might step on me. He'd had one forefoot on one side of my chest and the other foot on the other side. It sure scared me at first. When I saw that sergeant late in the day, I asked him if he'd seen that horse standing over me like that and he said yes, he saw 'im and that wasn't the first time. He said a number of times he had seen 'im standin' over me and if he tried to come closer than ten feet old Kidd would back his ears and bare his teeth and get ready to lunge at 'im. He told me he believed Kidd would tear a person to pieces if he tried to get to me when I was asleep.

"When the maneuvers were over in Louisiana we loaded up everything again—horses, equipment and men—and headed back to Fort Clark. We unloaded at the nearest railway stop which was about twenty miles away. All the riders had to lead some horses back to the fort. That is, all except me and Kidd. He'd have no horses led behind him! We got back to our old routine there and were at Fort Clark till June 1942.

"The things Kidd did while we were there would be a story in itself. He bullied the other horses and walked around like he was top sergeant himself. When we let them out in the little pasture nearby to graze, all I had to do was to call him at feed time and he and Stud would make a break for the stable where their stalls were. He got to where he would jump the gate, but Stud would run right up to it and stop, and I'd have to go let the bars down. Kidd would go into every stall and get a mouthful of oats out of every one before going to his own. As quick as he sampled the oats out of the others, he went right on to his own stall as though that was one of the regulations.

"It couldn't last long. We got orders to move to Fort McIntosh at Laredo, which was headquarters of the 56th Cavalry Brigade. It was understood that Kidd was to be shipped on to me at McIntosh and I left with the belief that he would soon be there with me. I needed 'im and I didn't want someone to hurt 'im, and I didn't want 'im to hurt somebody.

"After getting down there I watched for 'im every day, but Kidd never came. I knew I was going to Germany and I sure wanted that horse for overseas duty. All I ever could learn about 'im was just a rumor; I don't know if there was any truth in it or not and I never did get it verified. Someone told me that they had to kill 'im because he seriously injured two horseshoers and killed a third. If they had sent 'im on to me it never would have happened. I had built up his confidence and I have always wondered if some son-of-a-gun tore it down. One thing I know: if they mistreated 'im he fought back in the only way he knew how. I've always doubted that rumor. Maybe I didn't want to believe it, for Kidd is one of the most outstanding horses in my memory."

Dancing from a Distance

BUCK BRANNAMAN

One of the most interesting and important horses in my life was named Bif.

He came into my life during the summer of 1988. I was in despair over the ending of my first marriage, and I had been looking for months for ways to save myself. Once I started working with Bif, however, things began to look up. He was an important turning point in my life, and I damn sure was in his.

Because Bif was a dangerous horse to be around—he was lethal with his feet—I had to put so much of myself into working with him, not just to succeed, but to survive. It was hard to figure at the time, but Bif was quite a gift to me, all part of the healing process. He was also a validation of the approach to training horses that I had become associated with.

I named him Bif after Marty McFly's nemesis in *Back to the Future*, a popular movie at the time. The movie Bif was a big, tough, violent sort of person. ("Bif" was also an acronym for "Big Ignorant Fool," something my friends came up with when I started working with the horse.)

Bif had belonged to a horse outfit on the Madison River in Montana, an outfit that had a reputation for raising tough horses, broncs that tended to have problems with people. Rodeo stock contractors who knew about the horses figured anything with that outfit's brand had a pretty good chance of making a good bucking horse, a real draw at rodeos.

41

I was working on the other side of the river at the time, and I had been watching the outfit's cavvy of horses for several weeks. Bif stood out from the bunch. He was a big red thoroughbred-type Quarter Horse, and I knew he had some age on him—he looked to be four, maybe five years old. I needed a good gelding for the clinics I gave, so one day I rode across the Madison for a closer look.

The horse had a head that only a mother could love, and then only with a little effort. I could see he was pretty troubled and pretty scared. And I knew the reason why.

The folks who owned him had their own way to halter-break their horses. They'd put them in tie stalls and manhandle the halters on. This wasn't too hard to do when the horses were babies and were in tie stalls that measured only twelve by twelve feet. Then the horses would be kept tied up and away from food or water, sometimes for long periods of time, so that when they were untied, the young horses would readily lead to the stream to drink.

Even though the people had the best of intentions, the treatment was rough, and what came next was worse. Instead of teaching the horse how to give to pressure, one man would pull on his head as another one whipped him from behind. That's because the people thought the horse would associate getting a drink of water with leading. I don't know which brain trust thought this up, but it lacked a little in the logic department, not to mention how unkind it was.

You can only imagine the wrecks that resulted. Some horses couldn't handle the pressure, and when they'd try to pull away, they'd flip over backward. They'd begin kicking and striking and biting at the rope, with their ears pinned back.

Unfortunately, a lot of people still use this primitive method. They muscle their horses around and give "cowboys" a bad name.

Bif had been "trained" to lead this way. He'd also been branded and castrated during this time. Everything that had been done to him had been negative, and as far as he was concerned, humans were the enemy. But Bif was a survivor. His spirit didn't bend, and so rather than work with him, the horse handlers simply turned him out to pasture for a long period of time. This was a bad move all around. It meant he got to dwell on his negative exposure to humans.

That was the way Bif came back in from pasture when I met him. I could tell that he'd pretty much decided nothing like his past was ever going to happen to him again. But I still liked what I saw, and, after some thought, I bit the bullet and made the deal to buy him. I basically paid what is called "canner price," what the dog-food people would have paid.

The folks in the outfit ran him into a big pen, and I rode in on my saddle horse and roped him. I thought I'd try to lead him into the horse trailer, but at the time I didn't realize just how unhalterbroke he was.

There was a bunch of activity as we were getting the trailer positioned, and I had Bif stopped with the rope around his neck. I needed to check on the truck, so I asked someone in the corral to hold on to Bif. "Don't pull on him at all," I said, "just hold the rope, and keep it from getting down in the manure." The corrals at this outfit were really dirty, and the manure and mud were a couple of feet deep.

As soon as I started to walk away, Bif felt pressure from the rope and flipped over backward four times within about sixty seconds. It was awful. I ran back and got the rope off Bif's head, then urged him into the trailer free, just as you would load a cow.

As I hauled Bif away, I reflected on what a potential idiot I was for getting myself into another "project." I just couldn't have picked a nice easy one. Oh no, I needed to prove something.

When we got home, I chased Bif into an indoor round corral. A round corral is essential to the kind of training I do because there are no corners where a horse can run and hide. A round corral allows a horse to know that there is no place he can go where he can't move forward, no place where he can stop and lose his energy.

Bif stayed down at the west end, walking in and out of shafts of afternoon sunlight. I took a deep breath and walked toward him. Holding the tail of my halter rope, I tossed the halter harmlessly on the ground behind him. I was hoping he'd move his feet and step away, which would be a beginning. That's because a cornered horse instinctively moves his hindquarters toward whatever is threatening his safety. He stops his feet and prepares to kick (some studs will present their front end to be able to bite as well as rear up and strike with their forefeet).

To encourage a horse to overcome this instinct, you must show him that he can move his feet forward without feeling as if he's surrendering any of his defense mechanisms. He must also see that he can turn his head and look behind him with either eye; he needs to see you without feeling that you are going to take his life.

You then want to draw the horse's front quarters toward you. Getting him to turn his head and look at you is the preliminary step to his hindquarters falling away so the front end can come toward you (we call that untracking the hindquarters).

Looking at you is the equivalent of shifting into neutral, presenting himself in such a way that he's exposing his head to possible risk. You've not won him over yet: he's tolerant but not accepting. It's as though the horse still has a pistol, but he's lowering it instead of pointing it at you. In other words, you've climbed a small hill. You haven't climbed the mountain yet, but you've made a good start.

At this point, Bif saw me the same way he saw every other human. He figured I wanted to end his life, and he was going to make sure that didn't happen even if it meant taking mine. So instead of stepping away from the halter, he started kicking at it. Then he started kicking at me. He'd actually run backward at me and fire with both hind feet. This was quite a sight, especially from up close.

He'd kick at me and miss and kick some fence boards out of the corral. After a while there were splintered boards all over the place, like piles of kindling.

I spent the next ninety minutes reeling the halter in, and tossing it back at Bif's hindquarters, trying to encourage him to move his feet forward and not be so defensive. It took that long before I got one single forward step.

After another hour and a half, Bif was taking a few steps forward, then a few more, and it wasn't too long after that before I was driving him around the corral. That's not to say I could walk up to him. When I did, he'd try to paw me on top of the head or kick me. He wasn't a lover quite yet.

When working with a horse, particularly a troubled horse, you'll notice that he will spend a good portion of his time avoiding contact, physical and mental. By causing him to move, and then moving in harmony with him, you will slowly form a connection, as if you're dancing from a distance. Yet the horse may remain quite wary of you. When the distance between you and the horse becomes comfortable to him, you start to draw him in. You do this by moving away as he begins to acknowledge you with his eyes, ears, and concave rib cage (middle of rib cage arched away from you). At this moment you and the horse are "one." The farther you move from him, the closer he moves to you. This is known as "hooking on," and it's an amazing feeling. It's as if there is an invisible thread you're leading the horse with, and there's no chance of breaking it.

Before that first evening was over, after I'd spent about four hours in the corral, I finally did move up to Bif. That's when I was able to get him to "hook on" to me. He'd turn and face me, and then he'd walk toward me with his ears up. We were now making positive physical contact. What I was doing with Bif was similar to what Forrest had done with me on the day we met, the day he gave me the buckskin gloves. He didn't force his friendship on me. He maintained a comfortable distance until I was ready to come to him.

The experience also reminded me how much preparation and ground-work people need in order to give their horses—and themselves—a good foundation. They need to work on using the end of the lead rope to cause the front quarters and the hindquarters of their horses to move independently, whether the horse is moving forward or backward, right or left. The horse needs proper lateral flexion so that he can bend right or left while moving his feet at the same time. Horses need to be able to bend and give and yield, just as experienced dancers are able to bend and yield to their partner's lead.

Working a horse on the end of a lead rope, you may see tightness or trepidation when you ask him to move a certain way or at a certain speed or when using his front or hindquarters. Whenever you see it, you home in on that area until the horse becomes comfortable. Then you move on to something else. Just as important, through the directional movement that you put into the end of the lead rope, you can show the horse that he can let down his defenses, that he can move without feeling troubled, without feeling that he needs to flee. Rather than leave you, he can go with you, and both of you can dance the dance. Sometimes the music plays fast, sometimes it plays slow, but you must always dance together.

As long as I did it in a way that was fitting to Bif—that is, very, very carefully—I could touch him and rub him. One little wrong move on my part, and he'd have pawed my head off or kicked me in the belly. But I had to touch him, because that established the vital physical and emotional connection between horse and human. I rubbed him with my hand and with my coiled rope along his neck, rubbing him affectionately, the way horses nuzzle each other out in a pasture and especially the reassuring, maternal way a mare bonds with her foal.

I also rubbed Bif with my rope and my hands along his back and his flanks. That not only felt good to him, but it introduced him to the pressure he would feel when the saddle was on and the cinch was tightened.

When I got Bif saddled later that night, he put on a bucking demonstration like you've never seen. The stirrups were hitting together over his back with every jump. Watching him, I knew that if he bucked with me on his back, there was no way in the world I would ever be able to ride him, so I didn't even try. I just tried to get him a little bit more comfortable with a saddle on his back, then I unsaddled him and put him up. We ended on a good note, and I wanted him to sleep on it.

I was awake all night trying to figure out how I could help this horse. The next day I repeated the process. Bif was still very defensive, but we gained ground more quickly, to the point where I could step up on him and ride.

Bif never did buck with me. On the ground, he was one of the most treacherous horses I've ever been around, but it was because that bunch of hairy-chested macho cowboys got him started off on the wrong foot. With horses, as with people, you get only one opportunity to make a good first impression, and they missed theirs.

For the next couple of years I hauled Bif to my clinics, but I had to make sure people didn't get near my horse trailer. He'd have kicked or struck them before they knew they were within his range. Even if I was sitting on him, people had to keep their distance. Bif was sure of me, but he wasn't sure of anybody else. I could ride him, but that didn't mean he was gentle.

But for all that, whenever I'd leave Bif alone or in an unfamiliar setting, he'd whinny for me. Not the way a horse anticipates or asks for his feed or a treat, but the way an anxious horse calls out to its herd, its source of safety. Bif just didn't want to be without me. He'd always nicker, and it became a special thing between us.

Miles together can change things, and in time Bif got a lot better around people. Now, roughly ten years later, he's so gentle you'd never know that he had the kind of past he had. Bif's pretty much retired. I use him on the ranch once in a while, and sometimes my little five-year-old daughter, Reata, and I take him for a ride. He's had a good life, and he'll always have a home with me. He's got a heart the size of all outdoors.

I'll never be able to repay Bif for what he's taught me about working with horses. He represents a lot of horses and people, too, who simply got a bad deal at the start. He proves to me that you don't give up, and that even if you're going through something that makes you think your life is over, you can still have a future.

Mustangs

Tracks

ZANE GREY

The Stewart brothers were wild-horse hunters for the sake of trades and occasional sales. But Lin Slone never traded nor sold a horse he had captured. The excitement of the game, and the lure of the desert, and the love of a horse were what kept him at the profitless work. His type was rare in the uplands.

These were the early days of the settlement of Utah, and only a few of the hardiest and most adventurous pioneers had penetrated the desert in the southern part of that vast upland. And with them came some of that wild breed of riders to which Slone and the Stewarts belonged. Horses were really more important and necessary than men; and this singular fact gave these lonely riders a calling.

Before the Spaniards came there were no horses in the West. Those explorers left or lost horses all over the southwest. Many of them were Arabian horses of purest blood. American explorers and travelers, at the outset of the nineteenth century, encountered countless droves of wild horses all over the plains. Across the Grand Cañon, however, wild horses were comparatively few in number in the early days; and these had probably come in by way of California.

The Stewarts and Slone had no established mode of catching wild horses. The game had not developed fast enough for that. Every chase of horse or drove was different; and once in many attempts they met with success.

A favorite method originated by the Stewarts was to find a water-hole frequented by the band of horses or the stallion wanted, and to build round this hole a corral with an opening for the horses to get in. Then the hunters would watch the trap at night, and if the horses went in to drink, a gate was closed across the opening. Another method of the Stewarts was to trail a coveted horse up on a mesa or highland, places which seldom had more than one trail of ascent and descent, and there block the escape, and cut lines of cedars, into which the quarry was run till captured. Still another method, discovered by accident, was to shoot a horse lightly in the neck and sting him. This last, called creasing, was seldom successful, and for that matter in any method ten times as many horses were killed as captured.

Lin Slone helped the Stewarts in their own way, but he had no especial liking for their tricks. Perhaps a few remarkable captures of remarkable horses had spoiled Slone. He was always trying what the brothers claimed to be impossible. He was a fearless rider, but he had the fault of saving his mount, and to kill a wild horse was a tragedy for him. He would much rather have hunted alone, and he had been alone on the trail of the stallion Wildfire when the Stewarts had joined him.

Lin Slone awoke next morning and rolled out of his blanket at his usual early hour. But he was not early enough to say good-by to the Stewarts. They were gone.

The fact surprised him and somehow relieved him. They had left him more than his share of the outfit, and perhaps that was why they had slipped off before dawn. They knew him well enough to know that he would not have accepted it. Besides, perhaps they felt a little humiliation at abandoning a chase which he chose to keep up. Anyway, they were gone, apparently without breakfast.

The morning was clear, cool, with the air dark like that before a storm, and in the east, over the steely wall of stone, shone a redness growing brighter.

Slone turned his attention to the pack of supplies. The Stewarts had divided the flour and the parched corn equally, and unless he was greatly mistaken they had left him most of the coffee and all of the salt.

"Now I hold that decent of Bill an' Abe," said Slone, regretfully. "But I could have got along without it better 'n they could."

Then he swiftly set about kindling a fire and getting a meal. In the midst of his task a sudden ruddy brightness fell around him. Lin Slone paused in his work to look up.

The sun had risen over the eastern wall.

"Ah!" he said, and drew a deep breath.

The cold, steely, darkling sweep of desert had been transformed. It was now a world of red earth and gold rocks and purple sage, with everywhere the endless straggling green cedars. A breeze whipped in, making the fire roar softly. The sun felt warm on his cheek. And at the moment he heard the whistle of his horse.

"Good old Nagger!" he said. "I shore won't have to track you this mornin'."

Presently he went off into the cedars to find Nagger and the mustang that he used to carry a pack. Nagger was grazing in a little open patch among the trees, but the pack-horse was missing. Slone seemed to know in what direction to go to find the trail, for he came upon it very soon. The pack-horse wore hobbles, but he belonged to the class that could cover a great deal of ground when hobbled. Slone did not expect the horse to go far, considering that the grass thereabouts was good. But in a wild-horse country it was not safe to give any horse a chance. The call of his wild brethren was irresistible. Slone, however, found the mustang standing quietly in a clump of cedars, and, removing the hobbles, he mounted and rode back to camp. Nagger caught sight of him and came at his call.

This horse Nagger appeared as unique in his class as Slone was rare among riders. Nagger seemed of several colors, though black predominated. His coat was shaggy, almost woolly, like that of a sheep. He was huge, raw-boned, knotty, long of body and long of leg, with the head of a war charger. His build did not suggest speed. There appeared to be something slow and ponderous about him, similar to an elephant, with the same suggestion of power and endurance.

Slone discarded the pack-saddle and bags. The latter were almost empty. He roped the tarpaulin on the back of the mustang, and, making a small bundle of his few supplies, he tied that to the tarpaulin. His blanket he used for a saddle-blanket on Nagger. Of the utensils left by the Stewarts he chose a couple of small iron pans, with long handles. The rest he left. In his saddle-bags he had a few extra horseshoes, some nails, bullets for his rifle, and a knife with a heavy blade.

"Not a rich outfit for a far country," he mused. Slone did not talk very much, and when he did he addressed Nagger and himself simultaneously. Evidently he expected a long chase, one from which he would not return, and light as his outfit was it would grow too heavy.

Then he mounted and rode down the gradual slope, facing the valley and the black, bold, flat mountain to the southeast. Some few hundred yards from camp he halted Nagger and bent over in the saddle to scrutinize the ground.

The clean-cut track of a horse showed in the bare, hard sand. The hoof-marks were large, almost oval, perfect in shape, and manifestly they were beautiful to Lin Slone. He gazed at them for a long time, and then he looked across the dotted red valley up the vast ridgy steps, toward the black plateau and beyond. Then Slone slipped off the saddle and knelt to scrutinize the horse tracks. A little sand had blown into the depressions, and some of it was wet and some of it was dry. He took his time about examining it, and he even tried gently blowing other sand into the tracks, to compare that with what was already there. Finally he stood up and addressed Nagger.

"Reckon we won't have to argue with Abe an' Bill this mornin'," he said, with satisfaction. "Wildfire made that track yesterday, before sun-up."

Thereupon Slone remounted and put Nagger to a trot. The pack-horse followed with an alacrity that showed he had no desire for loneliness.

As straight as a bee-line Wildfire had left a trail down into the floor of the valley. He had not stopped to graze, and he had not looked for water. Slone had hoped to find a water-hole in one of the deep washes in the red earth, but if there had been any water there Wildfire would have scented it. He had not had a drink for three days that Slone knew of. And Nagger had not drunk for forty hours. Slone had a canvas water-bag hanging over the pommel, but it was a habit of his to deny himself, as far as possible, till his horse could drink also.

It took four hours of steady trotting to reach the middle and bottom of that wide, flat valley. A network of washes cut up the whole center of it, and they were all as dry as bleached bone. To cross these Slone had only to keep Wildfire's trail. And it was proof of Nagger's quality that he did not have to veer from the stallion's course.

It was hot down in the lowland. The heat struck up, reflected from the sand. But it was a March sun, and no more than pleasant to Slone. The wind rose, however, and blew dust and sand in the faces of horse and rider. Except lizards Slone did not see any living things.

Miles of low greasewood and sparse yellow sage led to the first almost imperceptible rise of the valley floor on that side. The distant cedars beckoned to Slone. He was not patient, because he was on the trail of Wildfire; but, nevertheless, the hours seemed short.

Slone had no past to think about, and the future held nothing except a horse, and so his thoughts revolved the possibilities connected with this chase of Wildfire. The chase was hopeless in such country as he was traversing, and if Wildfire chose to roam around valleys like this one Slone would fail utterly. But the stallion had long ago left his band of horses, and then, one by one his favorite consorts, and now he was alone, headed with unerring instinct for wild, untrammeled ranges. He had been used to the pure, cold water and the succulent grass of the cold desert uplands. Assuredly he would not tarry in such barren lands as these.

For Slone an ever-present and growing fascination lay in Wildfire's clear, sharply defined tracks. It was as if every hoof-mark told him something. Once, far up the interminable ascent, he found on a ridge-top tracks showing where Wildfire had halted and turned.

"Ha, Nagger!" cried Slone, exultingly. "Look there! He's begun facin' about. He's wonderin' if we're still after him. He's worried. . . . But we'll keep out of sight—a day behind."

When Slone reached the cedars the sun was low down in the west. He looked back across the fifty miles of valley to the colored cliffs and walls. He seemed to be above them now, and the cool air, with tang of cedar and juniper, strengthened the impression that he had climbed high.

A mile or more ahead of him rose a gray cliff with breaks in it and a line of dark cedars or piñons on the level rims. He believed these breaks to be the mouths of cañons, and so it turned out. Wildfire's trail led into the mouth of a narrow cañon with very steep and high walls. Nagger snorted his perception of water, and the mustang whistled. Wildfire's tracks led to a point under the wall where a spring gushed forth. There were mountain-lion and deer tracks also, as well as those of smaller game.

Slone made camp here. The mustang was tired. But Nagger, upon taking a long drink, rolled in the grass as if he had just begun the trip. After eating, Slone took his rifle and went out to look for deer. But there appeared to be none at hand. He came across many lion tracks and saw, with apprehension, where one had taken Wildfire's trail. Wildfire had grazed up the cañon, keeping on and on, and he was likely to go miles in a night. Slone reflected that as small as were his own chances of getting Wildfire, they were still better than those of a mountain-lion. Wildfire was the most cunning of all animals—a wild stallion; his speed and endurance were incomparable; his scent as keen as those animals that relied wholly upon scent to warn them of danger, and as for sight, it was Slone's belief that no hoofed creature, except the mountain-sheep used to high altitudes, could see as far as a wild horse.

It bothered Slone a little that he was getting into lion country. Nagger showed nervousness, something unusual for him. Slone tied both horses with long halters and stationed them on patches of thick grass. Then he put a cedar stump on the fire and went to sleep. Upon awakening and going to the spring he was somewhat chagrined to see that deer had come down to drink early. Evidently they were numerous.

Slone was packed and saddled and on his way before the sun reddened the cañon wall. He walked the horses. From time to time he saw signs of Wildfire's consistent progress. The cañon narrowed and the walls grew lower and the grass increased. There was a decided ascent all the time. Slone could find no evidence that the cañon had ever been traveled by hunters or Indians. The day was pleasant and warm and still. Every once in a while a little breath of wind would bring a fragrance of cedar and piñon, and a sweet hint of pine and sage. At every turn he looked ahead, expecting to see the green of pine and the gray of sage. Toward the middle of the afternoon, coming to a place where Wildfire had taken to a trot, he put Nagger to that gait, and by sundown had worked up to where the cañon was only a shallow ravine. Soon he was entering a forest where cedars and piñons and pines began to grow thickly.

Slone halted for the night. The air was cold. And the dampness of it gave him an idea there were snowbanks somewhere not far distant. The dew was already heavy on the grass. He hobbled the horses and put a bell on Nagger. A bell might frighten lions that had never heard one. Then he built a fire and cooked his meal.

In the early morning when all was gray and the big, dark pines were shadowy specters, Slone was awakened by the cold. His hands were so numb that he had difficulty starting a fire. He stood over the blaze, warming them. The air was nipping, clear and thin, and sweet with frosty fragrance.

Daylight came while he was in the midst of his morning meal. A white frost covered the ground and crackled under his feet as he went out to bring in the horses. He saw fresh deer tracks. Then he went back to camp for his rifle. Keeping a sharp lookout for game, he continued his search for the horses.

The forest was open and park-like. There were no fallen trees or evidences of fire. Presently he came to a wide glade in the midst of which Nagger and the pack-mustang were grazing with a herd of deer. The size of the latter amazed Slone. The deer he had hunted back on the Sevier range were much smaller than these. Evidently these were mule deer, closely allied to the elk. They were so tame they stood facing him curiously, with long ears erect. It was sheer murder to kill a deer standing and watching like that, but Slone was out of meat and hungry and facing a long, hard trip. He shot a buck, which leaped spasmodically away, trying to follow the herd, and fell at the edge of the glade. Slone cut out a haunch, and then, catching the horses, he returned to camp, where he packed and saddled, and at once rode out on the dim trail.

The wildness of the country he was entering was evident in the fact that as he passed the glade where he had shot the deer a few minutes before, there were coyotes quarreling over the carcass.

Slone could see ahead and on each side several hundred yards, and presently he ascertained that the forest floor was not so level as he had supposed. He had entered a valley or was traversing a wide, gently sloping pass. He went through thickets of juniper, and had to go around clumps of quaking aspen. The pines grew larger and farther apart.

The quiet of the forest thrilled Slone. And the only movement was the occasional gray flash of a deer or coyote across a glade. No birds of any species crossed Slone's sight. He came, presently, upon a lion track in the trail, made probably a day before. Slone grew curious about it, seeing how it held, as he was holding, to Wildfire's tracks. After a mile or so he made sure the lion had been trailing the stallion, and for a second he felt a cold contraction of his heart. Already he loved Wildfire, and by virtue of all his toil of travel considered the wild horse his property.

"No lion could ever get close to Wildfire," he soliloquized, with a short laugh. Of that he was absolutely certain.

The sun rose, melting the frost, and a breath of warm air, laden with the scent of pine, moved heavily under the huge, yellow trees. Slone passed a point where the remains of an old camp-fire and a pile of deer antlers were proof that Indians visited this plateau to hunt. From this camp broader, more deeply defined trails led away to the south and east. Slone kept to the east trail, in which Wildfire's tracks and those of the lion showed clearly. It was about the middle of the forenoon when the tracks of the stallion and lion left the trail to lead up a little draw where grass grew thick. Slone followed, reading the signs of Wildfire's progress, and the action of his pursuer, as well as if he had seen them. Here the stallion had plowed into a snow-bank, eating a hole two feet deep; then he had grazed around a little; then on and on; there his splendid tracks were deep in the soft earth. Slone knew what to expect when the track of the lion veered from those of the horse, and he followed the lion tracks. The ground was soft from the late melting of snow, and Nagger sunk deep. The lion left a plain track. Here he stole steadily along; there he left many tracks at a point where he might have halted to make sure of his scent. He was circling on the trail of the stallion, with cunning intent of ambush. The end of this slow, careful stalk of the lion, as told in his tracks, came upon the edge of a knoll where he had crouched to watch and wait. From this perch he had made a magnificent spring—Slone estimating it to be forty feet—but he had missed the stallion. There were Wildfire's tracks again, slow and short, and then deep and sharp where in the impetus of fright he had sprung out of reach. A second leap of the lion, and then lessening bounds, and finally an abrupt turn from Wildfire's trail told the futility of that stalk. Slone made certain that Wildfire was so keen that as he grazed along, he had kept to open ground.

Wildfire had run for a mile, then slowed down to a trot, and he had circled to get back to the trail he had left. Slone believed the horse was just so intelligent. At any rate, Wildfire struck the trail again, and turned at right angles to follow it.

Here the forest floor appeared perfectly level. Patches of snow became frequent, and larger as Slone went on. At length the patches closed up, and soon extended as far as he could see. It was soft, affording difficult travel. Slone crossed hundreds of deer tracks, and the trail he was on eventually became a deer runway.

Presently, far down one of the aisles between the great pines Slone saw what appeared to be a yellow cliff, far away. It puzzled him. And as he went on he received the impression that the forest dropped out of sight ahead. Then the trees grew thicker, obstructing his view. Presently the trail became soggy and he had to help his horse. The mustang floundered in the soft snow and earth. Cedars and piñons appeared again, making travel still more laborious.

All at once there came to Slone a strange consciousness of light and wind and space and void. On the instant his horse halted with a snort. Slone quickly looked up. Had he come to the end of the world? An abyss, a cañon, yawned beneath him, beyond all comparison in its greatness. His keen eye, educated to desert distance and dimension, swept down and across, taking in the tremendous truth, before it staggered his comprehension. But a second sweeping glance, slower, becoming intoxicated with what it beheld, saw gigantic cliff-steps and yellow slopes dotted with cedars, leading down to clefts filled with purple smoke, and these led on and on to a ragged red world of rock, bare, shining, bold, uplifted in mesa, dome, peak, and crag, clear and strange in the morning light, still and sleeping like death.

This, then, was the great cañon, which had seemed like a hunter's fable rather than truth.

It was the horse hunter's passion that reminded him of his pursuit. The deer trail led down through a break in the wall. Only a few rods of it could be seen. This trail was passable, even though choked with snow. But the depth beyond this wall seemed to fascinate Slone and hold him back, used as he was to desert trails. Then the clean mark of Wildfire's hoof brought back the old thrill.

"This place fits you, Wildfire," muttered Slone, dismounting.

He started down, leading Nagger. The mustang followed. Slone kept to the wall side of the trail, fearing the horses might slip. The snow held firmly at first and Slone had no trouble. The gap in the rim-rock widened to a slope thickly grown over with cedars and piñons and manzanita. The growth made the descent more laborious, yet afforded means at least for Slone to go down with less danger. There was no stopping. Once started, the horses had to keep on. Slone saw the impossibility of ever climbing out while that snow was there. The trail zigzagged down and down. Very soon the yellow wall hung tremendously over him, straight up. The snow became thinner and softer. The horses began to slip. They slid on their haunches. Fortunately the slope grew less steep, and Slone could see below where it reached out to comparatively level ground. Still, a mishap might yet occur. Slone kept as close to Nagger as possible, helping him whenever he could do it. The mustang slipped, rolled over, and then slipped past Slone, went down the slope to bring up in a cedar. Slone worked down to him and extricated him. Then the huge Nagger began to slide. Snow and loose rock slid with him, and so did Slone. The little avalanche stopped of its own accord, and then Slone dragged Nagger on down and down, presently to come to the end of the steep descent. Slone looked up to see that he had made short work of a thousand-foot slope. Here cedars and piñons grew thickly enough to make a forest. The snow thinned out to patches, and then failed. But the going remained bad for a while as the horses sank deep in soft red earth. This eventually grew more solid and finally dry. Slone worked out of the cedars to what appeared a grassy plateau inclosed by the great green-and-white slope with its yellow wall overhanging, and distant mesas and cliffs. He could look down to see the bare, worn rock, and a hundred yards from where he stood the earth was washed from its rims and it began to show depth and something of that ragged outline which told of violence of flood. Then he went down again, this time to come to a clear brook lined with willows. Here the horses drank long and Slone refreshed himself. The sun had grown hot. There was fragrance of flowers he could not see and a low murmur of a waterfall that was likewise invisible. For most of the time his view was shut off, but occasionally he reached a point where through some break he saw towers gleaming red in the sun. Toward the waning of the afternoon he began to climb to what appeared to be a saddle of land, connecting the cañon wall on the left with a great plateau, gold-rimmed and pine-fringed, rising more and more in his way as he advanced. At sunset Slone was more shut in than for several hours. He could tell the time was sunset by the golden light on the cliff wall again overhanging him. The slope was gradual up to this pass to the saddle, and upon coming to a spring, and the first pine-trees, he decided to halt for camp. The mustang was almost exhausted.

Thereupon he hobbled the horses in the luxuriant grass round the spring, and then unrolled his pack. Once as dusk came stealing down, while he was eating his meal, Nagger whistled in fright. Slone saw a gray, pantherish form gliding into the shadows. He took a quick shot at it, but missed.

"It's lion country, all right," he said. And then he set about building a big fire on the other side of the grassy plot, so to have the horses between fires. He cut all the venison into thin strips, and spent an hour roasting them. Then he lay down to rest, and he said: "Wonder where Wildfire is to-night? Am I closer to him? Where's he headin' for?"

In the gray dawn he arose refreshed. The horses were restive. Nagger snorted a welcome. Evidently they had passed an uneasy night. Slone found lion tracks at the spring and in sandy places. Presently he was on his way up to the notch between the great wall and the plateau. A growth of thick scrub-oak made travel difficult. It had not appeared far up to that saddle, but it was far. There were straggling pine-trees and huge rocks that obstructed his gaze. But once up he saw that the saddle was only a narrow ridge, curved to slope up on both sides.

The stretch of broken plateau before him grew wilder and bolder of outline, darker in color, weirder in aspect, and progress across it grew slower, more dangerous. There were many places Nagger should not have been put to—where a slip meant a broken leg. But Slone could not turn back. And something besides an indomitable spirit kept him going. Again the sound resembling thunder assailed his ears, louder this time. The plateau appeared to be ending in a series of great capes or promontories. Slone feared he would soon come out upon a promontory from which he might see the impossibility of further travel.

Four hours of turning and twisting, endlessly down and down, over boulders and banks and every conceivable roughness of earth and rock, finished the pack-mustang; and Slone mercifully left him in a long reach of cañon where grass and water never failed. In this place Slone halted for the noon hour, letting Nagger have his fill of the rich grazing. Nagger's three days in grassy upland, despite the continuous travel by day, had improved him. He looked fat, and Slone had not yet caught the horse resting. Nagger was iron to endure. Here Slone left all the outfit except what was on his saddle, and the sack containing the few pounds of meat and supplies, and the two utensils. This sack he tied on the back of his saddle, and resumed his journey.

He felt relieved down in the gullies, where he could not see far. He climbed out of one, presently, from which there extended a narrow ledge with a slant too perilous for any horse. He stepped out upon that with far less confidence than Nagger. To the right was a bulge of low wall, and a few feet to the left a dark precipice. The trail here was faintly outlined, and it was six inches wide and slanting as well. It seemed endless to Slone, that ledge. He looked only down at his feet and listened to Nagger's steps. The big horse trod carefully, but naturally, and he did not slip. That ledge extended in a long curve, turning slowly away from the precipice, and ascending a little at the further end. Slone drew a deep breath of relief when he led Nagger up on level rock.

Suddenly a strange yet familiar sound halted Slone, as if he had been struck. The wild, shrill, high-pitched, piercing whistle of a stallion! Nagger neighed a blast in reply and pounded the rock with his iron-shod hoofs. With a thrill Slone looked ahead.

There, some few hundred yards distant, on a promontory, stood a red horse.

"My Lord! . . . It's Wildfire!" breathed Slone, tensely.

He could not believe his sight. He imagined he was dreaming. But as Nagger stamped and snorted defiance Slone looked with fixed and keen gaze, and knew that beautiful picture was no lie.

Wildfire was as red as fire. His long mane, wild in the wind, was like a whipping, black-streaked flame. Silhouetted there against that cañon background he seemed gigantic, a demon horse, ready to plunge into fiery depths. He was looking back over his shoulder, his head very high, and every line of him was instinct with wildness. Again he sent out that shrill, air-splitting whistle. Then Wildfire plunged, apparently down, and vanished from Slone's sight.

A Half-Wild Horse and A Wild One

JAMES GALVIN

Hunched over on the tall kitchen stool with his head lowered, Mike listened to the telephone. He covered his eyes with his free hand and shook his head. "OK," he said, and "OK." It was Oscar on the phone, and he wanted to go over to the desert mesas and run wild horses.

Mike had mixed feelings about getting involved in Oscar's day. First there was Oscar's absolute lack of any instinct for self-preservation. He set a scary standard. And when it came to hours, he was out of the house by six and rarely home by ten. He lived on peanut butter sandwiches and Instant Breakfast. But Mike wanted to ride after wild horses, too.

The morning they'd agreed on dawned crisp and fine. Mike loaded Potatoes Browning into the trailer and drove up to Oscar's. Mike was surprised when he pulled into Oscar's yard. He was expecting to see Oscar's rope horse saddled and ready to load. It could be a long day. Instead it was just Oscar, who threw his saddle into the back of the pickup and said, "Let's go."

Mike almost said, Aren't you forgetting something? But didn't.

Oscar had a plan to catch the wave of fashion for paint horses without any cash outlay. Instead of buying a stud, he planned to capture a wild stallion and pasture-breed him to some good quarter horse brood mares.

The mares would be tame, so, once foaled out, he'd be able to bring the colts in and gentle them with the rest of his young horses. People who liked the idea of a paint, he figured, would love the idea of a wild sire for their pets.

Plus, it would give everyone something to talk about. "That Oscar." He never meant to break the stud horse—that is, probably not.

Finally Mike said, as he shifted into third, "You figure on just walking up to one of those mustangs and throw your saddle on him? Maybe you should have worn your sneakers."

"No, I'll just ride one of old Ronnie's ranch horses they aren't using."

Mike pushed back his sorry black hat and rubbed his forehead. He knew there was more.

"Yeah, there's this one horse hasn't been ridden for a while. Got some real good speed on him."

"How long has it been since anybody rode him?"

"Oh, couple of years."

Mike stared. "How come they don't ride him?"

"Oh, he bucks a little when you first get on him. But, man, is he fast. By now I reckon he's about half wild. Get two jobs done at once. And besides"—he looked at Mike—"what better way to catch a wild horse than with one that's half wild?" He grinned.

Mike sighed. "I guess."

They pulled into a big open pasture. Oscar held the gate. There were seven horses in the middle of a three-hundred-acre field, watching them tensely. There was no corral to run them into. The ground was boggy in places.

"It's that big gray gelding."

"Can you catch him with grain?"

"It'd be worth a try."

"Did you bring any grain?"

"Nope. Drive over there and pull your rig in next to the corner of the fence and make sort of a pen. Then unload your horse."

Mike pulled in and cut the motor. He got out.

Oscar took the lariat off his saddle and said, "OK. You got the horse. I'll wait here."

Mike thought he was getting set up. He just wasn't quite sure how yet. He said under his breath, "We all spend the day somehow."

He rode out in a big circle around the horses, then diagonaled toward them to ease them near the trailer. They stood their ground until he was close. The gray gelding snorted, and they all bolted and ran curving away.

Putting the steel to his horse, Mike took a line to cut them off at the fence. The seven horses blasted down the fence line and Potatoes raced to cut them off, which he managed, with a sliding stop to the fence. His chest was pushing against the wires when he stopped, and the rasty bunch reversed to the right direction, but way too fast.

Mike spun and quartered across the corner of the fence. Sure enough, they swerved away from the trailer, gray in the lead, and when they did, Mike turned them on the other fence.

Winded, they trotted toward the corner. When Mike saw Oscar's big grin—he was leaning against the trailer with the rope—he knew the game wasn't over.

He was bringing them down the fence line nicely, nearing the trailer, when the gray rolled back on his haunches, causing all the other to do the same. They came right over him, parting around him like a wave. He made a move on the gray but it was late.

The only thing to do with broomtails like these was wear them down, which he proceeded to do. After half an hour of running them up and down the fence line they quit. Mike walked them into the three-sided trap the horse trailer made in the corner. Oscar walked in behind them to hold them there, and they began to prance and mill nervously.

Then the gray ran right at Oscar and never shied when Oscar raised his arms to shoo him. The gray ran over him, knocking Oscar to the ground. Mike wasn't there to turn him, but they held the other horses till they calmed.

Mike went back after the gray. This time he came in easily because the others were there, and horses hate to be alone. As he passed Oscar to join his buddies, and before he could think up more mischief, Oscar threw a loop over his head and he froze.

Oscar started talking to him and easing up to him along the riata. The horse was a statue wired to explode. Oscar talked and scratched the horse's forehead. He kept talking as he eased his arm over the horse's neck and haltered him. He led him to the other side of the trailer and tied him to it. He ran his hand down the gray's neck and scratched behind his ears. They turned the other horses back into the pasture.

It could have been any horse any day of the year, the way Oscar threw the saddle on him. Oscar said, "We'd just as well ride from here," and gave the cinch an extra pull since he knew the horse was going to buck.

Mike sat Potatoes Browning and watched as Oscar bridled the gray horse and dropped the halter, leaving it hanging by the lead from the trailer. Holding the horse by the reins, he stepped over to the cab of the pickup and emptied his pockets of several small note pads and pens. He took his wallet out and slid it under the seat.

He flipped the off rein over the horse's neck, swung up, and quickly found the stirrup. He stayed ready. He knew what was coming. He nudged the horse, and both riders stepped smartly into the pasture. Mike was waiting for the explosion too.

Something passed between the two horses, an invisible communication, a threat, and Potatoes Browning shied and doubled under. Mike hadn't been expecting anything from his horse. He hit the ground hard and stood up, astonished.

Oscar started to chuckle, then laugh, then howl uncontrollably. He folded over in his saddle. The gray hadn't done anything. Then he did something so unusual, if it hadn't been witnessed it would never be believed.

As Mike described it, the horse kind of sucked himself in and kicked into something like a backward buck. Then Oscar was sitting on the ground, but he was still in the saddle. Stranger, he was still holding the reins in his hand and the bridle lay on the ground in front of him, like he was still riding but lacked the horse.

At first he thought the cinch had broken, but when he picked up the saddle and looked, the cinch was still cinched. And he was holding the reins. The horse had sucked himself out of the saddle, and the saddle going over his head had raked the bridle off.

The gray horse was running across the pasture to join the others where they grazed. They looked up, unimpressed.

Both men sat down where they were. Mike said, "At least my reins are attached to a horse."

Oscar said, "That would have made a good story, only no one would believe it."

"Isn't there some other way we could have done this?"

"Oh, yeah," Oscar replied. "There's lots of things we could have done, but compared to what we did, all of them are boring."

In the fifties, people started to acknowledge the wild horse problem. Without natural predators the wild herds were proliferating into thousands. They were mostly grazing unfenced on remote and poor public lands, running the grass down, eroding drainages, and threatening the livelihoods of ranchers by making the pasture useless for stock growing. That, and they were starving.

Catching wild horses had been a popular pastime among nervy horsemen, ever since there were wild horses. In the fifties and sixties, when they weren't running horses for sport or catching them to break, they'd round up and corral them by the hundreds and ship them off for dog food and glue.

As an idea, horses for dog food is not attractive to anyone in America. It was seen as a necessity. Sometimes, outside of necessity, there isn't much.

Oscar's family never had wild horses on their land, but there were herds nearby. When Oscar was little, his father and his uncle ignored the pleas of wives and daughters and went off together to rope wild horses.

Occasionally they'd bring one home to break and sell for a saddle horse, but the success rate and the profits on that deal never justified the time it took, so they had to call it a sport. Usually they'd just rope them and let them go. They lost a good many ropes on horses that plain wouldn't stop. Once they couldn't find any horses, so Oscar's uncle roped an elk. Wisely, he didn't try to dally. He just blew his riata a kiss.

Oscar was twelve when the two brothers first let him tag along on a wild horse chase. They located a herd on a mesa of rabbitbrush and deadfall from an ancient forest fire.

Oscar picked out a two-year-old and played his horse out, running around throwing loops at it. When he finally gave it up he didn't see where his father and uncle had gone. He crossed an arroyo and rode into an area that was like a natural corral of rocks. Wow! he thought. This would be the place to catch them.

He figured his uncle was a jump ahead when he saw him out in the middle of the rock enclosure, squatted down, with his back against a stump. He had his head down like he was rolling a cigarette. His horse was grazing peacefully nearby. And there was a wild horse, a white stallion like a pure Andalusian, roped and snubbed to the stump, still pulling back hard, his haunches rared under him, shaking his head like a hooked marlin.

"Yippee!" yelled Oscar, and loped up to where his uncle was calmly wait-ing for the stallion to choke himself into submission, waiting for Frank to come help hobble him and maybe take him home. Oscar never forgot the beauty of that white horse.

It wasn't until he was about ten feet away that he registered the numb stillness, not napping, not rolling a smoke, that shadowed his father's brother's face.

He saw the three coils of rope that were holding his uncle up in sitting position. One around his bent knees, one holding his upper arms tight against his sides, one around his broken neck.

The stallion had Oscar's uncle wound up like a gossamered fly, and he wasn't laying back on the rope to get away.

Oscar stood there dumb until his father rode up and cut the wild horse free.

So the next time Oscar and Mike got a free day they decided to chase mus-tangs. Mike made Oscar promise to bring a horse. They were unloading be-fore the sun came up over the mesa, which loomed like a sundered ocean liner.

Both horses were tense and prancing as they started up the red trail through the scrub. They could sense from their riders, in that horse-wise way, that this was no ordinary day of working and roping cows.

The men picked up fresh sign at a spring that wept out of the red side of the mesa and followed uphill through heavy brush and big red sandstone boulders. On steep pitches the horses' feet slipped in the scree, and their shoes sparked.

As they lunged and humped up the slope, Oscar riding behind, he told the story of how his uncle got himself hanged by a mustang. He still couldn't be exactly sure of what happened, but he wondered if the whole thing had been a trap, if a horse could have enough guile and meanness to lure a rider into what seemed like an easy place to catch him, then pull some premeditated whammy like that, and, if so, could he teach other horses the same trick or like ones. In any case, the long and small of the grisly tale was *pay attention.*

Oscar talked about what kind of horse they wanted: a big skewbald stal-lion with a lot of rear end, a thin neck, not too big of a head or too small of a tail, as one associated with Appaloosa stock.

They followed the tracks of unshod horses up a well-rutted trail, but they soon noticed there were as many tracks coming back down the trail as there were tracks ascending. It wasn't making sense. They decided to split up, Mike continuing upward, Oscar forking off to the top of the mesa directly to get a better overview.

They determined to meet at the rock corral in three hours. Neither carried a watch. Oscar rode for over two hours without seeing anything but deer, coyotes, eagles, and desert flora without end.

He was easing his horse down a steep rock slab above a three-hundred-foot drop. He took his feet out of the stirrups completely, half expecting the horse to lose his footing and disappear over the edge.

Then the ground got even worse. He worked along a narrow ledge that got narrower and narrower, then quit. There was no way to turn around, and backing the horse would have been double suicide. Oscar muttered, "Story of my life." Then he mentioned to the horse, whose ears were rotating like radar scanners, "Well, Spook, at least it ain't boring. You wouldn't want to be bored, would you?"

The only thing that suggested itself to do was to jump over a four-foot void to where the ledge picked up again and widened. It didn't look like a good idea, but it was the only one handy.

Oscar decided the idea was weak enough to need a backup idea, so he shook out one of the two lariats he was carrying, and lofted the straight end over a point of rock about ten feet above and three feet in front of him. He cinched the loop end over his saddle horn and held the loose end in his right hand.

Spook was less than enthusiastic about the leap. Oscar collected him and asked. Spook backed and pranced a bit, then squatted down and sprang. Oscar let the slack run out, and the horse gained the far ledge. The footing was treacherous, though, and once over he began to slip and scrabble. That's when Oscar dallied and held on till the horse got his feet under him and stood.

Oscar unwound his dally and pulled his rope off the spike of rock. He loosened the locked loop from his saddle horn and patted his horse on the neck. He exhaled a long breath, realizing he never remembered inhaling.

He re-coiled his rope as the horse stepped carefully along the resurrected ledge. The ledge ended and the slope eased, and he lunged his horse to the top of the pitch.

When he came over the top he saw them: twenty or so mustangs full tilt, manes and tails assuming the wind. Behind them a great ruckus of dust in which Mike disappeared and reappeared. Potatoes Browning, nose out, ears back, gaining.

Oscar spurred his horse, half galloping, half backpedaling, through the sand repose and off to join the chase.

Mike knew which mustang he wanted, so when various members of the herd swerved into coulees, he let them fall back until his horse had figured out his target.

It was a big paint stallion that looked like it had stamina, not a young horse. Mike knew wild horses don't have the staying power; they aren't the athletes that ranch-worked quarter horses are. Mike figured he could run him out. Indeed, he was closing, though he didn't know Oscar had joined the chase about two hundred yards back.

There were three horses running ahead of Mike now. They passed a row of sandrocks like teeth on his left. The stallion made a hard cut and leapt through a low gap in the geologic maw. Potatoes cut too and almost lost his rider. When Mike got back to the middle of the saddle he saw the rock formation encircled him. He had never seen it, but he knew it was the place Oscar had described, where they were to meet up, where Oscar's uncle had got bamboozled and hanged by a wild horse.

Mike saw the temptation of the old stump and decided to stay in the saddle no matter what.

The skewbald stallion slowed as if unsure what to do next, as if he'd got himself into a trap. He was forcing Mike's hand and Mike knew it. Now or never. Mike swung his loop twice, and by the third time Potatoes Browning was less than a length behind the mustang. An easy throw. The question now was what to do next, since the stallion didn't stop when the loop tightened around his neck; in fact he put on a burst of speed.

Mike made a dally but kept his horse following. Setting up would mean a wreck. They made a full turn inside the fairy ring of rocks. Then the stallion did something astonishing. He made a sliding stop, but before it was complete he doubled to the left and rolled back. Mike saw him charging as he pushed his own horse into the bit. Potatoes shied instinctively and kept the charging horse on his right side, turning to avoid a collision.

He rolled back as the stallion went by, which saved them but had the unfortunate effect of locking Mike's dally. Mike turned loose of his rope but it was too late. He was tied to the wild horse, who had made the same move again and was coming toward them.

Mike would have bailed but he felt the lariat clamp down on his thigh, tying him into the saddle. Potatoes again did the right thing, turning to face the mustang, again with disastrous results. The rope was now encircling Mike's waist, and the two horses were facing each other, hunkering down on their haunches. They were cutting Mike in half.

Then Mike felt the rope go slack and he could breathe. He slipped from the saddle and his horse stood. He saw Spook about thirty feet away, riderless, standing by his dropped reins.

Through the atmosphere of grit and his own grit-blinded eyes, he made out Oscar dropping his knife and building a loop from the rope he held in his left hand.

When the stallion raced past him, making for the opening in the rocks, Oscar wafted out a loop in front of the horse and roped the paint by the front legs, dropping him like a puppet flung to the ground, his momentum carrying him into a flip in an explosion of dust, legs, horsehair, and squeals. The mustang struggled to rise and run, and Oscar jerked him to the ground again. They did that seven times.

Oscar knew how dangerous it was for the horse, to be roped by the front legs at a gallop, but the son of a bitch had upped the ante and now Oscar wanted his ass.

Mike stood staring at the cut end of his own lariat, which was trailing from the stallion's neck. He wasn't quite sure what had happened. Oscar said, "Jump in any time, Mike."

Mike took a second lariat and a long cotton rope from his saddle. They scotch-hobbled the stallion, and he sat down in the dust to rest. Oscar picked up his knife, folded it, and sheathed it. They stood and watched for a good half hour as the stallion exhausted himself, struggling, falling, heaving by turns.

Nobody said anything. Then, when they picked up their horses again, Mike said, "Now what do we do?"

"I was just about to ask you the same thing."

What they did was tie the stallion's nose to his left hind leg so he had to hop with his head down.

Oscar led him with a rope around his neck, dallying and giving him a stretch when he fought. Mike rode behind with a line tied to the cotton rope that hobbled the stallion and kept his head down.

By and by they had an agreement, sort of. They loaded the stallion into the trailer with a steel cable and a come-along.

Mike said, "So now that you've caught this stallion, what will you do with him?"

Oscar said, "Turn him loose with some beautiful brood mares and let him screw his brains out."

The Pacing Mustang

ERNEST THOMPSON SETON

Jo Calone threw down his saddle on the dusty ground, turned his horses loose, and went clanking into the ranch-house.

"Nigh about chuck time?" he asked.

"Seventeen minutes," said the cook glancing at the Waterbury, with the air of a train-starter, though this show of precision had never yet been justified by events.

"How's things on the Perico?" said Jo's pard.

"Hotter'n hinges," said Jo. "Cattle seem O.K.; lots of calves."

"I seen that bunch o' mustangs that waters at Antelope Springs; couple o' colts along; one little dark one, a fair dandy; a born pacer. I run them a mile or two, and he led the bunch, an' never broke his pace. Cut loose, an' pushed them jest for fun, an' darned if I could make him break."

"You didn't have no refreshments along?" said Scarth, incredulously.

"That's all right, Scarth. You had to crawl on our last bet, an' you'll get another chance soon as you're man enough."

"Chuck," shouted the cook, and the subject was dropped. Next day the scene of the roundup was changed, and the mustangs were forgotten.

A year later the same corner of New Mexico was worked over by the roundup, and again the mustang bunch was seen. The dark colt was now a black yearling, with thin, clean legs and glossy flanks; and more than one of the boys saw with his own eyes this oddity—the mustang was a born pacer.

Jo was along, and the idea now struck him that that colt was worth having. To an Easterner this thought may not seem startling or original, but in the West, where an unbroken horse is worth $5, and where an ordinary saddle-horse is worth $15 or $20, the idea of a wild mustang being desirable property does not occur to the average cowboy, for mustangs are hard to catch, and when caught are merely wild animal prisoners, perfectly useless and untamable to the last. Not a few of the cattle-owners make a point of shooting all mustangs at sight, for they are not only useless cumberers of the feeding-grounds, but commonly lead away domestic horses, which soon take to the wild life and are thenceforth lost.

Wild Jo Calone knew a 'bronk right down to the subsoil.' "I never seen a white that wasn't soft, nor a chestnut that wasn't nervous, nor a bay that wasn't good if broke right, nor a black that wasn't hard as nails, an' full of the old Harry."

Since a mustang is worthless vermin, and a black mustang ten times worse than worthless, Jo's pard "didn't see no sense in Jo's wantin' to corral the yearling," as he now seemed intent on doing. But Jo got no chance to try that year.

The roundup circled down to the Canadian River, and back in the fall by the Don Carlos Hills, and Jo saw no more of the Pacer, though he heard of him from many quarters, for the colt, now a vigorous, young horse, rising three, was beginning to be talked of.

Antelope Springs is in the middle of a great level plain. When the water is high it spreads into a small lake with a belt of sedge around it; when it is low there is a wide flat of black mud, glistening white with alkali in places, and the spring a water-hole in the middle. It has no flow or outlet and yet is fairly good water, the only drinking-place for many miles.

This flat, or prairie as it would be called farther north, was the favorite feeding-ground of the Black Stallion, but it was also the pasture of many herds of range horses and cattle. Chiefly interested was the 'L cross F' outfit. Foster, the manager and part owner, was a man of enterprise. He believed it would pay to handle a better class of cattle and horses on the range, and one of his ventures was ten half-blooded mares, tall, clean-limbed, deer-eyed creatures, that made the scrub cow-ponies look like pitiful starvelings of some degenerate and quite different species.

One of these was kept stabled for use, but the nine, after the weaning of their colts, managed to get away and wandered off on the range.

A horse has a fine instinct for the road to the best feed, and the nine mares drifted, of course, to the prairie of Antelope Springs, twenty miles to the southward. And when, later that summer Foster went to round them up, he found the nine indeed, but with them and guarding them with an air of more than mere comradeship was a coal-black stallion, prancing around and rounding up the bunch like an expert, his jet-black coat a vivid contrast to the golden hides of his harem.

The mares were gentle, and would have been easily driven homeward but for a new and unexpected thing. The Black Stallion became greatly aroused. He seemed to inspire them too with his wildness, and flying this way and that way, drove the whole band at full gallop where he would. Away they went, and the little cow-ponies that carried the men were easily left behind.

This was maddening, and both men at last drew their guns and sought a chance to drop that 'blasted stallion.' But no chance came that was not 9 to 1 of dropping one of the mares. A long day of maneuvering made no change. The Pacer, for it was he, kept his family together and disappeared among the southern sandhills. The cattlemen on their jaded ponies set out for home with the poor satisfaction of vowing vengeance for their failure on the superb cause of it.

One of the most aggravating parts of it was that one or two experiences like this would surely make the mares as wild as the Mustang, and there seemed to be no way of saving them from it.

It was December 1893. I was new in the country, and was setting out from the ranch-house on the Pinavetitos, to go with a wagon to the Canadian River. As I was leaving, Foster finished his remark by: "And if you get a chance to draw a bead on that accursed mustang, don't fail to drop him in his tracks."

This was the first I had heard of him, and as I rode along I gathered from Burns, my guide, the history that has been given. I was full of curiosity to see the famous three-year-old, and was not a little disappointed on the second day when we came to the prairie on Antelope Springs and saw no sign of the Pacer or his band.

But on the next day, as we crossed the Alamosa Arroyo, and were rising to the rolling prairie again, Jack Burns, who was riding on ahead, suddenly dropped flat on the neck of his horse, and swung back to me in the wagon, saying:

"Get out your rifle, here's that — stallion."

I seized my rifle, and hurried forward to a view over the prairie ridge. In the hollow below was a band of horses, and there at one end was the Great Black Mustang. He had heard some sound of our approach, and was not unsuspicious of danger. There he stood with head and tail erect, and nostrils wide, an image of horse perfection and beauty, as noble an animal as ever ranged the plains, and the mere notion of turning that magnificent creature into a mass of carrion was horrible. In spite of Jack's exhortation to 'shoot quick,' I delayed, and threw open the breach, whereupon he, always hot and hasty, swore at my slowness, growled, 'Gi' me that gun,' and as he seized it I turned the muzzle up, and *accidentally* the gun went off.

Instantly the herd below was all alarm, the great black leader snorted and neighed and dashed about. And the mares bunched, and away all went in a rumble of hoofs, and a cloud of dust.

The Stallion careered now on this side, now on that, and kept his eye on all and led and drove them far away. As long as I could see I watched, and never once did he break his pace.

Jack made Western remarks about me and my gun, as well as that mustang, but I rejoiced in the Pacer's strength and beauty, and not for all the mares in the bunch would I have harmed his glossy hide.

There are several ways of capturing wild horses. One is by creasing—that is, grazing the animal's nape with a rifle-ball so that he is stunned long enough for hobbling.

"Yes! I seen about a hundred necks broke trying it, but I never seen a mustang creased yet," was Wild Jo's critical remark.

Sometimes, if the shape of the country abets it, the herd can be driven into a corral; sometimes with extra fine mounts they can be run down, but by far the commonest way, paradoxical as it may seem, is to *walk* them down.

The fame of the Stallion that never was known to gallop was spreading. Extraordinary stories were told of his gait, his speed, and his wind, and when old Montgomery of the 'triangle-bar' outfit came out plump at Well's Hotel in Clayton, and in presence of witnesses said he'd give one thousand dollars cash for him safe in a box-car, providing the stories were true, a dozen young cow-punchers were eager to cut loose and win the purse, as soon as present engagements were up. But Wild Jo had had his eye on this very deal for quite a while; there was no time to lose, so ignoring present contracts he rustled all night to raise the necessary equipment for the game.

By straining his already overstrained credit, and taxing the already over-taxed generosity of his friends, he got together an expedition consisting of twenty good saddle-horses, a mess-wagon, and a fortnight's stuff for three men—himself, his 'pard,' Charley, and the cook.

Then they set out from Clayton, with the avowed intention of walking down the wonderfully swift wild horse. The third day they arrived at Antelope Springs, and as it was about noon they were not surprised to see the black Pacer marching down to drink with all his band behind him. Jo kept out of sight until the wild horses each and all had drunk their fill, for a thirsty ani-mal always travels better than one laden with water.

Jo then rode quietly forward. The Pacer took alarm at half a mile, and led his band away out of sight on the soapweed mesa to the southeast. Jo fol-lowed at a gallop till he once more sighted them, then came back and in-structed the cook, who was also teamster, to make for Alamosa Arroyo in the south. Then away to the southeast he went after the mustangs. After a mile or two he once more sighted them, and walked his horse quietly till so near that they again took alarm and circled away to the south. An hour's trot, not on the trail, but cutting across to where they ought to go, brought Jo again in close sight. Again he walked quietly toward the herd, and again there was the alarm and flight. And so they passed the afternoon, but circled ever more and more to the south, so that when the sun was low they were, as Jo had expected, not far from Alamosa Arroyo. The band was again close at hand, and Jo, after starting them off, rode to the wagon, while his pard, who had been taking it easy, took up the slow chase on a fresh horse.

After supper the wagon moved on to the upper ford of the Alamosa, as arranged, and there camped for the night.

Meanwhile, Charley followed the herd. They had not run so far as at first, for their pursuer made no sign of attack, and they were getting used to his company. They were more easily found, as the shadows fell, on account of a snow-white mare that was in the bunch. A young moon in the sky now gave some help, and relying on his horse to choose the path, Charley kept him quietly walking after the herd, represented by that ghost-white mare, till they were lost in the night. He then got off, unsaddled and picketed his horse, and in his blanket quickly went to sleep.

At the first streak of dawn he was up, and within a short half-mile, thanks to the snowy mare, he found the band. At his approach, the shrill neigh of the Pacer bugled his troop into a flying squad. But on the first mesa they stopped, and faced about to see what this persistent follower was, and what he wanted. For a moment or so they stood against the sky to gaze, and then deciding that he knew him as well as he wished to, that black meteor flung his mane on the wind, and led off at his tireless, even swing, while the mares came streaming after.

Away they went, circling now to the west, and after several repetitions of this same play, flying, following, and overtaking, and flying again, they passed, near noon, the old Apache look-out, Buffalo Bluff. And here, on watch, was Jo. A long thin column of smoke told Charley to come to camp, and with a flashing pocket-mirror he made response.

Jo, freshly mounted, rode across, and again took up the chase, and back came Charley to camp to eat and rest, and then move on upstream.

All that day Jo followed, and managed, when it was needed, that the herd should keep the great circle, of which the wagon cut a small chord. At sundown he came to Verde Crossing, and there was Charley with a fresh horse and food, and Jo went on in the same calm, dogged way. All the evening he followed, and far into the night, for the wild herd was now getting somewhat used to the presence of the harmless strangers, and were more easily followed; moreover, they were tiring out with perpetual traveling. They were no longer in the good grass country, they were not grain-fed like the horses on their track, and above all, the slight but continuous nervous tension was surely telling. It spoiled their appetites, but made them very thirsty. They were allowed, and as far as possible encouraged, to drink deeply at every chance. The effect of large quantities of water on a running animal is well known; it tends to stiffen the limbs and spoil the wind. Jo carefully guarded his own horse against such excess, and both he and his horse were fresh when they camped that night on the trail of the jaded mustangs.

At dawn he found them easily close at hand, and though they ran at first they did not go far before they dropped into a walk. The battle seemed nearly won now, for the chief difficulty in the 'walk-down' is to keep track of the herd the first two or three days when they are fresh.

All that morning Jo kept in sight, generally in close sight, of the band. About ten o'clock, Charley relieved him near José Peak and that day the mustangs walked only a quarter of a mile ahead with much less spirit than the day before and circled now more north again. At night Charley was supplied with a fresh horse and followed as before.

Next day the mustangs walked with heads held low, and in spite of the efforts of the Black Pacer at times they were less than a hundred yards ahead of their pursuer.

The fourth and fifth days passed the same way, and now the herd was nearly back to Antelope Springs. So far all had come out as expected. The chase had been in a great circle with the wagon following a lesser circle. The wild herd was back to its starting-point, worn out; and the hunters were back, fresh and on fresh horses. The herd was kept from drinking till late in the afternoon and then driven to the Springs to swell themselves with a perfect water gorge. Now was the chance for the skilful ropers on the grain-fed horses to close in, for the sudden heavy drink was ruination, almost paralysis, of wind and limb, and it would be easy to rope and hobble them one by one.

There was only one weak spot in the program, the Black Stallion, the cause of the hunt, seemed made of iron, that ceaseless swinging pace seemed as swift and vigorous now as on the morning when the chase began. Up and down he went rounding up the herd and urging them on by voice and example to escape. But they were played out. The old white mare that had been such help in sighting them at night, had dropped out hours ago, dead beat. The half-bloods seemed to be losing all fear of the horsemen, the band was clearly in Jo's power. But the one who was the prize of all the hunt seemed just as far as ever out of reach.

Here was a puzzle. Jo's comrades knew him well and would not have been surprised to see him in a sudden rage attempt to shoot the Stallion down. But Jo had no such mind. During that long week of following he had watched the horse all day at speed and never once had he seen him gallop.

The horseman's adoration of a noble horse had grown and grown, till now he would as soon have thought of shooting his best mount as firing on that splendid beast.

Jo even asked himself whether he would take the handsome sum that was offered for the prize. Such an animal would be a fortune in himself to sire a race of pacers for the track.

But the prize was still at large—the time had come to finish up the hunt. Jo's finest mount was caught. She was a mare of Eastern blood, but raised on the plains. She never would have come into Jo's possession but for a curious weakness. The loco is a poisonous weed that grows in these regions. Most stock will not touch it; but sometimes an animal tries it and becomes addicted to it. It acts somewhat like morphine, but the animal, though sane for long intervals, has always a passion for the herb and finally dies mad. A beast with the craze is said to be "locoed." And Jo's best mount had a wild gleam in her eye that to an expert told the tale.

But she was swift and strong and Jo chose her for the grand finish of the chase. It would have been an easy matter now to rope the mares, but was no longer necessary. They could be separated from their black leader and driven home to the corral. But that leader still had the look of untamed strength. Jo, rejoicing in a worthy foe, went bounding forth to try the odds. The lasso was flung on the ground and trailed to take out every kink, and gathered as he rode into neatest coils across his left palm. Then putting on the spur the first time in that chase he rode straight for the Stallion a quarter of a mile beyond. Away he went, and away went Jo, each at his best, while the fagged-out mares scattered right and left and let them pass. Straight across the open plain the fresh horse went at his hardest gallop, and the Stallion, leading off, still kept his start and kept his famous swing.

It was incredible, and Jo put on more spur and shouted to his horse, which fairly flew, but shortened up the space between by not a single inch. For the Black One whirled across the flat and up and passed a soapweed mesa and down across a sandy treacherous plain, then over a grassy stretch where prairie dogs barked, then his below, and on came Jo, but there to see, could he believe his eyes, the Stallion's start grown longer still, and Jo began to curse his luck, and urge and spur his horse until the poor uncertain brute got into such a state of nervous fright, her eyes began to roll, she wildly shook her head from side to side, no longer picked her ground—a badger-hole received her foot and down she went, and Jo went flying to the earth. Though badly bruised, he gained his feet and tried to mount his crazy beast. But she was done for—her off fore-leg hung loose.

There was but one thing to do. Jo loosed the cinch, put Lightfoot out of pain, and carried back the saddle to the camp. While the Pacer steamed away till lost to view.

This was not quite defeat, for all the mares were manageable now, and Jo and Charley drove them carefully to the 'L cross F' corral and claimed a good reward. But Jo was more than ever bound to own the Stallion. He had seen what stuff he was made of, he prized him more and more, and only sought to strike some better plan to catch him.

Wild Jo never lacked energy. He meant to catch that Mustang, and when he learned that others were bestirring themselves for the same purpose he at once set about trying the best untried plan he knew—the plan by which the coyote catches the fleeter jackrabbit, and the mounted Indian the far swifter antelope—the old plan of the relay chase.

The Canadian River on the south, its affluent, the Piñavetitos Arroyo, on the northeast, and the Don Carlos Hills with the Ute Creek Cañon on the west, formed a sixty-mile triangle that was the range of the Pacer. It was believed that he never went outside this, and at all times Antelope Springs was his headquarters. Jo knew this country well, all the water-holes and cañon crossings as well as the ways of the Pacer.

If he could have gotten fifty good horses he could have posted them to advantage so as to cover all points, but twenty mounts and five good riders were all that proved available.

The horses, grain-fed for two weeks before, were sent on ahead; each man was instructed now to play his part and sent out to his post the day before the race. On the day of the start Jo with his wagon drove to the plain of Antelope Springs and, camping far off in a little draw, waited.

At last he came, that coal-black Horse, out from the sand-hills at the south, alone as always now, and walked calmly down to the Springs and circled quite around it to sniff for any hidden foe. Then he approached where there was no trail at all and drank.

Jo watched and wished he would drink a hogshead. But the moment that he turned and sought the grass Jo spurred his steed. The Pacer heard the hoofs, then saw the running horse, and did not want a nearer view but led away. Across the flat he went down to the south, and kept the famous swinging gait that made his start grow longer. Now through the sandy dunes he went, and steadying to an even pace he gained considerably and Jo's too-laden horse plunged through the sand and sinking fetlock deep, he lost at every bound. Then came a level stretch where the runner seemed to gain, and then a long decline where Jo's horse dared not run his best, so lost again at every step.

But on they went, and Jo spared neither spur nor quirt. A mile—a mile—and another mile, and the far-off rock at Arriba loomed up ahead.

And there, Jo knew fresh mounts were held, and on they dashed. But the night-black mane out level on the breeze ahead was gaining more and more.

Arriba Cañon reached at last, the watcher stood aside, for it was not wished to turn the race, and the Stallion passed—dashed down, across and up the slope, with that unbroken pace, the only he knew.

And Jo came bounding on his foaming steed, and leaped on the waiting mount, then urged him down the slope and up upon the track, and on the upland once more drove in the spurs, and raced and raced, and raced, but not a single inch he gained.

Ga-lump, ga-lump, ga-lump with measured beat he went—an hour—an hour, and another hour—Arroyo Alamosa just ahead with fresh relays, and Jo yelled at his horse and pushed him on and on. Straight for the place the Black One made, but on the last two miles some strange foreboding turned him to the left, and Jo foresaw escape in this, and pushed his jaded mount at any cost to head him off, and hard as they had raced this was the hardest race of all, with gasps for breath and leather squeaks at every straining bound. Then cutting right across, Jo seemed to gain, and drawing his gun he fired shot after shot to toss the dust, and so turned the Stallion's head and forced him back to take the crossing to the right.

Down they went. The Stallion crossed and Jo sprang to the ground. His horse was done, for thirty miles had passed in the last stretch, and Jo himself was worn out. His eyes were burnt with flying alkali dust. He was half blind so he motioned to his 'pard' to "go ahead and keep him straight for Alamosa ford."

Out shot the rider on a strong, fresh steed, and away they went—up and down on the rolling plain—the Black Horse flecked with snowy foam. His heaving ribs and noisy breath showed what he felt—but on and on he went.

And Tom on Ginger seemed to gain, then lose and lose, when in an hour the long decline of Alamosa came. And there a freshly mounted lad took up the chase and turned it west, and on they went past towns of prairie dogs, through soapweed tracts and cactus brakes by scores, and pricked and wrenched rode on. With dust and sweat the Black was now a dappled brown, but still he stepped the same. Young Carrington, who followed, had hurt his steed by pushing at the very start, and spurred and urged him now to cut across a gulch at which the Pacer shied. Just one misstep and down they went.

The boy escaped, but the pony lies there yet, and the wild Black Horse kept on.

This was close to the old Gallego's ranch where Jo himself had cut across refreshed to push the chase. Within thirty minutes he was again scorching the Pacer's trail.

Far in the west the Carlos Hills were seen, and there Jo knew fresh men and mounts were waiting, and that way the indomitable rider tried to turn the race, but by a sudden whim, of the inner warning born perhaps—the Pacer turned. Sharp to the north he went, and Jo, the skilful wrangler, rode and rode and yelled and tossed the dust with shots, but down a gulch the wild black meteor streamed and Jo could only follow. Then came the hardest race of all; Jo, cruel to the Mustang, was crueller to his mount and to himself. The sun was hot, the scorching plain was dim in shimmering heat, his eyes and lips were burnt with sand and salt, and yet the chase sped on. The only chance to win would be if he could drive the Mustang back to Big Arroyo Crossing. Now almost for the first time he saw signs of weakening in the Black. His mane and tail were not just quite so high, and his short half mile of start was down by more than half, but still he stayed ahead and paced and paced and paced.

An hour and another hour, and still they went the same. But they turned again, and night was near when Big Arroyo ford was reached—fully twenty miles. But Jo was game; he seized the waiting horse. The one he left went gasping to the stream and gorged himself with water till he died.

Then Jo held back in hopes the foaming Black would drink. But he was wise; he gulped a single gulp, splashed through the stream and then passed on with Jo at speed behind him. And when they last were seen the Black was on ahead just out of reach and Jo's horse bounding on.

It was morning when Jo came to camp on foot. His tale was briefly told:— eight horses dead—five men worn out—the matchless Pacer safe and free.

"'Taint possible; it can't be done. Sorry I didn't bore his hellish carcass through when I had the chance," said Jo, and gave it up.

Old Turkeytrack was cook on this trip. He had watched the chase with as much interest as anyone, and when it failed he grinned into the pot and said: "That mustang's mine unless I'm a darned fool."

Much persecution had made the Pacer wilder than ever. But it did not drive him away from Antelope Springs. That was the only drinking-place with absolutely no shelter for a mile on every side to hide an enemy. Here he came almost every day about noon, and after thoroughly spying the land approached to drink.

His had been a lonely life all winter since the capture of his harem, and of this old Turkeytrack was fully aware. The old cook's chum had a nice little brown mare which he judged would serve his ends, and taking a pair of the strongest hobbles, a spade, a spare lasso, and a stout post he mounted the mare and rode away to the famous Springs.

A few antelope skimmed over the plain before him in the early freshness of the day. Cattle were lying about in groups, and the loud, sweet song of the prairie lark was heard on every side. For the bright snowless winter of the mesas was gone and the springtime was at hand. The grass was greening and all nature seemed turning to thoughts of love.

It was in the air, and when the little brown mare was picketed out to graze she raised her nose from time to time to pour forth a long shrill whinny that surely was her song, if song she had, of love.

Old Turkeytrack studied the wind and the lay of the land. He selected a sedgy clump near some smooth, grassy ground, and first firmly sunk the post, then dug a hole large enough to hide in, and spread his blanket in it. He shortened up the little mare's tether, till she could scarcely move; then on the ground between he spread his open lasso, tying the long end to the post, then covered the rope with dust and grass, and went into his hiding place.

About noon, after long waiting, the amorous whinny of the mare was answered from the high ground, away to the west, and there, black against the sky, was the famous Mustang.

Down he came at that long swinging gait, but grown crafty with much pursuit, he often stopped to gaze and whinny, and got answer that surely touched his heart. Nearer he came again to call, then took alarm, and paced all around in a great circle to try the wind for his foes, and seemed in doubt. But the brown mare called again. He circled nearer still, and neighed once more, and got reply that seemed to quell all fears, and set his heart aglow.

Nearer still he pranced, till he touched Solly's nose with his own, and finding her as responsive as he well could wish, thrust aside all thoughts of danger, and abandoned himself to the delight of conquest, until, as he pranced around, his hind legs for a moment stood within the evil circle of the rope. One deft sharp twitch, the noose flew tight, and he was caught.

A snort of terror and a bound in the air gave Tom the chance to add the double hitch. The loop flashed up the line, and snake-like bound those mighty hoofs.

Terror lent speed and double strength for a moment, but the end of the rope was reached, and down he went a captive, a hopeless prisoner at last. Old Tom's ugly, little crooked form sprang from the pit to complete the mastering of the great glorious creature whose mighty strength had proved as nothing when matched with the wits of a little old man. With snorts and desperate bounds of awful force the great beast dashed and struggled to be free; but all in vain. The rope was strong.

The second lasso was deftly swung, and the forefeet caught, and then with a skilful move the feet were drawn together, and down went the raging Pacer to lie a moment later 'hog-tied' and helpless on the ground. There he struggled till worn out, sobbing great convulsive sobs while tears ran down his cheeks.

Tom stood by and watched, but a strange revulsion of feeling came over the old cowpuncher. He trembled nervously from head to foot, as he had not done since he roped his first steer, and for a while could do nothing but gaze on his tremendous prisoner. But the feeling soon passed away. He saddled Delilah, and taking the second lasso, roped the great horse about the neck, and left the mare to hold the Stallion's head, while he put on the hobbles. This was soon done, and sure of him now old Bates was about to loose the ropes, but on a sudden thought he stopped. He had quite forgotten, and had come unprepared for something of importance. In Western law the Mustang was the property of the first man to mark him with his brand; how was this to be done with the nearest branding-iron twenty miles away?

Old Tom went to his mare, took up her hoofs one at a time, and examined each shoe. Yes! One was a little loose; he pushed and pried it with the spade, and got it off. Buffalo chips and kindred fuel were plentiful about the plain, so a fire was quickly made, and he soon had one arm of the horse-shoe red hot, then holding the other wrapped in his sock he rudely sketched on the left shoulder of the helpless mustang a turkeytrack, his brand, the first time really that it had ever been used. The Pacer shuddered as the hot iron seared his flesh, but it was quickly done, and the famous Mustang Stallion was a maverick no more.

Now all there was to do was to take him home. The ropes were loosed, the Mustang felt himself freed, thought he was free, and sprang to his feet only to fall as soon as he tried to take a stride. His forefeet were strongly tied together, his only possible gait a shuffling walk, or else a desperate labored bounding with feet so unnaturally held that within a few yards he was inevitably thrown each time he tried to break away. Tom on the light pony headed him off again and again, and by dint of driving, threatening, and maneuvering, contrived to force his foaming, crazy captive northward toward the Piñavetitos Cañon. But the wild horse would not drive, would not give in. With snorts of terror or of rage and maddest bounds, he tried and tried to get away. It was one long cruel fight; his glossy sides were thick with dark foam, and the foam was stained with blood. Countless hard falls and exhaustion that a long day's chase was powerless to produce were telling on him; his straining bounds first this way and then that, were not now quite so strong, and the spray he snorted as he gasped was half a spray of blood. But his captor, relentless, masterful and cool, still forced him on. Down the slope toward the cañon they had come, every yard a fight, and now they were at the head of the draw that took the trail down to the only crossing of the cañon, the northmost limit of the Pacer's ancient range.

From this the first corral and ranch-house were in sight. The man rejoiced, but the Mustang gathered his remaining strength for one more desperate dash. Up, up the grassy slope from the trail he went, defied the swinging, slashing rope and the gunshot fired in the air, in vain attempt to turn his frenzied course. Up, up and on, above the sheerest cliff he dashed then sprang away into the vacant air, down—down—two hundred downward feet to fall, and land upon the rocks below, a lifeless wreck—but free.

Feral Heart

LAURA BELL

orning spills across the ridges like paint tipped over, its fingers of pale light reaching through the sage to flush from the leaves the cries of small birds. From a ragged spine of rock, my knot of a thousand sheep begins to loosen as, one by one, the ewes and lambs trickle off the edges in search of fresh feed. The air is awake, alive with movement. It is May, spring in northern Wyoming, and I am camped on the high benches of the McCullough Peaks.

At the edge of camp, my dogs sit on their haunches and lean out into the morning with a working dog's earnest air of responsibility. Lady is a red heeler, slight and speckled. A veteran queen of sheep camp. Louise is blue merle Aussie shepherd, younger, and owner of one blue eye that speaks of righteousness. Today, it says, sheep are leaving the bedground and your horse isn't saddled. We're ready. Send us. Their faces turn in quick attention from sheep to Willy eating his morning grain to me, coffee still in hand.

Picketed in a small clearing off from camp, Willy stands with his nose shoved deeply into his bucket of oats. I gather my saddle up from underneath the sheepwagon and pack it to him, heaving it to his back with a grunt. "Next life I'll be a tall woman," I say and pull the cinch up loose under his belly. Abruptly, his head swings up through the air, startled at some intrusion into the landscape. He stands frozen, watching so intently that for a moment he forgets to chew.

It's the horses that he sees, slipping down along the rim of the narrow canyon that falls from the peaks, widening and softening to spill into green feed below our camp. It's the bay stallion's band, one of three feral bands that range in the McCullough Peaks and whose paths we cross from time to time, sharing, as we do, the neighborhood.

They step lightly down the rim, coming closer to our camp and the sheep now streaming off the hill. There are seven mares, mostly bays and sorrels, two spring colts, and the stallion, moving off to the side of the group and slightly in its lead. Among them, there is no one animal that I would call beautiful. They are small and dense and rough, the shape of their bones buried under coats ragged still with winter. Like the gnarled firs that lean from the winds at timberline, these horses are carved by the elements in which they live, not by any breeder's idea of beauty.

Still, you should see them move. All grace and ease they make their way with full attention, their noses weaving through the air to catch our scent. Coming closer, they move like dancers seasoned side by side, their tough bodies one single expression of elegance, their effort one single chord of survival.

I have watched them bear a storm. With butts turned windward and heads hung low, they shift their warm weight into each other and stand through whatever the skies pour out to them. From the comfort of my sheepwagon stove, I have watched them bear a storm and found my pity grown to envy. Of their loyalty. Of their dependence on each other. Of the sureness it allows them in a landscape that does so little to shelter.

This morning they just stop above camp, not fifty yards from us, at the edge of the hungry wave of bleating sheep. The stallion stands with head high, watching Willy who watches him. About the mares, there is an air both wary and curious. Almost playful. One colt minces forward to sniff a woolly fleece, then leaps back from the surprise of it, stirring the mares into a ripple of snorts and skittering bucks. The stallion ducks his head, too, and shakes it in our direction like a dare. Unbearably tempted, Willy charges the end of his picket chain with a squeal.

A year ago they took him, called him away with whatever power their freedom holds. It had been a wilder, Marchy, morning with winds gusting against the flimsy tin of my sheepwagon roof. I woke to Willy, white-eyed and snorting, strained against his picket line that was snaked in a tangle through the brush. Following his eyes to the low hills above camp, I saw his torment in the three wild bands that had gathered in the coming storm to show out for each other, to strut in the electrical currents of air sweeping in from the northern skies. The hills were charged with their movement, the stallions circling and swinging, heads and tails high in the wind, around the edges of their mares. Willy was changed by his awareness of them, no longer the familiar member of my family, and I knew he would be gone if not for the chain that held him in camp.

So, I was careful as I saddled him. I led him away from camp to get on, but he reared and ducked his head, and because I was too stubborn to follow, the bridle slid from his head to the ground. For a moment, he stood between the two worlds, his eyes to the hills, one ear twitching slightly to the rattle of the oat bucket and the grain sifting through my fingers. With the stiff-legged staccato movements of exhilaration, he was gone, stirrups flapping like wings, into the hills. With his approach, the horses stirred into a rumble of confusion and disappeared, finally, over the ridge with Willy among them.

I remember standing for a long time watching the empty hills, awed that my life could change so in a moment. No phone to call with, no neighbor to flag down. Only a spidery track of dusty road whose miles would soon be impassable with the storm. I remember looking at my dogs and wondering if it were possible for them, too, to be drawn away from me by some experience more primally "dog." I thought not, and wondered at the difference in Willy that took him away.

I celebrated my twenty-fifth birthday on foot in the rain the next day, tearing a soggy tuna fish sandwich in pieces for Lady and Louise. For six days it rained, and on the seventh, my camptender chugged into camp at dawn chained up on all fours to get through the mud, worried about what he might find when he got there. Willy had been found out by the highway, lonesome and cut up and looking for oats. As a gelding, he'd had no place with the wild horses and had been fought out of the bands by the stallions. Through the back-range grapevine, John had gotten the news and showed up at first light with a spare horse loaded in the stockrack and an aging birthday cake on the front seat beside him.

That was a year ago. If Willy has memories of the beating he suffered, they are paled by the sparks and snorts flying across the distance this morning. Heads are up, and eyes are bright. In an air charged with invitation, I hang my weight into his head to draw him down, my own memories all too vivid. I turn to the horses up the hill, their spirits like bright lights beckoning, and realize that I, too, want to be gone away. More than anything else. More than the caution of my isolation. More than the wisdom of my losses. I want to shake my head back at them. I want to dare.

I fasten the bridle over his head and pull the cinch tight around his belly. Cheeking his head around to me, I dance his dance, pulling myself, finally, up into the saddle. Do we dare? In a sideways prance, we step gingerly into the sage, and the horses' heads fly high, their ragged manes catching the wind.

Can we dare not on a morning in spring run with our hearts stretched wide? And so I lean only slightly, shifting my weight to give him his head, and we are gone, hard and fast and wild through the sage toward the horses, already bolted and bucking up the hill. One hand a clutch of mane and reins, the other anchored to the horn, I pledge myself on for the ride, dogs yipping madly through the brush behind us. Below us the ground falls away unevenly and leaves us stumbling through the air over sage and rock and the holes of prairie dogs. I lose my sight to wind and tears and close my body around the center of what there is to trust and trust it.

For long moments, we ride their wake of dust and drumming hooves, suspended in the balance of fear and grace as hooves meet ground and the ground holds us up. As though there is no choice, we follow until our lungs and hearts can stand no more. Glittering and heaving, we pull up to watch them take the ridge. They snort and jump and stamp their feet at us, disappearing over the top with necks snaking and heads shaking in triumph.

Turning back, the morning is spread before us, raw and brilliant, tumbling for miles down to the desert basin below. The sheep are fanned in a great pale arc through the sage, and the birds cry out their morning songs. With corks popped off our sedated hearts, we fall from the slope, changed, and pick our trail back to camp and the rituals of our day.

The Luckiest Horse in Reno

DEANNE STILLMAN

When the men approached, the black foal might have been nursing. Or she might have been on her side, giving her wobbly legs a rest, leaning into her mother under the starry desert sky. The band of wild horses had only recently returned to this patch of scrub; the land had been stripped bare of forage by hordes of roaming cattle, and it was only in the past year that some edible plants—their seeds dropped here by migratory birds who knows when—began to green up the hills and provide nourishment for the critters that brought us all westward ho. At the sound of the vehicle, the band—all thirty-five horses—prepared to move and did move at once, for horses are animals of prey and so their withers twitched, their ears stiffened, their perfect, unshod hooves dug into the scrub for traction and then they began to run. The black foal might have taken a second or two longer than the others to rise. Perhaps the mare, already upright, bolted instantly, turning her head to see if the foal had followed. The headlights of the vehicle appeared over a rise. The men were shouting and then there was another bright light—it trained from atop the vehicle across the sunken bajada and it swept the sands, illuminating the wild and running four-legged spirits as their legs stretched in full perfect extension, flashing across their hides which were dun and paint and bay, making a living mural in 3-D in which the American story—all of it—was frozen here forever, in the desert as it always is, as bullets hissed from the vehicle through the patches of juniper and into the wild horses of the old frontier. It was Christmas. Two thousand years earlier, Christ had been born in a stable.

STATEMENT OF ACCUSED MARINE LANCE
CORPORAL —

January 14, 1999

I was home in Reno, Nevada on Christmas leave. On the 27th of December, 1998, approximately between 1900 and 2100 hours, I drove [my buddies] to Wal-Mart. We went inside and purchased one box, I believe, of 20 rounds of .270 caliber Winchester rifle ammunition, and two boxes of 12 gauge shotgun shells, brand unknown. The boxes of shotgun shells were green and yellow in color. The color of the shotgun shell itself is read [sic] plastic with brass bottoms. Also, we purchased a hand-held spotlight to spot rabbits in the dark so we could shoot them. We had approximately two to three six packs of beer with us. I drove up the construction road behind Rattlesnake Mountain. My pick up truck is a four-wheel drive, Ford Ranger, green 1992, with an open bed and toolbox in the back. When we left the road [my buddies] got into the bed of the truck so driving would be easier. The spotlight was plugged into the cigarette lighter and passed out the sliding rear window so they could shine it around the area of the truck as I drove. As I was driving, both of them pounded on the top of the truck to let me know to stop. I stopped the truck and got out to see what they were looking at. They said, "Hey, look, there is a horse."

Two months later on a cold and sunny afternoon, a man was hiking in the mountains outside of Reno. He saw a dark foal lying down in the sagebrush, not able to get up. A bachelor stallion had been watching from a distance and now came over and nibbled at the foal's neck. She tried to get up but couldn't, and the stallion rejoined his little band. The hiker called for help. A vet arrived and could find no injuries. As it grew dark, a trailer was pulled across the washes and gulleys until it approached the filly, about a hundred yards away and downhill. The stars were particularly bright that night and helped the rescue party, equipped only with flashlights, lumber across the sands and up the rocky rise where the filly was down. Four men lifted her onto a platform and carried her down the hill and into the trailer. "She was a carcass with a winter coat," said a rescuer. She was covered with ticks and parasites, weak and anemic. She was six months old. Two days later, at a sanctuary near Carson City called Wild Horse Spirit, two women helped her stand. But she kept falling. Over the weeks, they nourished her and she grew strong and regained muscle and she began to walk without falling down. But she was nervous, not skittish like a lot of horses are, especially wild ones, but distracted, preoccupied, perhaps even haunted. Because of her location when rescued, near Rattlesnake Mountain, and because she was starving, her rescuers reasoned that she had been a nursing foal who had recently lost her mother. Without mother's milk, a foal can last for a while in the wilderness, sometimes as long as a couple of months. And because a band of bachelor stallions had been nearby when she was found, her rescuers figured they had taken her in, looking after her until they could do it no longer, standing guard as she lay down in the brush to die. "Something made me stop," the hiker who found the filly would later say. As it turned out, the filly was the lone survivor of the Christmas massacre, and they called her Bugz. Like all survivors, she had a story to tell.

A visitor to the site of the massacre can know part of the story, just as a visitor to Gettysburg or Little Big Horn can bear witness but not fully. But here there are no texts to guide us; no oral histories passed down across time; just skulls and the cages of ribs and shins and intact hooves and manes and tails right where the wild horses were felled, forever preserved in the dry air of the Great Basin that birthed Nevada—mosh pit of America—godforsaken treasure chest of a state that lures big and small spenders alike with five-cent slots and high-roller events and hollow spectacles and all-night pawn and—yes!—"wild horses, just like in the Old West!" says the travel literature—"See them roam free just like they oughtta be!" But Bugz knows better and that's why Bugz is permanently spooked, not unlike another twitchy Nevada character, Bugsy Siegel, said to have been demon-possessed and therefore buggy. No doubt he was, having witnessed—and been the progenitor of—great rivers of desert carnage. But Bugz the horse is our real American hero, mute witness to the history of the West, important remnant of the dwindling wild horse population, help to man in the taming of the frontier, maker of trails, intrepid deliverer of urgent messages (yes, the Pony Express trail is now

Nevada Highway 95), fighter of battles, devoted member of the US cavalry, thrill-providing rodeo ride, license plate symbol, name of cool and desirable muscle car, fleet and wild heart of the American wanderer, tameable by no one yet a willing good friend who will carry you into hell if you ask.

"When we got the call, they said one horse was shot and wounded. Two others were dead," Betty Lee Kelly remembered, walking with me across the killing field. Betty and her partner Bobbi Royce are the founders of Wild Horse Spirit, a home for rescued, injured, abandoned, and abused wild horses. They gave their lives over to the horses fifteen years ago. When a wild horse is found shot or injured, which often happens in Nevada, they are usually the first contacted by animal control officers. Betty and Bobbi immediately drove from their home outside Carson City to the Virginia Range east of Reno, parking in a wash at Rattlesnake Mountain and meeting up with the Washoe County Sheriff and the man who had first happened upon the shootings and phoned law enforcement. The man led them to the injured horse whom they had been called to help. Betty guides me to the exact location. Four years after the massacre, a pair of equine leg bones lie crossed, as if running in repose, the cartilage of the hooves still intact. The bones are as white as white can get, radiating almost, a reverse silhouette of wildness frozen in movement and time. "She had probably been here for a day or two," Betty said. "She was lying in the sand. She had dug a small hole with her front legs, intermittently trying to get up. But she was shot in the spinal cord and her hind legs were paralyzed. An animal control officer put her to sleep." Betty and Bobbi would later name this filly Hope; police investigators would identify her as #7 in the final report. As the band of people explored the site, it quickly became clear that the incident was far more horrific—and way less routine—than the shooting of a few horses. Other murdered horses found that day included a nursing mare (#9) and her five- to six-month-old filly (#10) and two stallions (#8 and #11). And then there was the young colt, soon to be known in the Nevada court system as #4. Bobbi and Betty would call him Alvin. He was shot in the chest and then sprayed in the eyes, mouth, rectum, and genitals with a fire extinguisher, although at the time of the discovery, no one really knew what all the foamy white stuff was. Now, Alvin's carcass—the barrel of his chest—lies where he died, picked and blown clean by time, wind, and critters. The spine is flush against the sand and the ribs curve toward the sky. "There was a stallion watching us that day," Betty said. "Just standing at the perimeter as we found each dead horse. When the sun went down and we got in our cars, he trotted on down the road. His family had been wiped out but we still didn't know how bad it was."

When investigators returned the following morning to complete their report, they fanned out across the area. By the end of the second day, the death toll had climbed to thirty-four. Some horses had been shot—several times—in the head. Others—shot in the stomach—probably died more slowly. Somehow, Bugz had escaped, perhaps even returning to her mother's side to nurse as the mare lay dying on the desert sand. At the base of an old piñon pine lies a large cross of rocks and stones with the bullet-riddled skull of a wild horse at the top. Betty built the cross two years after the massacre, the day the killers went on trial in Virginia City, a blood-soaked frontier town that feeds on its own mythology, charging two bucks to tour a brothel museum wherein, legend has it, a prostitute's hand is entombed in a jar, sliced off when its owner tried to steal from the till. Shortly after the massacre, a state senator rose to make a speech on the Nevada house floor. "If a wild horse comes to your property," he said to much applause, "shoot him." Eventually the killers would plead guilty to a misdemeanor, despite evidence such as a photograph of one of them standing proudly with his foot atop the colt who came to be known as Alvin. But Bugz knows what happened on Rattlesnake Mountain that awful Christmas day. Bugz saw the stallions, mares, fillies, and colts that were her band make their last stand in the West that they made ours and where they still—occasionally—roam.

Cow Ponies
&
Other Workhorses

A Horse to Brag About

MAX EVANS

I reckon just about every human in the world that was raised on a cow ranch, worked as a cowboy, or just plain rode for pleasure knew and loved a horse like Old Snip. In the memory of us all there is one old pony that comes to mind more often than all the others. A horse to do a little braggin' about. That's the kind of horse Old Snip was.

The first time I saw the little stocking-legged, blazed-face, snip-nosed bay, a long-legged bronc stomper named Robert Ian was hanging the steel in his shoulders. It was in a big pole corral at Cow Springs, New Mexico, and the dust was fairly boiling from under Old Snip. He bucked hard, mighty hard, with long, ground-bustin', neck-poppin' jumps, straight ahead till he hit one side of the corral, then he turned and put out all he had till he hit the other side. He bucked straight just like he did everything else in his life. But that was the only time he ever bucked.

Gradually he slowed and then quit altogether. Robert Ian worked him in and out around the corral letting him get used to the weight on his back, the steel in his mouth, the rein on his neck, letting him know that these things wouldn't hurt him if he behaved himself. The little old pony caught on quick and by the fourth saddling, Robert Ian decided he'd turn him over to me. He said, "Here, boy, get your saddle on this here Old Snip. He's gentle as a loggin' horse."

I was just a gawky, freckled-face kid hanging around the outfit wranglin' horses, patching fences, anything Robert Ian happened to think of that he thought I wouldn't mess up. Mainly I hung around to get a few square meals, listen to the tall yarns cowboys have a habit of spinning and maybe to learn a little something.

"You think he's broke gentle?" I asked cautiously eyeing the bay.

"Why, boy," he said, "this here horse would do to go to preachin' on."

I saddled up, gathered the reins up tight in my left hand, grabbing the heavy black mane at the same time. I took hold of the saddle horn with my right and stuck my left knee in his shoulder, swung my right leg smoothly over his back, and Old Snip moved out with a nice running walk. Right away I breathed easy again. I've never known a horse to pick up a fast running walk that quick. He was a natural at it. A running walk will carry a cowboy a lot of miles in a day and bring him back without his tonsils shook loose. Sittin' up there on him I felt just as good as an old coat that a feller's worn a long time and hates to throw away. He was already beginning to rein. The least pressure and he turned smooth as new grass, just where you wanted him.

"Now, listen, boy," Robert Ian said when I came back, "I owe Ed Young twenty dollars and I promised him this here horse in payment." My heart turned mighty cold at these words for I thought he was giving the horse to me.

"You been wanting to go over on that San Cristobal outfit and hunt arrowheads, ain't you?"

I said, "Yeah."

"All right, here's your chance. You can leave about daylight in the mornin' and you'll be at the Indian ruins right around ten. I'll make out a bill of sale from me to Ed," he added. "You can stay at the old line camp across from Long Draw tomorrow night and make it in to Ed's the next day."

"Yeah," I said, not liking the sound of that *bill of sale* business.

"Something else," Robert Ian said, "If you keep your mouth shut, listen hard and work like hell you might get a job with the San Cristobal outfit. A regular payin' job."

That last sounded good because all I'd got in the way of pay around there was a dollar Robert Ian gave me when we went to Santa Fe one time. That seemed like a lot of money then but I was a year older now and wanted to put on the dog a little.

Me and Old Snip were out on a piñon-crowded trail heading lickety-split for the San Cristobal Ranch when the sun came up. Boy, it was a mighty fine morning. A bunch of deer jumped up out of some oak brush and went tearing up the hill. A coyote crossed our trail and the magpies started screaming. The bluejays flew from tree to tree.

By nine o'clock we crossed the highway between Cline's Corners and Lamy, New Mexico, and were well into the ranch property itself. The highway is fenced now, but then she was wide open. The August sun was warming up fast. I figured it was going to get hotter than blue blazes before noon. Sure enough it did. I didn't care though. Here I was mounted on a little animal that I figured the good Lord had made especially for me and I saw those sky-high, white and red bluffs sticking up like a bunch of cathedrals.

I took the worn out catch rope Robert Ian had given me and tied Old Snip to a piñon tree with a knot that wouldn't slip and choke him later on if he got boogered at something. Then I started out across those ruins with my head down and my eyes peeled expecting any second to see a perfect arrowhead.

Some college feller told me years later that these ruins were five or six hundred years old. They were brand spanking new to me that day in August. You could still see the outlines of the sandstone houses built in a big square. Out in the middle was the round kiva—a sort of church for the Indians. Broken pottery with designs painted on them in real bright colors was scattered about everywhere. There were lots of broken arrowheads and pieces of flint all over.

Then I found what I'd been looking for, a great big perfect arrowhead made out of black glassy obsidian. Man! Chills ran all over me and I knew what a prospector must feel like when he pans a big gold nugget for the first time. I got to walking so fast trying to find another one that I probably stepped over several unseen. Boy, I had a pocket just smack full of flint pieces, arrowheads, and bright colored pottery.

Then I saw another one, white and small, a bird point. Just as I bent to pick it up I noticed a shadow spread across the ground around me. It was a cloud. As I straightened up I looked into the sky. There were lots of clouds, black and heavy with water. They hadn't begun to get together yet so I figured I had plenty of time to hunt.

Between the cathedrals and the line camp where I aimed to spend the night was a lot of barren, badly eroded ground and one deep-cut arroyo called Long Draw. Flash floods in the mountains caused these to fill with water and sometimes made crossing impossible. I was so wrapped up in what I was doing, I didn't pay the clouds much attention.

Then she hit—an earbustin' clap of thunder! I raised up quick-like and looked over to where Snip was tied. He was so wide-eyed you could see the white showing. It's not natural for a cow pony to get excited over a little rain storm brewing. But when Old Snip looked over at me and blasted out with a long loud nicker, I figured it was time to leave. I still swear to this day that horse was smarter than me and was just giving warning it was high time to drag out of there before it was too late. Sure enough it almost was.

Over to the east in the higher mountains, the clouds were having a family reunion and the more lively members were spitting out forked fire and deep down, rumbling noises. I could see the blue white sheets of rain pour out into the canyons and foothills. The storm was moving on out towards the flats and us, fast-like.

I buckled on my spurs, missing the hole with the buckle tongue a couple of times because I was getting a little excited. I untied Old Snip and mounted up. I leaned over in the saddle and away we went. Snip seemed to understand that the whole idea was to get across all that barren ground before the rain reached us. If it did, we might have to sleep out on this side of the arroyo all night without any shelter. He was really moving now, up and down . . . straining hard with his hindquarters on the upgrade and keeping his forelegs out in front on the downgrade.

We didn't quite make it. About a quarter of a mile out in the eroded flats, the rain caught us. I pulled up and took a look. There wasn't much to see, the rain was so heavy. As we moved out again I could feel the cold wetness already soaked through to the skin and the water running from the brim of my hat like it was coming off a tin roof.

Old Snip was beginning to slip and slide in the slick, muddy clay. We kept going just the same. I was so wet now I didn't feel the coldness so much. We finally made it to Long Draw. I reined down a gradual slope out into the gravel covered bottom. Water was running in little muddy rivers everywhere. Then all of a sudden I could see nothing but water. A solid stream of reddish, muddy churning water! We were in real trouble! The heavy rain up in the mountains was just now reaching this part of Long Draw.

Before I had time to think, the water swirled up around my boot heels. Then it hit, a great big wall of mud, water, piñon sticks, pine needles, and everything else that grows in the mountains. I dropped the reins and grabbed the saddle horn with both hands. My arms felt like they had been stretched out as long as a wagon tongue. I couldn't see and it felt like a whole ocean of water had spilled right on top of us. I knew for sure this was it. I wanted to do some praying but I couldn't get my mind on it for worrying about holding on to that saddle horn.

I began to strangle, and a lot of red, light and black spaces seemed to jump out of my head. I got a big suck at a bunch of air. It was mighty wet air as far as that goes but there wasn't quite enough water in it to drown a feller. We went splashing under again, up and out, down and under, over and over. After this had gone on for what seemed like about two long years I happened to remember hearing one old cowboy say a horse could swim better if you hung onto his tail instead of the saddle horn. They are only about two yards apart, but getting from that horn to that tail wasn't any simple act.

I had to take the gamble. If I missed I was a gone dog and I knew it. I turned loose and grabbed! One hand caught tail hair! I was washed sideways and every other way. By this time I was sure there was as much water in me as there was out of me. Somehow I hung on and got hold with my other hand. Everything was muddy at this point, including my memory.

A long time later, at least it seemed a long time later, I noticed a horse's hind leg next to my face. I counted one, two, three, four horse's legs. Then I realized I was lying in the mud and Old Snip was standing there with his head down, his sides bellowing in and out, breathing hard. I didn't mind that old sticky mud. No, siree, not one bit. I rightly loved it. I got up and put my arm across that bay pony's neck. I didn't say anything. I didn't have to. I knew he understood.

We stayed all night over at the line camp. Even if we were hungry and a little cold I didn't mind and I hope Old Snip didn't.

The next day about noon I rode up to Ed Young's place and let out a yell. He walked out, or I should say a hat came out with him walking under it, because he wore the biggest hat I ever saw. It was a real, honest-to-goodness old-time cowboy hat.

I said, "Robert Ian sent you this here horse," and I handed him the bill of sale. The best eyes in the world couldn't have made out what that piece of paper said. That old Long Draw mud and water had seen to that. "Reckon you'll have to get him to make you out another one," I said, tickled plumb to death. I figured I still had a chance somehow to come up with the wherewithal to own Old Snip for my very own. I told Ed what had happened, then I said, "Say, Robert Ian said you might be needing a hand."

"I might," he said, looking at me with those gleaming blue eyes across that hawk-looking, humped-up nose. "What can you do, boy?" he asked pointblank.

"Hell," I said, "I can do anything."

Several weeks later I knew that this was not exactly the whole truth. I know now that I stayed on at Ed's in the beginning because I wanted to be with Old Snip, but later on I liked it all the way around. That evening I helped him feed the horses and milk the cows. After supper I got up and helped his wife with the dishes.

This set real good with Mother. All the cowboys in the country called her Mother Young because she was such a top-notch cook, doctor, and anything else a woman had to be to make a good wife and mother thirty miles from town right smack dab in the middle of all outdoors.

Ed had some good horses in his own right. He had broken broncs for the old Waggoner outfit in the early days and a lot of other big outfits, and he wouldn't have anything but good horses around him.

I got to ride and work with them all. There was Old Sut, a coal black twelve-year-old. You could ride him all day and he'd never even break a sweat. Then there was Flax, the golden-maned sorrel—a good range roping horse; Apache, the big hard-bucking paint; Raggedy Ann, the little brown mustang that Ed had roped and broke himself; and Fooler, a blaze-faced chestnut—Ed's favorite. When the cowboys spoke about Fooler they would always say, "That Fooler's quite a horse, yep, he's one hell of a horse."

But none of them compared with Old Snip. As time went on he just got better and better. You could ride him all day without wearing him out because of his fast easy gait. He reined like a regular cutting horse, quick, but smooth and easy. Boy, that stop he had! Those hind legs would slide way up under him with his forelegs shoved out in front and you didn't feel hardly any jar at all. He learned to work a rope. He kept his head looking down the rope all the time and the slack pulled out.

I learned to heel calves on him. Ed and I worked a lot just by ourselves. It sure makes a calf easier to throw and brand if you rope him by the heels. I was getting so I hardly missed a loop when riding Old Snip.

One day Ed said, "We're going down to Eldon Butler's and help him brand about fifty head. He's interested in buying Old Snip. We've got plenty of horses around here and I need the money."

As we worked our way down out of the mountains towards Butler's I felt sort of sick. I cleared my throat and said, "Ed, how much you asking for Old Snip?"

"Aw, around a hundred I reckon the way he's turning out." He added, "Now, I really want you to show off what a heeling horse he is. That'll do more to sell him than anything else."

We cut the calves out from the mother cows and held them in a pole corral. The mothers bawled to beat sixty and stirred up a lot of dust. The branding irons were heating in an open tire. Eldon was getting the black leg vaccine ready and Ed was sharpening his knife getting ready to castrate the bull calves, except one they picked out for a breeding bull because of his good conformation and markings.

I was thinking, a hundred dollars, at the rate I was getting paid, I would be a hundred years old before I had it saved up. I really didn't feel any extra love in my heart right at that moment for Eldon Butler. He was a fine feller too.

Ed yelled, "We're ready, boy."

I rode out among the calves on Old Snip. He eased in till we had one in the right position, then I dropped a slow loop under one of the big bull calves. Most fellers make the mistake of throwing too fast a loop to be good heelers. You've got to kinda let it float down. Then just as the hind legs move against the loop you pull the slack and you've got him. The big calf began bucking and bellering but I turned Old Snip and dragged it to the fire. Eldon ran up and got hold of his tail and over he went.

Pretty soon you could smell the hair burning where they put the brand to him. Ed castrated, earmarked, and vaccinated him while Eldon held. I let them have the slack, and the finished product got up shaking his head wondering what in the world had happened to him.

I caught four in a row and felt kind of proud of myself until I noticed Eldon looking at Old Snip with mighty admiring eyes. I don't know what happened after that but it was the worst branding I ever attended. It took me about nine loops to catch every calf and even when I did, it looked like Old Snip and me couldn't keep from getting tangled up in the rope.

It was something or other all the time. I reckon that's the sorriest work we ever did together. I could see the disgusted look on Eldon's face. Ed was downright pale after all the braggin' he'd done about Old Snip. I guess we were all glad to get the job over with.

It was after dark when we unsaddled that night. I told Ed to go on in the house and wash for supper if he wanted to, I'd take care of the horses. I shucked out several ears of corn and forked some hay in the manger. I stood there in the dark awhile and smelled Old Snip. He smelled just like a horse, but not just any old horse.

There always seems to be just a little bit of fun mixed up with all the trouble we have, like the time I sat up on Old Snip and looked at a white faced cow as if she were some sort of varmint. The fall before, we had moved all Ed's cows down out of the mountains to the home pasture for the winter. We didn't move them all at one time, I can tell you that.

Ed had a grazing permit on national forest land and those cows were scattered out in small bunches over about 200,000 acres of mountains, hills, canyons, rocks and timber, but all the rest of his herd put together was easier to round up than this one old cow. She always took off into the thickest timber or down some rough canyon. She was nothing but trouble, so that's what we named her.

Now there she was out in the bog. There was plenty of grass on the outside but she had to go fall off in it, and now if I didn't drag her out pretty soon she'd sink out of sight. I took the leather loop from the saddle horn and unwound the three wraps from the catch rope. I tied one end of the rope to my saddle horn and built a loop in the other end.

I whirled it a couple or three times and let it go. I had to catch her horns if I was going to be able to let her loose by myself. The loop settled down just where I wanted it and I spurred Old Snip in the opposite direction. Nothing moved. Old Trouble was really bogged down. I began to do some solid cussin' and sweatin'.

After awhile the old fool inched up out of the bog a little bit. "Now, Snip!" I yelled, "Now!" Old Snip threw all his weight against that rope and out she came. She struck dry ground running and hit the end of the rope hard. Old Snip was braced. I felt the back of the saddle raise and pull the flank cinch tight against Old Snip's belly.

Now, in the first place I should never have tried this by myself. In the second place I should never have got off Old Snip without somebody around, but that's exactly what I did. Old Snip backed fast, moving right and left trying to keep the rope tight. I worked in from the side trying to get to Trouble's head slightly behind her horns. She was slobbering at the mouth, shaking her head, and straining with all she had against the rope. Her main idea was to run one of those sharp horns right square through me.

I finally got to her and gripped down with all my strength on her muzzle with one hand, twisting and holding a horn with the other. She slung me around, but I stayed with her and pretty soon when she made a run forward there was some slack in the rope. I jerked hard and the loop came off her horns. I made a run for Old Snip and Trouble made a run for me. I could feel the breeze across my hind end as she went by.

To this day I've never mounted as fast. Even then I was a mite slow. Trouble turned back and ran her horns under Old Snip's flank. He leaped up and away! I almost fell off. She made a couple more wild passes at us before she turned and trotted. I reckon that was her way of thanking us for saving her life.

Old Snip learned to work in timber. It got so I could tell when and what he smelled even when we couldn't see it. For instance, if it was a coyote or some other varmint out in the brush, he would throw one ear forward and then the other while looking toward the scent. If it happened to be cattle hiding in the brush, his neck would arch and he would pull over toward them. This saved lots of riding and looking in rough country. If it was a bunch of horses, he got a little extra excited and quickened his gait.

One day we got lost. I did, anyway. Suddenly I didn't know exactly where we were. The country looked different than I'd ever seen it. I noticed the fast-moving clouds above. Then everything was solid gray.

The wind came first in big gusts, then the snow. It hit wet, cold, and mean. It was a blowing snow. I turned back down out of the high country, but I didn't really know where we were headed. First, the ground covered over; then the tree limbs began to pick it up. Every once in a while a big shower of snow would fall on us out of the trees when the wind shook it loose. My hands were getting numb in my thin leather gloves, and my nose and ears were beginning to sting. The snow came on thicker and thicker.

I reined Old Snip this way, then that. It just didn't do any good. I had to admit I was completely lost. The blizzard never let up, in fact, it was just getting started. Before long I could just barely see Old Snip's thick black mane out in front of me. He was plowing along with his head low. The snow was drifting. Sometimes we'd go in up over my boot tops.

Finally I let Old Snip have his head. I just sat in the saddle and hoped he didn't fall off a sheer bluff. Soon I didn't feel anything. It wasn't so bad.

Then I remembered hearing that was the time of greatest danger. So, I began to move my arms back and forth, back and forth, faster and faster, until I couldn't hold them up any longer. Then there was just a world of cold white, with Old Snip and me right in the middle of it.

I sat a long time wondering why Old Snip didn't keep moving. Maybe he'd frozen stiff standing up! Then there it was—a gate, by doggies. It was the horse pasture gate into Ed Young's Rafter E Y Outfit.

After I fed Old Snip about three times as much as he could eat and stood with my hind end so close to the fireplace it just about scorched, I ate the biggest batch of Mother Young's hot biscuits, sow belly, and pinto beans that a man ever wrapped himself around. That was twice Old Snip had saved my life. I don't know how he found his way down out of that world of frozen white, but he did.

I worked for the San Cristobal outfit for two years and then somebody got the idea I should go off and get some book learnin'. I had to leave Old Snip behind.

Ed sold him after I left to some rich Texas ranchers. Of course Ed didn't know him as well as I did or he'd never have done it.

I never did get a bill of sale to Old Snip, but I felt he was mine just the same. He belonged to me then and he does now—wherever he is.

Teammates

LAURIE WAGNER

Harnessing up at 5 degrees in February—the frigid air sparkles with snow crystals and the sun is just beginning to brighten the eastern sky.

When I enter the barn, the cats pop out of the hay-stuffed manger to meow at my feet, their black, gray and white coats fuzzed up like furry hand muffs.

I pour food in their chipped crockery bowls and stroke each arched back while they purr and contentedly crunch the dry morsels.

Rays of sun reach through the small sawed out windows giving the barn the feel of a cathedral with dappled dark corners and stained glass light. It's hushed and silent inside.

Outside, the calves begin to bellow at the sight of my husband, Mick, bringing buckets of pellets to their feed bunks. After filling the horses' grain boxes, I grab the long, cotton lead ropes off a wooden peg sunk in a log beam and head out to catch up Jack and Jill, the half-Arab/half-Percheron cross team that have belonged to Mick for 16 of their 18 years.

Jack and Jill came out of Canada, purchased as yearlings by Mick's friend and fellow draft horse owner, Dick Ennos, of Cass City, Michigan. Dick was attending a sale in Reaboro, Ontario, in January, 1978, when he called Mick long distance to tell him about the snappy black gelding and mare. When Mick gave Dick the OK to purchase the team, Dick forked over just $850 for the pair. At home on his farm, Dick worked the young team a little, getting them used to the harness. Not long after, bringing a load of Belgians to the West Coast for Japanese buyers, Dick hauled the blacks to Mick's Wyoming ranch.

Green broke but hot-blooded, the blacks, known in Canada as Carriage Horses, were the perfect medium size and weight for the deep snow and narrow feed trails on the O Bar Y. Mick was raised with draft horses and had driven his own teams for over 20 years. He was used to working with each horse's individual personality. The gelding, whom he named Jack, was calm and steady with a ton of try and the will to work. The mare, Jill, spooked-up easily, was prone to sudden hissy fits and often let Jack take up her share of the slack. In the beginning, Mick used the blacks separately, hitching them up one at a time to a pair of older Clydesdales, Donnie and Clyde. Each day he drove to feed his cow herd and also 500 head of elk for the Fish and Game. The trek to the elk feedground was two miles over and two miles back on a sled trail that hovered three feet off the snow covered ground.

It was then that Jack, going one day, and Jill, going the next, learned the basic commands and how to stand steady when hay was loaded on the feed-sled. Jack fared fairly well, but Jill had serious problems facing the 165-foot bridge that spanned the Green River. Horrified at the hollow sound of hooves on the old wooden structure, she balked and froze, locked her legs and, blowing and snorting, let the team literally drag her across to safe ground on the other side. Soon though, Mick was working the Clydes and the blacks four abreast. By the end of the winter, Jack and Jill were going solo, graduates extraordinaire.

Come summer, Jack and Jill were used to being hitched and driven together. Quite often, Mick hooked them up to a small rubber-tired wagon he had hand-built and used them to ferry the family on picnics or to take salt up to the cattle in the high country where they foraged on forest grass. With their glossy black coats and flashy, fancy demeanors, Jack and Jill soon won a favorite and permanent place in Mick's heart.

The following winter, Mick used Jack and Jill as well as Donnie and Clyde and an older Percheron team of mares, Nell and Bell. He traded off teams as often as necessary to keep them from wearing down too much in the deep snow and under heavy hay loads. It was toward spring the next year, in May of 1980, during the ash fall out of Mount St. Helen, that Mick had his first and only major wreck with Jack and Jill. He was hauling hay on a wagon, trundling across the frozen manure and rough, half-iced feedground to reach the cows and new calves in the west pasture. Nearing Mud Creek, the steel doubletree's bolt hole wore through and sent the doubletree smashing smack into the horses' hocks. Mick yelled "whoa," grabbed for all the line he could lay claim to before the team's frantic forward dash hit a deep irrigation ditch head on and broke the neckyoke. The blow jerked Mick off, over the front of the wagon, onto the tongue and into the snow. By then, with the doubletree's banging against their back legs and the wagon left behind, the team took off in a frenzied all out gallop, dragging Mick. He lost one line but had them turned in a tight right circle until he couldn't hang on any longer and lost the other line. The unfettered team headed straight for the bull pasture fence, broke through the wire and, one on each side of the posts, continued head-long in fright. All Mick could do was close his eyes. When the sound of snapping wire and breaking posts stopped, he staggered to his feet, bruised and battered and calmly cussing. The team was shut down, huddled in a terrible tangle of posts, woven and barbed wire, tattered harness and broken hames. Mick approached them slowly, talking softly but disparagingly all the while: "Well, you no good, good-for-nothin', crow bait numbskulls . . . don't you know what 'whoa' means yet?"

As he cut them out of the mess and led them back to the barn, Mick was amazed that Jill had escaped unscathed and Jack had only one long nasty cut on his left hind cannon bone. The vet was called to stitch up Jack and Mick took a snowmachine out to run in Nell and Bell as a replacement team. By the time he took the John Deere crawler over to retrieve the wagon, the cows had discovered the load of hay and blithely helped themselves to the feast. All that was left for Mick to do was pick up the scattered baling wire and count his blessings.

When I met Jack and Jill in the fall of 1982, they'd been working for Mick for almost five years. Jack had helped Mick break a team of tall, stocking-legged mules to work in 1981; his calm, steady attitude made him a perfect equine teacher. Jill could still be goofy and unpredictable, especially if she thought she saw a "booger" or got a "bee in her bonnet" over something silly. During the early years I was on the O Bar Y, I often helped harness Jack and Jill and occasionally held the lines while Mick doctored a calf or got in a heavy cow. I never drove. They were just too much of a handful for my inexperienced hands. I made myself useful by opening gates, loading hay and kicking off bales to the cows.

There were two near wrecks I experienced with Jack and Jill. The first was the spring of 1986. We'd had a lot of snow in February and the feed trails were the only way to travel except for the four mile long snowmachine trail out to the highway. A cow moose and her last year's calf had holed up in the hay stack we were feeding from. When we pulled in to load bales, Mama Moose decided to defend what she thought of as her hay. Jack and Jill were veterans in moose encounters by then and seemed unafraid, but when we pulled in closer, the cow charged them head on. The team reared and tried to back up, Mick yelled "whoa" and the cow retreated, her tongue wagging and her hackles raised; even her scrawny calf imitated her every obnoxious move. There was plenty of room for the cow and calf to go around the sled and out the stackyard gate, but she refused to budge. Over and over again we tried to pull in—only to have her charge and retreat.

Each time, Jack and Jill got more flustered and flighty.

"Come on, you stupid cow," Mick hollered at the moose, "Get the hell out of the way."

The cow and calf eased around the corner of the stack into deep snow and we thought we'd won the battle when, suddenly, the moose lunged back into view, charged full bore between Jack and Jill astraddle the tongue.

She was nearly in our faces and we thought she was coming right over the front of the sled when she scrambled through the tug chains and was gone out the gate with her calf pacing behind her. The reek of moose urine hung heavy in the air. Jack and Jill shook like aspen leaves in the wind and broke out into an icy sweat. But, they held steady and with a final "giddap," we pulled in to load hay.

The second near wreck occurred one fall after a new snow. Mick and I were still using the small rubber tired wagon to feed with and every morning we drove into a windbreaked yard by the cow barn for hay. The night before, Mick had taken his John Deere crawler down to doze out the stacks and left it parked by the inner corral gate, with a canvas covering the hood and seat. Jack and Jill had placidly entered the yard for the past 10 days. That particular morning, though, seeing the canvas draped crawler, Jill convinced herself that the thing was a monster in wait.

She shied sideways, reared and tried to turn around in the meantime, boogering up our usually calm Jack. Mick had his hands full trying to control the team while I staggered to and fro trying to maintain my balance in the rocking wagon.

After several hectic minutes of "whoas" and "giddaps," with Jill refusing to go one step closer to the crawler, she lunged sideways, pushing Jack over until they were at a 90 degree angle to the wagon. Feeling the off side tug tight against his back leg, Jack came unglued and let go a mighty double-legged kick. I heard Mick holler, "Jump," and as I catapulted off the back of the wagon, Jack's hooves hit home and took out the entire sideboard where I'd been standing. Wood splinters and pieces of 2x12 flew through the air. Luckily, the shattered wagon stayed upright, the team righted them-selves and calmed down and we rolled into the stack with Jill still prancing, dancing and rolling her eyes at the crawler monster.

In 1988, when Mick sold the Wyoming ranch and we moved to our new home in Colorado, we made a dozen trips back and forth hauling furniture, household goods, ranch supplies and equipment. Our last trip in late Sep-tember brought our saddle horses and Jack and Jill. The other teams and older saddle horses we had reluctantly, but necessarily, sold at auction. Some-how, having Jack and Jill to begin over again with gave us a sense of conti-nuity, of hope. Jack and Jill are going through their fifth winter here, patient and willing partners in our desire to continue ranching.

Age and experience have eased Jill's temperament, though she still hates crossing bridges and can't tolerate too much wind harassing her. Today she stands docilely when I walk up to clip the lead onto her worn halter. She even snuffles my gloved hand, looking for hidden treats. I'm careful to talk to Jack and let him know I'm there before reaching for his halter. He's nearly blind now and sudden movements frighten him.

"Are you guys ready to go to work?" I ask.

"Huh, huh, huh," Jack nickers back and I lead them back to the barn.

Greedy for their grain, Jack and Jill bury their heads in the boxes, unwill-ing to move or shift their weight as I squeeze between them to brush last evening's crusted snow off their broad backs and scrape the icicles off their manes and tails. They're quiet as I hook the collars around their necks and heave the harnesses up and over, fasten the hames, snap the quarter straps to the breast strap and tighten the belly band. As I pull their long tails up through the britchins, I pat them each on their massive butts and murmur endearments.

I stand for awhile in the open sunny doorway, watching steam rise from their nostrils, and listen to them munch their grain. I'm thankful for this win-ter that they've been my responsibility to handle, harness and drive while Mick feeds. Now that they're old, reliable and mostly gentle, Mick trusts them to my care.

I'm honored.

I realize that this is most likely their last year to help us feed. Jack is sore shouldered and stove-up. His blindness is getting worse, to the point that he follows Jill wherever she goes. We've even seen her tenderly herd him to the river bank waterhole and on over to their feed. I hate to even think about the time to come when Jack will die or have to be put down, leaving Jill without her lifetime, trusty mate. So I brush the thought from my mind and concentrate on today.

I untie their ropes and lead them outside in the crisp, below zero sunshine to bridle. Mick comes over to help. We unfurl the lines and hook Jack and Jill together for the umpteenth time. They walk slowly side by side through the corral gates to the waiting wagon. Jill steps daintily over the tongue and Jack sidles over into his accustomed place. I hook up the neck yoke and we both fasten back the tugs. The team flicks their ears back and forth until "giddap" echoes out over the snow-covered pasture. They lean into their collars and walk off in unison. There are cows waiting for feed!

Corazón

GEORGE PATULLO

With manes streaming in the wind, a band of bronchos fled across the grama flats, splashed through the San Pedro, and whirled sharply to the right, heading for sanctuary in the Dragoons. In the lead raced a big sorrel, his coat shimmering like polished gold where the sun touched it.

"That's Corazón," exclaimed Reb. "Head him or we'll lose the bunch."

The pursuers spread out and swept round in a wide semicircle. Corazón held to his course, a dozen yards in advance of the others, his head high. The chase slackened, died away. With a blaring neigh, the sorrel eased his furious pace and the entire band came to a trot. Before them were the mountains, and Corazón knew their fastnesses as the street urchin knows the alleys that give him refuge; in the cañons the bronchos would be safe from man. Behind was no sign of the enemy. His nose in the wind, he sniffed long, but it bore him no taint. Instead, he nickered with delight, for he smelled water. They swung to the south, and in less than five minutes their hot muzzles were washed by the bubbling waters of Eternity Spring.

Corazón drew in a long breath, expanding his well-ribbed sides, and looked up from drinking. There in front of him, fifty paces away, was a horseman. He snorted the alarm and they plunged into a tangle of sagebrush. Another rider bore down and turned them back. To right and left they darted, then wheeled and sought desperately to break through the cordon at a weak spot, and failed.

Wherever they turned, a cowboy appeared as by magic. At last Corazón detected an unguarded area and flew through it with the speed of light.

"Now we've got 'em," howled Reb. "Don't drive too close, but keep 'em headed for the corral."

Within a hundred yards of the gate, the sorrel halted, his ears cocked in doubt. The cowboys closed in to force the band through. Three times the bronchos broke and scattered, for to their wild instincts the fences and that narrow aperture cried treachery and danger. They were gathered, with whoops and many imprecations, and once more approached the entrance.

"Drive the saddle bunch out," commanded the range boss.

Forth came the remuda of a hundred horses. The bronchos shrilled greeting and mingled with them, and when the cow-ponies trotted meekly into the corral, Corazón and his band went too, though they shook and were afraid.

For five years Corazón had roamed the range—ever since he had discovered that grass was good to eat, and so had left the care of his tender-eyed mother. Because he dreaded the master of created things and fled him afar, only once during that time had he seen man at close quarters. That was when, as a youngster, he was caught and branded on the left hip. He had quickly forgotten that; until now it had ceased to be even a memory.

But now he and his companion rovers were prisoners, cooped in a corral by a contemptible trick. They crowded around and around the stout enclosure, sometimes dropping to their knees in efforts to discover an exit beneath the boards. And not twenty feet away, the dreaded axis of their circlings, sat a man on a horse, and he studied them calmly. Other men, astride the fence, were uncoiling ropes, and their manner was placid and businesslike. One opined dispassionately that "the sorrel is shore some horse."

"You're damn whistlin'," cried the buster over his shoulder, in hearty affirmation.

Corazón was the most distracted of the entire band. He was in a frenzy of nervous fear, his glossy coat wet and foam-flecked. He would not stand still for a second, but prowled about the wooden barrier like a jungle creature newly prisoned in a cage. Twice he nosed the ground and crooked his forelegs in an endeavor to slide through the six inches of clear space beneath the gate, and the outfit laughed derisively.

"Here goes," announced the buster in his expressionless tones. "You-all watch out, now. Hell'll be poppin'."

At that moment Corazón took it into his head to dash at top speed through his friends, huddled in a bunch in a corner. A rope whined and coiled, and, when he burst out of the jam, the noose was around his neck, tightening so as to strangle him. Madly he ran against it, superb in the sureness of his might. Then he squalled with rage and pain and an awful terror. His legs flew from under him, and poor Corazón was jerked three feet into the air, coming down on his side with smashing force. The fall shook a grunt out of him, and he was stunned and breathless, but unhurt. He staggered to his feet, his breath straining like a bellows, for the noose cut into his neck and he would not yield to its pressure.

Facing him was the man on the bay. His mount stood with feet braced, sitting back on the rope, and he and his rider were quite collected and cool and prepared. The sorrel's eyes were starting from his head; his nostrils flared wide, gaping for the air that was denied him, and the breath sucked in his throat. It seemed as if he must drop. Suddenly the buster touched his horse lightly with the spur and slackened the rope. With a long sob, Corazón drew in a life-giving draught, his gaze fixed in frightened appeal on his captor.

"Open the gate," said Mullins, without raising his voice.

He flicked the rope over Corazón's hind quarters, and essayed to drive him into the next corral, to cut him off from his fellows. The sorrel gave a gasp of dismay and lunged forward. Again he was lifted from the ground, and came down with a thud that left him shivering.

"His laig's done bust!" exclaimed the boss.

"No; he's shook up, that's all. Wait awhile."

A moment later Corazón raised his head painfully; then, life and courage coming back with a rush, he lurched to his feet. Mullins waited with unabated patience. The sorrel was beginning to respect that which encircled his neck and made naught of his strength, and when the buster flipped the rope again, he ran through the small gate, and brought up before he had reached the end of his tether.

Two of the cowboys stepped down languidly from the fence, and took position in the center of the corral.

"Hi, Corazón! Go it, boy!" they yelled, and spurred by their cries, the horse started off at a trot. Reb tossed his loop—flung it carelessly, with a sinuous movement of the wrist—and when Corazón had gone a few yards, he found his forefeet ensnared. Enraged at being thus cramped, he bucked and bawled; but, before Reb could settle on the rope, he came to a standstill and sank his teeth into the strands. Once, twice, thrice he tugged, but could make no impression. Then he pitched high in air, and—

"NOW!" shrieked Reb.

They heaved with might and main, and Corazón flopped in the dust. Quick as a cat, he sprang upright and bolted; but again they downed him, and, while Reb held the head by straddling the neck, his confederate twined dexterously with a stake-rope. There lay Corazón, helpless and almost spent, trussed up like a sheep for market: they had hog-tied him.

It was the buster who put the hackamore on his head. Very deliberately he moved. Corazón sensed confidence in the touch of his fingers; they spoke a language to him, and he was soothed by the sureness of superiority they conveyed. He lay quiet. Then Reb incautiously shifted his position, and the horse heaved and raised his head, banging Mullins across the ear. The buster's senses swam, but instead of flying into a rage, he became quieter, more deliberate; in his cold eyes was a vengeful gleam, and dangerous stealth lurked in his delicate manipulation of the strands. An excruciating pain shot through the sorrel's eye: Mullins had gouged him.

"Let him up." It was the buster again, atop the bay, making the rope fast with a double half-hitch over the horn of the saddle.

Corazón arose, dazed and very sick. But his spirit was unbreakable. Again and again he strove to tear loose, rearing, falling back, plunging to the end of the rope until he was hurled off his legs to the ground. When he began to weary, Mullins encouraged him to fight, that he might toss him.

"I'll learn you what this rope means," he remarked, as the broncho scattered the dust for the ninth time, and remained there, completely done up.

In deadly fear of his slender tether, yet alert to match his strength against it once more, should opportunity offer, Corazón followed the buster quietly enough when he rode out into the open. Beside a sturdy mesquite bush that grew apart from its brethren, Mullins dismounted and tied the sorrel. As a farewell he waved his arms and whooped. Of course Corazón gathered himself and leaped—leaped to the utmost that was in him, so that the bush vibrated to its farthest root; and of course he hit the earth with a jarring thump that temporarily paralyzed him. Mullins departed to put the thrall of human will on others.

Throughout the afternoon, and time after time during the interminable night, the sorrel tried to break away, but with each sickening failure he grew more cautious. When he ran against the rope now, he did not run blindly to its limit, but half wheeled, so that when it jerked him back he invariably landed on his feet. Corazón was learning hard, but he was learning. And what agonies of pain and suspense he went through!—for years a free rover, and now to be bound thus, by what looked to be a mere thread, for he knew not what further tortures! He sweated and shivered, seeing peril in every shadow. When a coyote slunk by with tongue lapping hungrily over his teeth, the prisoner almost broke his neck in a despairing struggle to win freedom.

In the chill of the dawn they led him into a circular corral. His sleekness had departed; the barrel-like body did not look so well nourished, and there was red in the blazing eyes.

"I reckon he'll be mean," observed the buster, as though it concerned him but little.

"No-o-o. Go easy with him, Carl, and I think he'll make a good hoss," the boss cautioned.

While two men held the rope, Mullins advanced along it foot by foot, inch by inch, one hand outstretched, and talked to Corazón in a low, careless tone of affectionate banter. "So, you'd like for to kill me, would you?" he inquired, grinning. All the while he held the sorrel's gaze.

Corazón stood still, legs planted wide apart, and permitted him to approach. He trembled when the fingers touched his nose; but they were firm, confident digits, the voice was reassuring, and the gentle rubbing up, up between the eyes and ears lulled his forebodings.

"Hand me the blanket," said Mullins.

He drew it softly over Corazón's back, and the broncho swerved, pawed, and kicked with beautiful precision. Whereupon they placed a rope around his neck, dropped it behind his right hind leg, then pulled that member up close to his belly; there it was held fast. On three legs now, the sorrel was impotent for harm. Mullins once more took up the blanket but this time the gentleness had flown. He slapped it over Corazón's backbone from side to side a dozen times. At each impact the horse humped awkwardly, but, finding that he came to no hurt, he suffered it in resignation.

That much of the second lesson learned, they saddled him. Strangely enough, Corazón submitted to the operation without fuss, the only untoward symptoms being a decided upward slant to the back of the saddle and the tucking of his tail. Reb waggled his head over this exhibition.

"I don't like his standing quiet that away; it ain't natural," he vouchsafed. "Look at the crick in his back. Jim-in-ee! he'll shore pitch."

Which he did. The cinches were tightened until Corazón's eyes almost popped from his head; then they released the bound leg and turned him loose. What was that galling his spine? Corazón took a startled peep at it, lowered his head between his knees, and began to bawl. Into the air he rocketed, his head and forelegs swinging to the left, his hind quarters weaving to the right. The jar of his contact with the ground was appalling. Into the air again, his head and forelegs to the right, his rump twisted to the left. Round and round the corral he went, blatting like an angry calf; but the thing on his back stayed where it was, gripping his body cruelly. At last he was fain to stop for breath.

"Now," said Mullins, "I reckon I'll take it out of him."

There has always been for me an overwhelming fascination in watching busters at work. They have underlying traits in common when it comes to handling the horses—the garrulous one becomes coldly watchful, the Stoic moves with stern patience, the boaster soothes with soft-crooned words and confident caress. Mullins left Corazón standing in the middle of the corral, the hackamore rope strung loose on the ground, while he saw to it that his spurs were fast. We mounted the fence, not wishing to be mixed in the glorious turmoil to follow.

"I wouldn't top ol' Corazón for fifty," confessed the man on the adjoining post.

"Mullins has certainly got nerve," I conceded.

"A buster has got to have nerve." The range boss delivered himself laconically. "All nerve and no brains makes the best. But they get stove up and then—"

"And then? What then?"

"Why, don't you know?" he asked in surprise. "Every buster loses his nerve at last, and then they can't ride a pack-hoss. It must be because it's one fool man with one set of nerves up ag'in a new hoss with a new devil in him every time. They wear him down. Don't you reckon?"

The explanation sounded plausible. Mullins was listening with a faintly amused smile to Reb's account of what a lady mule had done to him; he rolled a cigarette and lighted it painstakingly. The hands that held the match were steady as eternal rock. It was maddening to see him stand there so coolly while the big sorrel, a dozen feet distant, was a-quake with dread, blowing harshly through his crimson nostrils whenever a cowboy stirred—and each of us knowing that the man was taking his life in his hands. An unlooked-for twist, a trifling disturbance of poise, and, with a horse like Corazón, it meant maiming or death. At last he threw the cigarette from him and walked slowly to the rope.

"So you're calling for me?" he inquired, gathering it up.

Corazón was snorting. By patient craft Reb acquired a grip on the sorrel's ears, and, while he hung there, bringing the head down so that the horse could not move, Mullins tested the stirrups and raised himself cautiously into the saddle.

"Let him go."

While one could count ten, Corazón stood expectant, his back bowed, his tail between his legs. The ears were laid flat on the head and the forefeet well advanced. The buster waited, the quirt hanging from two fingers of his right hand. Suddenly the sorrel ducked his head and emitted a harsh scream, leaping, with legs stiff, straight off the ground. He came down with the massive hips at an angle to the shoulders, thereby imparting a double shock; bounded high again, turned back with bewildering speed as he touched the earth; and then, in a circle perhaps twenty feet in diameter, sprang time after time, his heels lashing the air. Never had such pitching been seen on the Anvil Range.

"I swan, he just misses his tail a' inch when he turns back!" roared a puncher.

Mullins sat composedly in the saddle, but he was riding as never before. He whipped the sorrel at every jump and raked him down the body from shoulder to loins with the ripping spurs. The brute gave no signs of letting up. Through Mullins' tan of copper hue showed a slight pallor. He was exhausted. If Corazón did not give in soon, the man would be beaten. Just then the horse stopped, feet a-sprawl.

"Mullins,"—the range boss got down from the fence—"you'll kill that hoss. Between the cinches belongs to you; the head and hind quarters is the company's."

For a long minute Mullins stared at the beast's ears without replying.

"I reckon that's the rule," he acquiesced heavily. "Do you want that somebody else should ride him?"

"No-o-o. Go ahead. But, remember, between the cinches you go at him as you like—nowhere else."

The buster slapped the quirt down on Corazón's shoulder, but the broncho did not budge; then harder. With the first oath he had used, he jabbed in the spurs and lay back on the hackamore rope. Instead of bucking, Corazón reared straight up, his feet pawing like the hands of a drowning man. Before Mullins could move to step off, the sorrel flung his head round and toppled backward.

"No, he's not dead." The range boss leaned over the buster and his hands fumbled inside the shirt. "The horn got him here, but he ain't dead. Claude, saddle Streak and hit for Agua Prieta for the doctor."

When we had carried the injured man to the bunk-house, Reb spoke from troubled meditation:

"Pete, I don't believe Corazón is as bad as he acts with Mullins. I've been watching him. Mullins, he didn't—"

"You take him, then; he's yours," snapped the boss, his conscience pricking because of the reproof he had administered. If the buster had ridden him his own way, this might not have happened.

That is how the sorrel came into Reb's possession. Only one man of the outfit witnessed the taming, and he would not talk; but when Reb came to dinner from the first saddle on Corazón, his hands were torn and the nail of one finger hung loose.

"I had to take to the horn and hang on some," he admitted.

Ay, he had clung there desperately while the broncho pitched about the river-bed, whither Reb had retired for safety and to escape spectators. But at the next saddle Corazón was less violent; at the third, recovering from the stunning shocks and bruisings of the first day, he was a fiend; and then, on the following morning, he did not pitch at all. Reb rode him every day to sap the superfluous vigor in Corazón's iron frame and he taught him as well as he could the first duties of a cow-horse. Finding that his new master never punished him unless he undertook to dispute his authority, the sorrel grew tractable and began to take an interest in his tasks.

"He's done broke," announced Reb; "I'll have him bridle-wise in a week. He'll make some roping horse. Did you see him this evening? I swan—"

They scoffed good-naturedly; but Reb proceeded on the assumption that Corazón was meant to be a roping horse, and schooled him accordingly. As for the sorrel, he took to the new pastime with delight. Within a month nothing gave him keener joy than to swerve and crouch at the climax of a sprint and see a cow thrown heels over head at the end of the rope that was wrapped about his saddle-horn.

The necessity of contriving to get three meals a day took me elsewhere, and I did not see Corazón again for three years. Then, one Sunday afternoon, Big John drew me from El Paso to Juarez on the pretense of seeing a grand, an extraordinary, a most noble bull-fight, in which the dauntless Favorita would slay three fierce bulls from the renowned El Carmen ranch, in "competency" with the fearless Morenito Chico de San Bernardo; and a youth with a megaphone drew us both to a steer-roping contest instead. We agreed that bull-fighting was brutal on the Sabbath.

"I'll bet it's rotten," remarked Big John pessimistically, as we took our seats. "I could beat 'em myself."

As he scanned the list, his face brightened. Among the seventeen ropers thereon were two champions and a possible new one in Raphael Fraustro, the redoubtable vaquero from the domain of Terrazas.

"And here's Reb!" roared John—he is accustomed to converse in the tumult of the branding-pen—"I swan, he's entered from Monument."

Shortly afterwards the contestants paraded, wonderfully arrayed in silk shirts and new handkerchiefs.

"Some of them ain't been clean before in a year," was John's caustic comment. "There's Slim; I KNOW he hasn't."

They were a fine-looking body of men, and two of my neighbors complained that I trampled on their feet. The horses caught the infection of excitement from the packed stands and champed on their bits and caracoled and waltzed sideways in a manner highly unbecoming a staid cow-pony.

There was one that did not. So sluggish was his gait and general bearing, in contrast to the others, that the crowd burst into laughter. He plodded at the tail-end of the procession, his hoofs kicking up the dust in listless spurts, his nose on a level with his knees. I rubbed my eyes and John said, "No, it ain't—it can't be—"; but it was. Into that arena slouched Corazón, entered against the pick of the horses of the Southwest; and Reb was astride him.

We watched the ropers catch and tie the steers in rapid succession, but the much-heralded ones missed altogether, and to John and me the performance lagged. We were waiting for Reb and Corazón.

They came at last, at the end of the list. When Corazón ambled up the arena to enter behind the barrier, the grandstand roared a facetious welcome; the spectacle of this sad-gaited nag preparing to capture a steer touched its risibilities.

"Listen to me," bawled a fat gentleman in a wide-brimmed hat, close to my ear. "You listen to me! They're all fools. That's a cow-horse. No blasted nonsense. Knows his business, huh? You're damn whistlin'!"

Assuredly, Corazón knew his business. The instant he stepped behind the line he was a changed horse. The flopping ears pricked forward, his neck arched, and the great muscles of his shoulders and thighs rippled to his dainty prancing. He pulled and fretted on the bit, his eyes roving about in search of the quarry; he whinnied an appeal to be gone. Reb made ready his coil, curbing him with light pressure.

Out from the chute sprang a steer, heading straight down the arena. Corazón was frantic. With the flash of the gun he breasted the barrier-rope and swept down on him in twenty strides. Reb stood high in the stirrups; the loop whirled and sped; and, without waiting to see how it fell, but accepting a catch in blind faith, the sorrel started off at a tangent.

Big John was standing up in his place, clawing insanely at the hats of his neighbors and banging them on the head with his programme.

"Look at him—just look at him!" he shrieked.

The steer was tossed clear of the ground and came down on his left side. Almost before he landed, Reb was out of the saddle and speeding toward him.

"He's getting up. HE'S GETTING UP. Go to him, Reb!" howled John and I.

The steer managed to lift his head; he was struggling to his knees. I looked away, for Reb must lose. Then a hoarse shout from the multitude turned back my gaze. Corazón had felt the slack on the rope and knew what it meant. He dug his feet into the dirt and began to walk slowly forward— very slowly and carefully, for Reb's task must not be spoiled. The steer collapsed, falling prone again, but the sorrel did not stop. Once he cocked his eye, and seeing that the animal still squirmed, pulled with all his strength. The stands were rocking; they were a sea of tossing hats and gesticulating arms and flushed faces; the roar of their plaudits echoed back from the hills. And it was all for Corazón, gallant Corazón.

"Dam' his eyes—dam' his ol' eyes!" Big John babbled over and over, absolutely oblivious.

Reb stooped beside the steer, his hands looping and tying with deft darting twists even as he kept pace with his dragged victim.

"I guess it's—about—a—hour," he panted.

Then he sprang clear and tossed his hands upward, facing the judges' stand. After that he walked aimlessly about, mopping his face with a handkerchief; for to him the shoutings and the shifting colors were all a foolish dream, and he was rather sick.

Right on the cry with which his master announced his task done, Corazón eased up on the rope and waited.

"Mr. Pee-ler's time," bellowed the man with the megaphone presently, "is twenty-one seconds, ty-ing the world's re-cord."

So weak that his knees trembled, Reb walked over to his horse. "Corazón," he said huskily, and slapped him once on the flank.

Nothing would do the joyous crowd then but that Reb should ride forth to be acclaimed the victor. We sat back and yelled ourselves weak with laughter, for Corazón, having done his work, refused resolutely to squander time in vain parade. The steer captured and tied, he had no further interest in the proceedings. The rascal dog-trotted reluctantly to the center of the arena in obedience to Reb, then faced the audience; but, all the time Reb was bowing his acknowledgments, Corazón sulked and slouched, and he was sulking and shuffling the dust when they went through the gate.

"Now," said John, who is very human, "we'll go help Reb spend that money."

As we jostled amid the outgoing crowd, several cowboys came alongside the grandstand rail, and Big John drew me aside to have speech with them. One rider led a spare horse and when he passed a man on foot, the latter hailed him:

"Say, Ed, give me a lift to the hotel?"

"Sure," answered Ed, proffering the reins.

The man gathered them up, his hands fluttering as if with palsy, and paused with his foot raised toward the stirrup.

"He won't pitch nor nothing, Ed?" came the quavered inquiry. "You're shore he's gentle?"

"Gentler'n a dog," returned Ed, greatly surprised.

"You ain't fooling me, now, are you, Ed?" continued the man on the ground. "He looks kind of mean."

"Give him to me!" Ed exploded. "You kin walk."

From where we stood, only the man's back was visible. "Who is that fellow?" I asked.

"Who? Him?" answered my neighbor. "Oh, his name's Mullins. They say he used to be able to ride anything with hair on it, and throw off the bridle at that. I expect that's just talk. Don't you reckon?"

A Colt with Some Heart

CAROLYN DUFURRENA

Thunderheads drifted through the summer afternoon, their shadows darkening the ridges of the Pine Forest Range. Peggy sat at the kitchen counter, coffee and a cigarette in front of her. Two four-year-old boys, my son and her grandson, played in the shallow ditch just outside the window, building endless mud pies. I watched while Peggy folded laundry. We talked and talked the hours away, as she broke an egg into a bowl of flour, stirring up a batch of rolls for dinner. She set them on the pilot light to rise and put the laundry away. We had another cup of coffee. Merv was only a little late. It wasn't near time to get worried. Still, her blue eyes scanned the ridge every few minutes.

Merv snaked the big bay colt down over the rocky, brush-choked trail, through the lightning-blackened pines rimming the cirque's headwall ridge, down slopes thickly masked by mountain mahogany and aspen. The trail had led him from the headquarters west, up a rocky canyon, across a big high meadow—a little soggy even this late in summer—and up again, out of the sagebrush and into the pines. He had a pretty good scatter on the cattle: fifty head each in the several little basins on the eastern side, fifty head over the ridge. There was room on the top of this mountain for a lot of cows. It was great place to start a young horse, and he was happy with this one.

126

The glacial lake was dark green at midday, and mossy light brocaded the jumble of granite boulders beneath the surface. He stepped off in a grassy place near the icy water and cautiously slipped the hobbles around the colt's hocks. He stood, and stretched. He walked to the shore through a skiff of long pine needles over fine sand.

Swifts skimmed the wavelets, hunting the afternoon hatch. The wind freshened. The grizzled cowboy breathed, lifting the terrible, old, used-to-be-white hat off his forehead.

A couple of fly fishermen eyed him curiously, a figure out of a Western novel riding into the twentieth century. The fishing population had changed here since the government had declared this a wilderness. Not many locals now chose to hike the jeep trail they'd driven over in years past, and these men were from someplace else. One of them came over.

"How's the fishin'?" Merv inquired politely, fishing his own can of Copenhagen out of a blue shirt pocket. They discussed the merits of angling in the middle of the day, dubious at best, and shot the breeze for a while. The fisherman said he'd better work his way around the backside.

He eyed the bay, half-asleep in the warm sun as he passed by. "What's your horse's name?"

"Roller."

Merv did not explain how the horse had earned his name. The colt loved his life, loved his work. He loved to chase cows, and worked up a pretty good sweat doing it. When the saddle came off at the end of the day, he would roll and roll in the pasture, as many as six or seven times.

"Nice horse," the fisherman commented, walked past, and smacked him on the rump.

Merv's eyes widened as Roller—still hobbled—came out of his doze with a snort. He took one, then two sideways jumps toward the lake. Merv moved as carefully as he could toward the colt's head, but Roller was panicked, and too quick. Every yank on those hobbles scared him worse. Next thing Merv knew, Roller had bucked himself, saddle, snaffle bit, hobbles and all, into the icy green water.

Glaciers carve a steep profile, and the water is deep close to shore. The terrified horse lunged, struggling for his life. The hobbles kept the colt's front hocks close together: handcuffs. Waves surged from his shoulders as he heaved against the weight of the soaked saddle and blankets, the split reins tangling around his feet. Easy enough for him to tip over and drown. Merv could only stand helplessly on the shore, watching. "Goddammit, Roller. . ." he cursed, or perhaps it was closer to prayer.

The colt's eyes showed white. He snorted and coughed, kicked and kicked at the hobbles. Finally, somehow, he broke free. Still hauling the heavy blankets, the soaking wet saddle, he lunged through the hidden underwater boulders toward shore. Power doubled, he clawed his way back up through the rocks until with one final desperate heave, he stood, dripping and quivering on the grass.

Merv reached out slowly, took the reins, eased off the cinch and slid the sopping saddle to the ground.

For a while he didn't say anything. Then, "Well, hell, Roller. Might as well have a little siesta while these blankets dry, and then ease on home." He looked at the trail leading up the headwall ridge, seeing the trip back across the big meadow, across the far side of the mountain toward home, and sighed. Roller shook his massive shoulders like a dog, and sighed too. He dropped his head to the grass. He was hungry.

The sun had left Peggy's lawn, and the children played horses on the living room rug. Peggy took one deep breath as she saw Merv and the big bay colt emerge from the shadows of the rocky canyon. She poured her cold coffee down the sink and turned the dough out to punch down into rolls for his dinner.

Merv shook his head as he finished telling his wife the story of his day. "That old Roller. I thought I was gonna lose him, by God. By God colt's got some heart to him, don't he."

Roller was still alive in 2001—he would have been twenty that year. He worked for Merv on high desert ranches for years, helping with branding, running mustangs, chasing cows, until Merv retired. Merv's son Gary had him for a while, then passed him to granddaughter Lacey. Last she heard of him, he was traded to team penners from California.

Horses of the Badlands

THEODORE ROOSEVELT

We breakfast early—before dawn when the nights have grown long, and rarely later than sunrise, even in midsummer. Perhaps before this meal, certainly the instant it is over, the man whose duty it is rides off to hunt up and drive in the saddle-band. Each of us has his own string of horses, eight or ten in number, and the whole band usually split up into two or three companies. In addition to the scattered groups of the saddle-band, our six or eight mares, with their colts, keep by themselves, and are rarely bothered by us, as no cowboy ever rides anything but horses, because mares give great trouble where all the animals have to be herded together. Once every two or three days somebody rides round and finds out where each of these smaller bands is, but the man who goes out in the morning merely gathers one bunch. He drives these into the corral, the other men (who have been lolling idly about the house or stable, fixing their saddles or doing any odd job) coming out with their ropes as soon as they hear the patter of the unshod hoofs and the shouts of the cowboy driver. Going into the corral, and standing near the center, each of us picks out some one of his own string from among the animals that are trotting and running in a compact mass round the circle; and after one or more trials, according to his skill, ropes it and leads it out. When all have caught their horses the rest are again turned loose, together with those that have been kept up overnight. Some horses soon get tame and do not need to be roped; my pet cutting

129

pony, little Muley, and good old Manitou, my companion in so many hunting trips, will neither of them stay with the rest of their fellows that are jam-
ming and jostling each other as they rush round in the dust of the corral, but
they very sensibly walk up and stand quietly with the men in the middle, by
the snubbing-post. Both are great pets, Manitou in particular; the wise old
fellow being very fond of bread and sometimes coming up of his own accord
to the ranch house and even putting his head into the door to beg for it.

If any horses have strayed, one or two of the men will be sent off to look
for them; for hunting lost horses is one of the commonest and most irksome of
our duties. Every outfit always has certain of its horses at large; and if they remain out long enough they become as wild and wary as deer and have to be
regularly surrounded and run down. On one occasion, when three of mine had
been running loose for a couple of months, we had to follow at full speed for
at least fifteen miles before exhausting them enough to enable us to get some
control over them and head them towards a corral. Twice I have had horses ab-
sent nearly a year before they were recovered. One of them, after being on the
ranch nine months, went off one night and traveled about two hundred miles
in a straight line back to its old haunts, swimming the Yellowstone on the way.
Two others were at one time away nearly eighteen months, during which time
we saw them twice, and on one occasion a couple of the men fairly ran their
horses down in following them. We began to think they were lost for good, as
they were all the time going farther down towards the Sioux country, but we finally recovered them.

In the spring, mud-holes cause very serious losses among the cattle, and are
at all times fruitful sources of danger; indeed, during an ordinary year more cattle die from getting mired than from any other cause. In addition to this they
also often prove very annoying to the rider himself, as getting his steed mired
or caught in a quicksand is one of the commonest of the accidents that beset a
horseman in the far West. This usually happens in fording a river, if the latter is
at all high, or else in crossing one of the numerous creeks; although I once saw
a horse and rider suddenly engulfed while leisurely walking over what appeared
to be dry land. They had come to an alkali mud-hole, an old buffalo-wallow,
which had filled up and was covered with a sun-baked crust, that let them
through as if they had stepped on a trap-door. There being several of us along,
we got down our ropes and dragged both unfortunates out in short order.

When the river is up it is a very common thing for a horseman to have
great difficulty in crossing, for the swift, brown water runs over a bed of deep

quicksand that is ever shifting. An inexperienced horse, or a mule—for a mule is useless in mud or quicksand—becomes mad with fright in such a crossing, and, after speedily exhausting its strength in wild struggles, will throw itself on its side and drown unless the rider gets it out. An old horse used to such work will, on the contrary, take matters quietly and often push along through really dangerous quicksand. Old Manitou never loses his head for an instant; but, now resting a few seconds, now feeling his way cautiously forward, and now making two or three desperate plunges, will go on wherever a horse possibly can. It is really dangerous crossing some of the creeks, as the bottom may give way where it seems hardest; and if one is alone he may work hours in vain before getting his horse out, even after taking off both saddle and bridle, the only hope being to head it so that every plunge takes it an inch or two in the right direction.

Nor are mud-holes the only danger the horseman has to fear; for in much of the Bad Lands the buttes are so steep and broken that it needs genuine mountaineering skill to get through them, and no horse but a Western one, bred to the business, could accomplish the feat. In many parts of our country it is impossible for a horseman who does not know the land to cross it, and it is difficult enough even for an experienced hand. The whole country seems to be one tangled chaos of canyon-like valleys, winding gullies and washouts with abrupt, unbroken sides, isolated peaks of sandstone, marl, or "gumbo" clay, which rain turns into slippery glue, and hill chains the ridges of which always end in sheer cliffs. In such a place the rider dismounts and leads his horse, the latter climbing with cat-like agility up seemingly inaccessible heights, scrambling across the steep, sloping shoulders of the bluffs, sliding down the faces of the clay cliffs with all four legs rigid, or dropping from ledge to ledge like a goat, and accepting with unruffled composure an occasional roll from top to bottom. But, in spite of the climbing abilities of the ponies, it is difficult, and at times— for our steeds, at any rate—dangerous work to go through such places, and we only do it when it cannot be avoided. Once I was overtaken by darkness while trying to get through a great tract of very rough land, and, after once or twice nearly breaking my neck, in despair had to give up all attempts to get out, and until daybreak simply staid where I was, in a kind of ledge or pocket on the side of the cliff, luckily sheltered from the wind. It was midsummer and the nights were short, but this particular one seemed quite long enough; and though I was on the move by dawn, it was three hours later before I led the horse, as hungry, numb, and stiff as myself, out on the prairie again.

The afternoon's tasks are usually much the same as the morning's, but this time is often spent in doing the odds and ends; as, for instance, it may be devoted to breaking-in a new horse. Large outfits generally hire a bronco-buster to do this; but we ourselves almost always break our own horses, two or three of my men being pretty good riders, although none of them can claim to be anything out of the common. A first-class flash rider or bronco-buster receives high wages, and deserves them, for he follows a most dangerous trade, at which no man can hope to grow old; his work being infinitely harder than that of an Eastern horse-breaker or rough-rider, because he has to do it in such a limited time.

Some of the things he teaches his horse would be wholly useless to an Eastern equestrian: for example, one of the first lessons the newly-caught animal has to learn is not to "run on a rope"; and he is taught this by being violently snubbed up, probably turning a somersault, the first two or three times that he feels the noose settle round his neck, and makes a mad rush for liberty. The snubbing-post is the usual adjunct in teaching such a lesson; but a skillful man can do without any help and throw a horse clean over by holding the rope tight against the left haunch, at the same time leaning so far back, with the legs straight in front, that the heels dig deep into the ground when the strain comes, and the horse, running out with the slack of the rope, is brought up standing, or even turned head over heels by the shock. Cowboys are probably the only working-men in the world who invariably wear gloves, buckskin gauntlets being preferred, as otherwise the ropes would soon take every particle of skin off their hands.

A bronco-buster has to work by such violent methods in consequence of the short amount of time at his command. Horses are cheap, each outfit has a great many, and the wages for breaking an animal are but five or ten dollars. Three rides, of an hour or two each, on as many consecutive days, are the outside number a bronco-buster deems necessary before turning an animal over as "broken." The average bronco-buster, however, handles horses so very rudely that we prefer, aside from motives of economy, to break our own; and this is always possible, if we take enough time. The best and quietest horses on the ranch are far from being those broken by the best riders; on the contrary, they are those that have been handled most gently, although firmly, and that have had the greatest number of days devoted to their education.

Some horses, of course, are almost incurably vicious, and must be conquered by main force. One pleasing brute on my ranch will at times rush at a man open-mouthed like a wolf, and this is a regular trick of the range-stallions. In a great many—indeed, in most—localities there are wild horses to be found, which although invariably of domestic descent, being either themselves runaways from some ranch or Indian outfit, or else claiming such for their sires and dams, yet are quite as wild as the antelope on whose domain they have intruded. Ranchmen run in these wild horses whenever possible, and they are but little more difficult to break than the so-called "tame" animals. But the wild stallions are, whenever possible, shot; both because of their propensity for driving off the ranch mares, and because their incurable viciousness makes them always unsafe companions for other horses still more than for men. A wild stallion fears no beast except the grizzly, and will not always flinch from an encounter with it; yet it is a curious fact that a jack will almost always kill one in a fair fight. The particulars of a fight of this sort were related to me by a cattle man who was engaged in bringing out blooded stock from the East. Among the animals under his charge were two great stallions, one gray and one black, and a fine jackass, not much over half the size of either of the former. The animals were kept in separate pens, but one day both horses got into the same inclosure, next to the jack-pen, and began to fight as only enraged stallions can, striking like boxers with their fore feet, and biting with their teeth. The gray was getting the best of it; but while clinched with his antagonist in one tussle they rolled against the jack-pen, breaking it in. No sooner was the jack at liberty than, with ears laid back and mouth wide open, he made straight for the two horses, who had for the moment separated. The gray turned to meet him, rearing on his hind legs and striking at him with his fore feet; but the jack slipped in, and in a minute grasped his antagonist by the throat with his wide-open jaws, and then held on like a bull-dog, all four feet planted stiffly in the soil. The stallion made tremendous efforts to shake him off: he would try to whirl round and kick him, but for that the jack was too short; then he would rise up, lifting the jack off the ground, and strike him with his fore feet; but all that he gained by this was to skin his foe's front legs without making him loose his hold. Twice they fell, and twice the stallion rose, by main strength dragging the jack with him; but all in vain. Meanwhile the black horse attacked both the combatants, with perfect impartiality, striking and kicking them with his hoofs, while his teeth, as they slipped off the tough hides, met with a snap like that of a bear-trap. Undoubtedly the jack would have killed at least one of the horses had not the men come up, and with no small difficulty separated the maddened brutes.

One Good Turn

WILL JAMES

Croppy was a little gray horse I'd traded for while riding through a settlement on my way to another range country. I traded because I felt sorry for the horse, not because I needed him, for I already had a string of six good horses, all excepting one.

I was riding along and keeping my horses in a good walking pace when, glancing over my shoulder, I sees a horse and rider coming my way at the speed of a runaway engine. It didn't take the rider long to catch up with me, and I was surprised that instead of going on like I thought he would, on account of he'd seemed to be in such a hurry, he jerked his sweaty and panting horse, in a showing-off way, to a walk alongside of mine.

As we howdydoed I could tell by one glance at the rider that he was out to play cowboy. His outfit, from the rattlesnake hatband on his big hat to his leather cuffs and chaps, was all decorated up with nickel spots; there was more nickel spots on his saddle and bridle, and from all about him I figured that all his riding was done at showing-off in the settlement and none at all on the range.

"The way you're riding," I says, as we begin talking, "I thought sure you was headed to a fire, or maybe a funeral somewhere."

He grins and looks at me kind of blank:

"No," he says "I was just going after the mail."

"Oh, I see, Pony Express rider." I went on: "But I still think you was headed for a funeral."

"Funeral?" he asks, surprised. "What makes you think so?"

"Well," I says, grinning sarcastic. "The way you ride that horse of yours there'll soon be a funeral, a horse funeral. Doggone shame, too, because he's a right pretty little horse."

"Yes," agrees the would-be cowboy, "he is a pretty little horse, and a good one, too, but I think he's too small for me."

We rode along, not talking much, and I noticed that that feller was sure sizing up my saddle horses, even the one I was riding. I had a hunch as to what that meant and I figured he would soon be talking trade to me, so I prepared for that and I sized his horse up mighty quick. I could tell he was a good horse and not too little for any man who knows how to sit a horse and treat him right. He was poor and tired looking, but he was young and sound, and with a rest on good feed he would be a mighty good little horse. I couldn't tell how well broke he was or how much he knowed, but I could see he was willing and not at all stiff-necked or stubborn. He seemed to be only anxious to do all he could to please his rider, and when I seen that his mouth was bleeding from the crazy looking bit he was packing, I decided to help that little horse and trade for him, if possible.

But I didn't want to let on that I would trade or the big hunk of nickel-plated meat that slopped on the little gray might of made the trading hard. I figured to let him be the first to talk trade, and from the way he acted I didn't think I'd have long to wait.

And I didn't. He spoke right up, and, pointing to a big buckskin in my string, he asked how I'd trade him for his little gray. The buckskin was a good-looking horse but about as worthless as he was good to look at. He was too slow and lazy to catch cold, no spur could faze his thick hide and a feller sure had to work his way on him. He was stiff-necked and cold-jawed, and it was near as hard to turn him by pulling on a rein as it would of been by pulling on his tail. He was no young horse either, and outside of a ring bone that was started, and a sprained tendon, he was fairly sound. To a greenhorn he would look sound enough.

I used the horse very little, only to pack once in a while, but never to ride, for I'd rode him once and that had been enough for me. So I kept him for a trading horse. I'd got him that way a couple of month before, and even though I'd got stung a little in that trade I figured I'd more than make that up in some other trade with him. The looks of him would sure do the work if I run acrost the right party to trade with, and now I thought I sure had that party.

I acted kind of surprised and not at all interested when the nickel-spotted feller pointed at my buckskin and asked how I'd trade for his gray.

"Why," I says, grinning, "you ain't riding nothing that would make trade, and you'd have to give me so much to boot with that skinny little gray of yours that you'd just about be buying that buckskin of mine."

That seemed to set that feller to thinking and feeling kind of cheap as he looked down at his horse, for that poor little gray did look mighty puny as compared to my big buckskin. But I knowed that the little gray was easy worth two of the buckskin any time or place.

I didn't feel no remorse as I went on with my trading talk; instead I felt pleased with the hope that I could make him pay for the way he treated the little gray, and the more I could make him pay the better I'd like it.

"That buckskin of mine is some horse," I bragged on, "as good a look-ing horse as you'll find anywhere. He'd make you proud of being seen on him, and he'll go as far as you want to ride him any time."

That all was sure the truth, and 'specially the last part, because, with going any long distance, the rider would be more tired in making the horse go than the horse would in travelling the distance.

"He's a showy horse," I says, as I guessed the feller's caliber, "and would set off your fancy outfit nice. And another thing, if you want to show off in front of your girl and your friends once in a while, all you have to do is 'thumb' him (running both thumbs stiff along neck muscles) and he'll give a pretty fair exhibition of bucking, but not hard enough to buck off any average rider." That was only trade talk, for I didn't think the horse would ever buck.

"I know you sure can ride him, easy," I went on, not believing that he would ride any horse that bucked much. But that remark done its work and it sure pleased him.

The big buckskin, travelling ahead with my other horses, sure did look good. He carried his head up well and he showed good enough action. I no-ticed how the nickel-plated feller kept a-looking at him, and being as I had that feller's pedigree pegged down I sort of guessed what was running in his mind as he looked at the horse. I figured how he pictured himself parading on the showy buckskin in the little town of the settlement, making him buck in front of the pool hall or post office or wherever there would be people to watch him. Yep, he'd have a great time playing cowboy of evenings.

We rode on, neither of us saying anything for quite a spell, then, as we came closer to the little town, I guess he got sort of nervous at the thought I'd be riding on, and I could see he'd decided that he just had to have that buckskin of mine.

"How much would you want to boot with this horse of mine for that buckskin of yours?" he blurted out.

"Well," I says, acting surprised again. "I never thought of parting with that horse." I lied. "Wouldn't any of the others do?"

I wouldn't of parted with any of the others. But I knowed I was safe there, and he says: "No, the buckskin is the one I want."

"You sure know a good horse when you see one," I says, grinning to myself. "The buckskin is right classy and with just one look at him anybody can see he's a hundred-and-fifty-dollar horse, plum gentle, too."

"But I couldn't give you no hundred to boot," he says, showing his hand, "I only paid fifty dollars for this gray, but he's a good horse, too, and worth more."

"I don't think he's worth fifty now," I says, eyeing the gray, "but," I went on, like I was doing some tall figuring, "being I'm about broke and need some money to travel on I'll trade with you if you'll give me sixty dollars to boot."

If that feller'd had the money with him, I think he'd given me the sixty right then and there, but he didn't have it. He said he was getting only forty a month and board on the construction job where he was working, but he would do his best to borrow the money from some friends he had in town.

I said I would stay in town for the night and give him a chance to rake up the money. I was going to stay in town anyway, and he rode along with me to the feed lot of a livery stable.

There he left me, and, without even trying the buckskin, he hit for other parts of town to dig up the money. He'd gone by the good looks of the buckskin all together. That seemed to be about all that mattered to him.

I unpacked and unsaddled and left my horses loose to the hay manger, and, being it was near sundown, I hit for where I could get me a big steak. When I got back to the stable my trade victim was in the feed lot and looking the buckskin over some more. He looked kind of downhearted as he seen me and said that all he could rake up was thirty dollars.

"There's no splitting the difference in this trade," I says. "It's sixty to the boot or no trade."

I was running my bluff to the limit. I had a good chance and I took advantage of it, not only to please myself as a horse trader but to sort of even scores for the little gray.

He was bound to get my buckskin, and now he wanted to try him. From that I got the idea that he could rake up more money but he wanted to make double sure of the horse first.

The buckskin was gentle as a house cat, and as the feller put his saddle on him I remarked that I'd been riding the horse pretty hard and steady, that he was tired and maybe wouldn't show off so good right now.

"But to look at him," I says, "you wouldn't think he'd been rode much. He's a mighty tough horse."

The feller climbed in the saddle, and the buckskin showed lively enough as he was rode around the manger-ful of hay in the big lot; he was even made to break into a trot and then a lope without much spurring, and I remarked once as the feller rode him past me that the horse sure looked good under that fancy outfit of his. That went well.

Another time that feller rode by me I told him to "goose" the horse and make him buck a little. I said he couldn't buck hard, and fact is I didn't think he'd buck at all. The feller looked at me kind of like he was leary to try, and when I just laughed, he got up enough gumption to run both his thumbs along the horse's neck.

To my real surprise the horse did buck, not exactly buck but crow-hopped in a few long lazy-like jumps and, of course, the feller rode him easy enough. That sure clinched the deal and the feller was as tickled as a baby with a new rattle. He seemed so pleased and surprised to be still on the horse after the last jump, that after he took a breath on that he thumbed him again and the buckskin crowhopped some more.

Then I thought that had gone far enough, for I figured that horse might loosen up, really buck and throw him off, and I wanted to get my boot money and make the trade before that happened. It was getting dark, too, and he still had to go back to the construction camp.

He got off the buckskin and, as I had made it plain that there would be no trade unless he raked up the sixty dollars, he rushed out saying that he'd somehow get thirty dollars more to add to the thirty he already got. I figured he'd sure try hard this time.

I told him I'd wait in the stable office. I waited for about an hour, and then here he come back on the run. He hadn't been able to rake up over twenty dollars more, and I knowed that he'd sure done his best. That made fifty dollars all together, and I accepted. I think I'd accepted even if I hadn't wanted to trade because he sure begged for me to let him have that buckskin.

We shook hands and he rode away happy on that horse, leaving me with the little gray and fifty dollars to boot.

If it had come to a showdown I'd of been glad to trade my buckskin even up for the gray, and given some boot myself, if I'd had to, and though I didn't need the gray, I liked him a heap better than the buckskin, and I wanted to save that good little horse from more abuse. I'd evened up scores for him, and as for the buckskin, that horse's hide and head was too thick to feel any abuse. He'd be sure to always take good care of himself.

It was early the next morning when I lined out, the little gray free with my other horses and with no other meat to pack but what little was on his own bones. I took some grain along in the pack for him, and when the settlement was left behind and I made camp in open country again, I gave him a good feed of that grain before I hobbled him out to graze. I hated to hobble him but he was still too close to where he'd been used to and I was afraid he might go back or wander away.

When I first got the little gray I decided to name him Croppy on account that both his ears were cropped; half of 'em had froze off during some blizzard and only stubs was left. The feller I'd got him from called him Prince, I think, or some such fancy name, but Croppy, as a name, fitted him well for me.

Croppy was the closest horse to my camp when I woke up and looked around the next morning, and I gave him another good feed of grain before starting out for the day's travel. He was still free to nip at the scattered bunch grass as he went along with my other horses and he had nothing to pack but his own self.

A few days' travel from the settlement and I come to the round-up camp of a big cow outfit. I went to work for that outfit, turned my horses in the "caviada" (saddle horse bunch) and they had nothing to do but eat and rest and pile on fat while I rode the outfit's horses on round-up. That was a good outfit and I stayed on for some months, longer than I usually stayed with any outfit, because the fever to drift on to new ranges would most always hit me after I was with an outfit for a couple of months.

I didn't neglect little Croppy as I rode on for the outfit. Him and my other horses was in the caviada which was corraled two or three times a day while we changed horses and I got to see him every time the caviada was corraled. Croppy didn't need no care but being he was a little poor at first and I run out of grain, I begin feeding him pieces of biscuits which the riders throwed away after they got through eating. The little son of a gun got to liking 'em real well, and come a time when there wasn't enough pieces of biscuits on the ground, I'd nip a few from the Dutch oven, and sometimes, when the caviada would be turned out of the corral, he'd hang around camp till I gave him a biscuit before he'd join the bunch to graze.

I never was much to make a pet of any horse. I always take the best care of a horse and I leave him alone when I don't need him. Most pets are only doggone nuisances and spoiled, sniffing in pockets or chewing on saddle leather. None of my best horses ever cared to be petted.

Croppy could of been spoiled into a pet easy enough, but I wanted to keep him dependable, and the closest I wanted him to be to a pet was to have him so he would let me walk up to him any time or place, whether he was in a corral or out grazing with other horses. I couldn't do that with my other horses, and a horse that can be walked up to when he's out loose is mighty handy at times.

With Croppy liking biscuits the way he did, gave me a good chance to train him to let me walk up to him when loose and even when he might of wanted to run away to other horses. I'd ride through the caviada every chance I had and finally got him so I could walk up to him and he'd wait for me even if the other horses around loped away. Sometimes, coming in from a long ride, I didn't have no biscuits to give him and he'd let me catch him just the same, but I'd make up for that at other times. He'd got to be quite a camp horse, too, and often stuck around close, when the caviada was grazing a mile away.

There come many times when my training Croppy not to run away from me when loose turned out to be mighty handy, and the first time was when I quit the outfit and hit out for other ranges. Croppy, like my other horses, was now fat as a seal.

I was a couple of days' ride away from the outfit's range, and night was coming on when I made camp by a corral and up in some hills above a spring. The best feed was up there, but it was scarce most everywhere in that country, and I was careful to hobble all my horses so they wouldn't drift too far, all but Croppy, for he never tried to lead the horses away nor would he leave them. I gave him a cold flapjack which I'd cooked that morning and then he went to grazing.

When I crawled out of my bedding the next morning I couldn't see any of my horses anywhere, but I didn't think much of that because, as often happened, they would only be around the point of some hill and close by. So I took my time to cooking myself a breakfast and getting my stuff ready to pack before I went to looking for them.

I picked up their tracks and followed 'em to where they'd grazed over a low ridge. I thought sure of finding them on the other side, but they wasn't there, and they wasn't on the other side of the next ridge either, nor the next. I got up on top of another ridge and from there the tracks headed straight for a wide valley where there was no feed for a horse to stop and graze. I could of seen horses or their dust for ten miles and there was no sight of either. They'd sure hit out. I was afoot, and in a mighty big country. But there was nothing for me to do but keep on their trail all I could, and when I found one and then another broken rope hobble which had wore thin on the stiff brush, I sort of lost all hope of ever seeing my horses again, for I figured I'd find more broken hobbles along the trail and I'd never be able to catch up with 'em, not afoot.

I'd always prided myself of never being left afoot, but this was one time when it happened.

I started picking my way down the rocky ridge, my thoughts far from cheerful, when, coming around the point of a rocky ledge what do I see, and only a rope's length from me, but my little Croppy horse.

How I felt at the sight of him can't be described with words, only that if a feller had come to me right then and wanted to trade me a hundred buckskins for that little gray, I'd been apt to take a shot at him.

That little horse had left the other horses go on and was coming back to my camp to get his biscuits, but biscuits or no biscuits I don't think he'd ever come back to the feller I'd got him from.

It was only a couple of miles back to my camp. I rode him there bareback, and without even a string on his head. I'd left a couple of flapjacks on a rock for him, and while he et them I saddled him and then started on the trail of my other horses. I was well mounted on little Croppy and by the time night come I had them runaways back to my camp. I made sure of new hobbles which I cut off a heavy cotton rope for 'em, and I "sidelined" two of the leaders to make double sure I'd have 'em when morning come.

Croppy didn't get no hobbles, only an extra mess of flapjacks. If I done that little horse a good turn when I got him away from the horse-killing hombre he sure more than repaid me, not only that once but more times after that and in other ways.

Racers
&
Buffalo Runners

Five-Hundred-Mile Horse Race

N. HOWARD THORP

There was always a horse race brewing or in prospect when cowhands got together. The usual kind, which was for a short distance, such as a half mile or less, could be gotten up almost anywhere, in a few minutes, impromptu, with no jockey club rules to worry about. The boys would go to a level place, step off the distance, strip their ponies to save weight, and ride. Whoever had money bet on the outcome. Lacking money, almost anything else of value would do for what our English highness, Lord Lincoln, usually called a wager. I remember a race I saw in the little town of Pecos when I was coming back from my first song hunt. The "race track" was the main street of the town, and the "grandstands" were the sidewalks, which were lined with dozens of cowboys from different outfits. The two horses contending for honors were cow horses owned locally, and several thousand dollars, not to mention saddles, silver-mounted bridles, hair ropes, spurs, and what-have-you, changed hands in a few minutes on the outcome. I personally bet all my cash capital except five dollars, naturally on the wrong horse.

One completely impromptu race was run the day the Englishman, Mc-Queen, announced he was going to have a horse sale, old-country style. Mc-Queen raised trotting horses which were fast enough, but of no earthly use as cow horses; however, in announcing the sale, he promised free "breakfasts" for all—meaning high-noon breakfast, of course, but cowboys from ranches near and far began showing up soon after sunup. They found McQueen and his flunkies dressed in English riding clothes, carrying little rattan sticks in their hands, and there was plenty of champagne and other alcoholic dynamite on hand for the flunkies to pour. I have known cowpunchers to get loaded when they had to fill their own glasses, but when there were flunkies to do the filling, kid o' mine! Some of them told McQueen that they had decided to initiate him into the Cowpunchers' Union, and did so in the stables, the main part of the ceremony being that he had to take eleven drinks, one after another, swaller for swaller, with each of the brothers present, a feat which didn't tend to sober him. He was then introduced to the game of fuzzy-guzzy*, which was new and fascinating to him, and at which he lost all his ready cash, then his silver flask, and finally his watch, and after that a horse race was proposed, which to a cowhand was like a gold-mounted invitation to set the boss's good-looking daughter. McQueen agreed to run a big fat mare he owned with a colt by her side, against a smoky horse owned by a cowboy named Tobe, the distance half a mile, terms horse for horse, colt thrown in.

Now, there was a little exercise track in front of the house, and all of Mc-Queen's horses knew that track like a book from much use of it, but it was no race track to them, just a place to jog and have fun. The route for the race was laid out with the track as part of it, and when the handkerchief was dropped, McQueen's fat mare shot far ahead of Tobe's horse until she came to the track, but there she dropped back into a jog and couldn't be whipped or cussed into going faster. Tobe reached the finish line all alone, McQueen's horse ending up at the tables where the drinks were laid out.

"I say, old chaps," said McQueen, "I hardly call that a fair test, don't yer know." And he insisted on running the race again.

The result was the same, not only the second time, but each of half a dozen times. In fact, they might be running the same race yet if McQueen hadn't got so drunk he couldn't ride any more, and finally admitted, to the tune of "God Save McQueen," that he was beat.

There were all sorts of crazy horse races run in the West, one of the craziest being one that was proposed and won by Calamity Jane herself. She was sitting in front of a saloon beside her horse, Jim, when a stranger rode up and

---

*Played with a small top with four sides on which are marked the letters A, N, W, and L— meaning all, nothing, win, lose.

invited her to trade horses. He was willing, he said, to prove that his horse could outrun hers under any conditions, for money, marbles, or whiskey. She said the idea of a race sort of appealed to her and inquired if she might name the distance and conditions. The stranger said he was willing, and each of them put one hundred dollars in the hands of a stake holder, winner to take all. Calamity Jane then had a notary write down the terms of the race, and it was signed and witnessed by two passing gamblers. The terms she dictated were as follows: "We'll start twenty feet back of the platform where the horses are now standing, jump the horses up on the platform, ride into the saloon, take a drink, ride out through the back door, enter the next saloon by the back door, have a drink there, and out the front, enter the next saloon, and so on all the way down the street until all eleven saloons and dance halls on that side of the street are visited in turn. First horse at the bar of the last saloon gets the money." Her horse had been trained to do this stunt and had done it for years, and when he got to a bar, he could even take a bottle in his teeth, up-end it, and drink just like a man—and with about the same physical consequences. Calamity Jane won the race by three saloons and four drinks.

There was a different class of horse race entirely, the outcome of which depended very little on flashy speed or tricks, and very much on the stamina of the horse and the horsemanship of the rider. Cowboys' endurance races are a thing of the past now, but in their day, sponsored by different people and especially Buffalo Bill, they had a peculiar place in the West and were a picturesque part of the life. I got the detailed story of one such race, which was run in the early eighties, from Jack Best, who was one of the contestants. He rode in this race, he told me, the year he went north with a trail herd from southern New Mexico, which was about the time when my brother and I had a ranch south of Stanton, Nebraska, on Maple Creek. The conditions of the race were as follows: it was to start at Deadwood, South Dakota, and finish at Omaha, Nebraska. No horse entered would be over fifteen hands. He must be a qualified cow horse, and carry a rider and saddle, six-gun and chaps, all to weigh not less than one hundred and ninety pounds. The nearest distance from Deadwood to Omaha was approximately five hundred and thirty miles, but the riders could choose their routes to suit themselves. Each rider was allowed a helper to drive his buckboard or hack, which went along to carry chuck, horse feed, and bedding. Creeks and rivers had to be forded as they were come to. Starting time was a Saturday morning at six o'clock, in Deadwood, and the contestants had to check in at the fair grounds at Omaha not later than midnight the following Saturday in order to qualify. The condition of the horse on arrival was supposed to count 60 per cent, the time of arrival 40 per cent. There were four purses. The first prize was one thousand dollars in cash, and Buffalo Bill in person was to hand the money to the winner.

Following is the account of the ride Jack Best made in that race, in my words but as if he were telling it, as in fact he did tell it to me.

A bucking horse reared high, and pitched through the crowd that had gathered to see the first stage of the big race, which was just about to start. Suddenly the bucker fell. Somebody piled on his head to prevent his scrambling to his feet and trampling the rider, who was pinned underneath. When they worked the horse off, it was found that the rider, Hank Singleton, had a broken leg. That was a hard line of luck for Hank, who was one of the ten entrants in the race. What had happened was that he had left the corral riding the young horse which bucked, and leading Once Again, the horse he meant to ride in the race. The noise of the crowd frightened the young horse, and whirling, he got the rope of the led horse under his tail, clamped down on it, became more frightened, started pitching, then lost his footing and fell.

Hank, with a broken leg, was out of the race before it began. But his sister was following on another horse, intending to lead the young saddle horse back to the corral; however, as soon as she saw that her brother was being cared for, she went to the judges and asked for a chance to take his place. They gave her permission to do so. When we started, therefore, there were nine men riders, and one girl.

I don't remember the names of all the horses that lined up at the start, but the four that went the whole way and finished were a black named Coaly, a bay named Ranger, a sorrel named Hornet, and my own little horse, Johnnie Dun. Of all ten horses in the race, Johnnie Dun was the smallest in height, standing just fourteen-two hands. He had a dark line down his back, a black mane and tail, was glass-eyed, wore a naught-size shoe, and was branded Diamond A. He had a fast walk, a good running fox trot, an easy lope, and like all of his color and kind, a lot of bottom. For a month before the race, Dunnie had been getting his exercise daily to make him hard and fit. Starting at ten miles a day, with three feeds of oats and good mountain hay, I had increased the training distance daily, and the week before the start of the event he was going thirty miles every day, and was as hard as rocks.

A good deal of fun was poked at Johnnie Dun when we lined up to start, because he was so small; the other horses were all around fifteen hands. Now my own idea was that some of them were too fat, and others too long coupled, to stand a long, hard grind. However, the gamblers thought otherwise. They were makin' books and layin' all kinds of odds, and at Deadwood, Ranger and Hornet seemed to be the general favorites. Once Again, ridden now by Singleton's sister, was also carrying a lot of money to win. But Johnnie Dun was the joke horse of the race, as far as the gamblers went, and nobody was willing to make a bet on such a long shot except one old cowhand who, a year or so previously, had ridden Dunnie up the trail from New Mexico, and had a feeling of affection for him. More because of that than any real belief that he could win, this feller placed a twenty-five-dollar bet that I would finish in the money, that is, that I'd be one of the first four. The gamblers gave him odds of four to one that number eight, which was Dunnie's number that I wore on a card on my back, wouldn't show.

Amid a lot of shouting and excitement, we received our final instructions, and got away. Three of the ten starters went off in a high lope, cutting a great swath, throwing dust and gravel as they sped down the flat. Five galloped, trotted, or fox-trotted. Dunnie was fishing at the bit and wanted to make as showy a start as anybody. But I figured that a five-hundred-mile race wasn't going to be won in the first mile, and I held him down to a flat-foot walk. The Singleton girl, whose number was nine, did the same thing with her mount, Once Again; in fact, she rode at my side, taking it easy, and we chatted and got acquainted. Her father, she said, was driving her hack; he had a pair of spotted ponies hitched to it. I told her that my brother Bill was driving our outfit, and he had a pair of long-legged mules that could walk around five miles an hour and not worry. Bill, I might as well remark here, carried a keg of water, plenty of food, a few bales of hay, and two sacks of oats; also a bucket and sponge, a bottle of rubbing alcohol, and a blanket for Dunnie in case the nights were cold or rainy. The girl asked what I thought of her horse. I had to tell her the truth, which was that I was afraid he was too soft and fat. "But if you hold him down the first few days," I said, "you might have a chance. Don't expect me to pull you out of any bogs, though!" Helping a girl was one thing, but that thousand-dollar purse at the end of the long grind was another.

"Cowboy," she said, understanding perfectly well what I was thinking, "this is a hoss race!"

At eleven o'clock, five hours after the start, she and I were still riding along together, and my original opinion about her horse was unchanged. My hack had stopped, and when I came up to it, Bill was cooking up a meal. "Good luck!" I said, and pulled off the road. The girl went on to overtake her own outfit.

I unsaddled Dunnie, fed him, had a good dinner myself, and rested. The five-hour ride hadn't been more than a good morning's exercise for either of us, but I once read about a party of men who were left afoot in the desert, with very little food, at a place where they were at least fifty miles from water. If they had lost their heads thinking about it, they might have tried to get to that moisture quick and died of exhaustion. But their leader had a watch, and he made a rule that the party should walk fifteen minutes, then rest ten, walk fifteen and rest ten, and keep it up; and by not ever lettin' any of the party tire themselves out, he got them through to water safely. My idea in this race was something like that for Dunnie. By one o'clock I was saddled and on my way again. We had covered almost twenty-five miles, and had left the town of Calcite some distance behind.

The tracks of the hacks showed that all of the riders, like ourselves, were making a beeline for the town of Interior. However, I didn't catch up with any of them that first afternoon; they seemed to smell the Omaha "moisture," and were making for it as fast and hard as they could go. My brother, with our hack, passed me with his mules at a trot, and handed me a couple of doughnuts he had brought from Deadwood. "I'll camp about six," he said. "That should bring us five miles or so beyond Box Elder Creek, and I'll have supper ready when you come." He whipped up and drove on. I held Dunnie to his slow and steady pace. About an hour after getting out of the hills, I came to Box Elder Creek, and here both Dunnie and I had a good drink. He stood in the water for a few minutes, cooling off his legs and feet. Refreshed by this short rest, we rode on several miles more and reached the camp which Bill had made in a mott of timber.

On the wheel of the buckboard, Bill had rigged up what he called a buggy-o-meter, by means of which he could figure out more or less correctly the miles we traveled. It was based on the number of revolutions of the wheel, times its circumference. After consulting this contraption and doing the necessary multiplying, Bill announced that we had covered something more than forty-eight miles so far. I was well satisfied with that. After watering Dunnie, I threw him some hay, stripped off the saddle, threw a sheet over him, then ate my own supper. I must say that Bill, without being a regular *cocinero*, could toss up some mighty fine grub over a campfire, and it sure tasted good to a feller who half the time was hungrier than a red-headed woodpecker.

After we ate, Bill and I went into a huddle. As I said, I had a general idea how I meant to run the race, and of how I thought a man and a horse might win it. You probably gathered that my plan did not depend very much on speed in any given short distance, but I knew, from long experience with cow ponies, that a horse that was given specially good care, many times would travel a long distance faster and in better shape than a naturally better horse that was ridden harder and faster for short distances, but wasn't given equal care. My main thought, accordingly, was to keep Dunnie going, not fast or hard, but steadily, for just as much of the time as was possible without wearing him down, letting him rest frequently. That first evening, therefore, knowing that the moon would soon be up, I decided to put a few more miles behind me as soon as Dunnie finished his supper. By nine o'clock I felt good and rested, and Dunnie looked as fit as when we started, so I saddled him and pulled out. Within five miles, Bill caught up and passed me. Soon I saw a rig camped beside the road. Behind the buckboard and the spotted ponies was the Singleton girl's fat horse, Once Again. The girl and her father were apparently fast asleep, so I kept right on, and in another six miles or so, came to the camp Bill had made. He said that some other outfit was camped immediately ahead, but whose it was he didn't know. He also said that according to the buggy-o-meter we had put fifty-nine miles behind us, just about half the distance to our first goal, the town of Interior.

I offered Dunnie water, but he didn't want any. I sponged off his back, legs, and shoulders with alcohol, rubbed him dry, and threw a sheet and blanket over him, then broke out some good hay for him, fed him grain, and finally turned into my own hot-roll for a good night's sleep.

Bill called me at four. I smelled the coffee and bacon he had ready and waiting, and he told me that he had already given Dunnie a good rubbing with a flannel cloth to take out any stiffness that the first day's trip might have caused. Now as part of my equipment I was carrying two double Navajo saddle blankets. One had been used the day before, and was sweaty and liable to cause chafing. I gave that one to Bill and asked him to wash it out at the first creek he came to. The other one, which was clean, I put under the saddle. On a long ride, no horse is better than his back, and I meant to keep Dunnie's back in good shape if it was in my power to do so.

In the course of the first two miles or so that morning, I came to a camp and saw the horse, Ranger, which carried number one in the race. His rider and helper were just eating breakfast as I went by at an easy trot. About a mile further on I passed number ten, and close by, numbers two and six. I was fox-trotting along easily when the sorrel horse named Hornet (number three in the race) came out of the brush, and his rider and I rode along together for a while. This feller was long and skinny, and when he was standing on the ground he looked like a rattlesnake on stilts. Some distance on we passed number seven, then in a little while number four, who was just saddling up. Most of those horses had gone a lot faster while they were going, the day before, than Dunnie. Yet here we were, right along with them. Hornet's rider remarked that the weather was sure cool. Yes, I agreed, it sure was. He remarked that I was traveling pretty slow, wasn't I? Yes, I said, I reckon I was. He said he guessed he would try to make better time. I told him not to let me stop him. So he struck out at a high lope, and as I watched horse and rider disappear, I thought of a saying of my old Swiss grandmother:

A long race,
A slow pace.

Dunnie and I weren't going to be hurried. We continued to keep our slow and easy gait, and one after another, all the horses in the race, except Once Again, with the Singleton girl aboard, caught up and passed us.

Bill and I camped for grub and rest at eleven o'clock, and it was close to noon before Once Again finally put in an appearance, following close behind the girl's rig, and carrying his head low. I knew by the look of him that he wasn't going to get much farther. Father and daughter pulled up close to us.

"Light an' take a load off your saddle," I said.

Bill invited them to eat dinner with us. The girl seemed discouraged as she looked after her horse, but declared she would keep going till that night anyhow. Then if Once Again didn't perk up, she said, she would drop out. I rode off from that camp at about one o'clock. But before I went, the Singleton girl had a talk with Bill and me that showed her heart was in the right place.

"Jack," she said, "from what you've told me, you live a long ways from here, an' don't know a whole lot about people in these parts."

I told her I was practically born poppin' longhorns out o' the tornial along the Rio Grande.

"Well," she said, "all the horses in this race are local horses, except Coaly and your Johnny Dun. Coaly is supposed to have been sent here by a ring of gamblers, to win the race. He's a clean thoroughbred, and his rider has a reputation for winning, no matter how. Ranger and Hornet are carryin' most of the Deadwood gamblers' money, but the big money has been bet in Lincoln and Omaha on this big black horse, Coaly.

"If you don't think Coaly is fast," she went on, "you don't know the feel of cactus when you're settin' in the middle of it. If those other riders ever find that you fellers have any sort of a look-in to win, they won't stop at much. At least, that's my notion. They'll try to dope or cripple your horse, if they can, or they'll put you out some other way. Keep your eyes peeled. Remember that there's probably a hundred thousand dollars at stake."

Her own horse, she admitted, was in no condition to compete. "I'll probably drop out; but I wish you boys luck. That's why I'm warnin' you to be on the lookout. Take care of yourself, and your horse."

Bill and I felt grateful, and said so.

"That's all right," she replied. "I may hop the train and see you in Omaha. *Adios.*"

I climbed aboard Dunnie and rode off, and never saw her again.

The next few days were a steady grind of riding, resting, eating, riding, resting, eating, with a few highlights and incidents along the way. Nearly every night we made our last camp ahead of the others, or got an earlier start next day, and nearly every morning the others passed me, one by one, until Dunnie and I were again at the tail of the procession. On Monday morning, for example, I left camp at five o'clock, and in the next two hours passed seven of the outfits camped along the road. I was just thinking that another horse must be ahead or dropped out, when suddenly I passed Coaly's camp as the rider and his helper were having breakfast.

"Come and have coffee," they called.

I shook my head and thanked them, saying I had eaten, and kept right on. Shortly after crossing Pass Creek, the brown horse, number seven, galloped by under a full head of steam. His rider waved. "I'll order supper for you in Omaha!" he shouted.

I felt like saying, "Brother, you'll never get to Omaha on *that horse!*"—but I didn't. And as a matter of fact, neither did he—get to Omaha, I mean.

They all passed me, horses and rigs both. As Bill went by, he called, "I'm goin' to stop at nine today, Jack, an' we'll have some coffee and rest a while." That was our regular routine—ride, rest, ride. And whenever we were making one of those rests, even a short one, I would sponge Dunnie's head, wash out his nostrils, take off the saddle, give him an alcohol rub, and let him munch some hay. In half an hour we would be going again, refreshed like a prize fighter after the rest between rounds. I gave the horse every attention I could think of that would keep him fit, and anybody with eyes could see that under that kind of treatment he was standing up well; but I was thinking a lot, and very seriously, about that thoroughbred, Coaly, and about what the Singleton girl had said about the money that was down on him, and about those other horses, Ranger and Hornet, both of which were built bigger and stronger than Dunnie. I figured that the load of money on these three would not have been wagered unless it was supposed that one of them was almost sure to win. However, neither Bill nor I ever had any notion of quitting. We were raised with horses, and we felt that if any of the other riders thought they could run any rani-cum-boogerie on us, they were welcome to try. It was real competition that we were up against. Dad, who had been a horseman all his life, used to say, when he matched one of his horses in a race, "I may not win myself, but I'll sure make the other feller think he has been to a hoss race."

We passed Norris on Black Pine Creek in the middle of Monday morning, and got to White River at about eleven o'clock. All the other riders were bunched up there, afraid of the water, but Bill never even stopped; he drove right in, hollering to me to keep on the lower side of the team. Twice we struck swimming water, but it didn't cause us any trouble, in fact, Dunnie seemed to enjoy the swim and the look and feel of the clear water. We went into camp on the far side, and soon all the other riders came across. I laid up here till one-thirty, and when I pulled out, some of the other riders trailed along with me. Soon, however, my speed proved too slow for their liking, and they galloped on ahead. Bill and I camped at six on the other side of Mission, about a hundred and seventy-five miles from Deadwood, laid up till eleven, then rode for another hour, camping at midnight at Rock Creek, where we found seven other outfits camped. This was the only night when so many of us were together. The missing outfits, I discovered, were numbers seven and nine, one being the Singleton girl on Once Again, and the other the rider who had promised when he passed me, to order supper for me in Omaha. There was one other casualty. Number ten, who was camped next to us, said his horse had been sick half the night with colic, and he would have to drop out and turn back. That left only seven of us.

Next day Bill and I had a piece of luck, the only important bit of luck that came our way from first to last in all the five hundred miles of the race. I left at five o'clock, just as most of the others were lighting their campfires; and eight o'clock saw me crossing the Keyapaha River. Bill caught up and passed me there. Nine miles further on he was waiting for me; none of the other riders had caught up yet.

"We're campin' here till they pass," he said.

He had news.

One by one the riders went by us, and when the last one was out of sight, we went too—but by a different road. The news Bill had picked up was that for many miles the straight road ahead was a quagmire. He and I turned to the left, paralleling the muddy stretch on higher ground. Our way was a few miles farther, but the going was fine, and when we hit the Niobrara that evening at the town of Riverview, and got Nebraska instead of Dakota under our feet, we learned that we were ahead of everybody. And by eleven that night when we set out again and put ten more miles behind us, none of the other riders had yet appeared. In fact, it was not till nine o'clock next morning that I saw any of them. At that time Hornet and Ranger caught up with me. The two horses were coated with dried mud up to their knees, and looked drawn and tired, and the riders told me they had pulled through twenty miles of heavy bog mud the day before, and that all the hacks but one got stuck. They said there was another horse right behind, but they didn't know which one it was, and two more of the riders had dropped out.

Tired though Hornet and Ranger were after that hard mud, their riders could not long bear to crawl along at the slow and steady pace which I made Dunnie take. They galloped on ahead. But when I reached Bill's camp at eleven o'clock, there they were, waiting for their own hack (they were both using the same one now), and smelling Bill's coffee with hungry looks. They ate with us, and before we were through, their hack came along.

Following my usual routine, I pulled out again at one-thirty, walking Dunnie for an hour, then fox-trotting him for another hour. We camped again at six. About nine, three riders and two hacks passed—the horses were Ranger, Coaly, and Hornet. They all camped near us, but Bill and I pulled out again at eleven, and as I was passing, Hornet's rider told me that another horse had now dropped out and there were only four of us left in the race. Covering another ten miles in the dark before turning in for the long sleep, we found we were about three hundred and ten miles on our journey, and we had Thursday, Friday, and Saturday yet to go. Those next two hundred miles, we knew, would furnish the real test. Coaly already looked awful; Ranger and Hornet seemed to be dead tired. Dunnie, thanks to the care I constantly gave him, looked fine. But he probably wasn't as much of a horse, I knew, as the others were. The race, I told myself, was still far from over.

The others overtook me the next day at about nine o'clock, as usual, and I let them go ahead.

"Don't hurry," Bill said, grinning like a mountain cat over a fresh-killed deer, "we've got 'em licked."

But no rooster ever ought to crow till his chickens are hatched. It was eleven o'clock when I next caught up with Bill; and I didn't find him at the side of the road with a fire built, and coffee on to boil, and beans in the pan, and biscuits comin' up.

> *Bacon in the pan,*
> *Coffee in the pot;*
> *Get up an' get it—*
> *Get it while it's hot.*

No, his hack was standing in the middle of the road, tip-tilted like a stovepipe hat on a drunk's head. He had hit a boulder and knocked every spoke out of the right hind wheel.

"So we've got 'em licked, have we!" says I, lighting to inspect the damage. Without Bill and the hack to take care of all the little chores and leave me free to care for Dunnie, I knew I wouldn't stand any chance at all of taking the race. "*Now* what are we going to do?"

"*We* aren't goin' to do a thing," said Bill, who was peeled down to his undershirt and sweatin' with an ax. "You fork your horse an' hit the road. I'll have this fixed an' beat you in to O'Neill yet."

I never thought he could do it, but he sure did. He cut a long pole and tied it on top of the front axle and under the rear one, with the end of the pole dragging along behind. The hack sagged a little on the pole corner, but it stayed up, and when Bill waved his whip and spoke kind words to those long-legged mules of his, riding on three wheels and a bob-sled, he split the breeze about as fast as on four wheels. When I got to O'Neill I found him strutting around like a turkey gobbler in a hen pen, admiring the hack, which now had four good wheels and looked the same as ever. Bill had rustled an old wheel from somebody's buggy shop, and though it had taken our last cent of cash money to buy it, once more we had hopes of shaking the hand of Buffalo Bill and sharing the promised purse. O'Neill was called three hundred and forty miles from Deadwood.

I left there at one o' clock, riding along the Elkhorn River. Bill passed me, but none of the other riders or hacks came in sight. At six-thirty I rode into the camp Bill had made, and smelled something that made my stomach get right up and wave its hat. As a special celebration, Bill had borrowed a chicken and fried it for our supper. I took good care of my half of the fowl, as well as Dunnie, giving the little horse an alcohol rub and bandaging his legs with wet cloths. We went on again after eleven for about an hour and a half, the buggy-o-meter tallying three hundred and eighty miles when we stopped for the night. One hundred and fifty miles still to go, and two days to make it in!

Next day none of the riders appeared until Bill and I were nooning. Then all three came by together, trailing behind their two hacks, and when they saw us, they camped a little beyond. Their horses, with heads hanging, looked gaunt and tired. Presently the three riders strolled over to where we were.

"Keep your eyeballs oiled," said Bill, when he saw them coming. But a cowhand foaled in Texas and busted out in New Mexico didn't need that warning.

It was easy to see that the three had some serious business on their minds. I hunkered down near Dunnie, just in case their intentions had any reference to him. But as it turned out, they were mostly interested in mathematics and long division. They started edging into the subject by pointing out what all of us knew by heart, namely, that there were four prizes offered for this race—$1,000, $500, $300, and $200—making a grand total of $2,000.

"Cut the deck deeper, fellers," said Bill, "Jack and I don't *sabe*."

"Only four of us," Hornet's rider pointed out, "are left, and it's still anybody's race." He then went on to say that $2,000 could be cut four ways, making four even piles of $500 each. "Why not make a pool of it," he said, "we can let the horses take it easier. We'll cut cards to see who comes in first, but whatever the cards say, we'll split the money four ways even. That's the way she lays with us. How about you two?"

A certain kind of smell always means a skunk. This Hornet feller had been friendly enough to me, even if he was so skinny that a man would need an extra batch of luck to hit him with a handful of gravel, but his talk wasn't the kind I liked to trouble my ears with. I'm no professor with a deck of cards, but I have met people who can make them act real educated. It passed through my mind that tens of thousands of dollars had been bet on each of the other three horses left in the race, and only twenty-five dollars on Dunnie; and it seemed as plain as plowed ground that if we did cut cards with those three, there was one rider present who would not cut the high card, and the name of his horse was Johnny Dun. I shook my head, and Bill, backing me up, said "No!"

"It's still a hoss race, fur's I'm concerned," I said.

"Reckon I know how you feel," said Hornet's rider smoothly. "That prize money is warm in your pocket already, ain't it? But," rising to his feet, "you know there's never any certainty in a hoss race—*is* there?"

That was the end of the parley. "We'll have to watch those *hombres* like hawks," said Bill when we were alone again. "If I ever heard a plain warnin', that's it."

"An' we're only two against five."

"They may not try to pull anything; and again, they may. We won't camp near them again. And nobody hangs around our camp any time, day or night. Whenever you use the water bucket, Jack, put it away in a gunnysack an' tie the end good—don't give 'em any possible chance to dope Dunnie."

Now it was that same afternoon as I was passing through the town of Neleigh, that a crowd cheered me. One fellow came running out and thrust a bottle of whiskey into my hand. "Go it, old Diamond-A!" he yelled, adding that he used to work for that outfit down in Deming, New Mexico. About five miles farther on I caught up with Bill and offered him a jolt of the rye, and I sure didn't have to twist his arm to make him take it. We ate supper, and I hit the hay, Bill keeping one eye wide open. At nine-thirty he called me. We went eight miles farther, passing Warnersville before we made our last night camp. About midnight the hacks of our rivals pulled up and passed, and presently the three riders trailed along too. We saw them apparently make camp at a little distance, but we did not call attention to ourselves in any way. I think Bill slept with one eye open all night, expecting somebody to creep up out of the dark and try something on Dunnie. I turned in and told him to call me at four.

Well, we were expecting a surprise from those other riders, but not the surprise we got.

Dunnie and I at this point had only seventy miles to go to the fair grounds at Omaha, and we had until twelve o'clock midnight to do it—just twenty-four hours. Easy? After the grind we had been through? Don't you think it!

I was up and ready to go at four-thirty next morning. It was still only half light, and I saw no signs of activity in the camp of the other riders. Since it was the last big day, I tied a bright new silk handkerchief around my neck, and pulled out aboard Dunnie all dressed up for the home stretch. The little horse still looked good. Nothing had happened to us so far; maybe nothing would. As Hornet's rider had said, the prize money was already hot in my pocket. And then I passed the camp of the other riders.

It wasn't a camp any more. In fact, it was as quiet as a hoss-thief after the hanging—not because the other riders weren't awake yet, but because they had gone. In the dark of the night they had stolen a march on us. At what time they had left, neither Bill nor I had any idea. But gone they were, and by now they might be ten, twenty, or even twenty-five miles ahead. Bill saw the possibilities at a glance; and with his mules at a keen trot left me behind.

"Keep your eyes open," he hollered. "I might leave a message for you at the station in Nickerson."

I figured my chances as I rode. If those riders had traveled all night, as seemed likely, even if their horses couldn't strike a lope and hold it, I realized that maybe just by walking they could make it to the fair grounds ahead of me. I had a powerful itch to make Dunnie lay out his legs and run. Though he was tired, I knew he still had a lot up his sleeve. But I decided against changing my style of riding, even if I was to lose the race for it. I walked the little horse for an hour, then fox-trotted him for an hour, then walked him, and kept it up, like the party in the desert walking fifteen minutes and resting ten.

Two farmers came out of a cross lane. "Here comes another cowboy from the Black Hills," they yelled, wavin' their hats. "Go it, sonny!"

A little later I met a team and buggy coming towards me, and I hailed the driver. "Seen anything of three men on horseback," I asked, "an' a couple o' hacks?"

Yes, he said with a grin, he had seen 'em.

"How far ahead?"

"About ten miles."

"How are they makin' it?"

"A slow walk, an' about played out."

"*Bueno!*" I went on feeling a little better.

I caught up with Bill about thirty miles from the last night's camp. It was then ten-thirty in the morning. He had met a fellow who told him that the other riders were now only about four miles ahead and going very slowly. It was hard to sit down for two hours and a half in the face of those facts, and just do nothing but rest, knowing that every minute carried them yards closer to the winning line and the big prize; but that's what we did, for I knew what the rest would do for Dunnie. He had lost some flesh during the long grind, but he still didn't look drawn or gaunt. When I left that camping place, at one o'clock, I had forty-odd miles to go, and eleven hours to make it in.

Bill and I passed through Nickerson together at about four. He then went on ahead, and when I caught up with him at six, he had a good supper cooked. He had passed the other outfits, he said, and they had passed him in turn while he was fixing supper. He said they looked about all in, and were urging their dead-tired horses for all they were worth.

This was our last camp. I fed Dunnie once more, and gave him a final rubdown with the last few drops of alcohol. But we were up and off at seven. Bill hit a six-mile gait and I stayed alongside till we came to the last hack. Right ahead of it we saw the other one. It was then nine-thirty, with thirteen miles to go. At ten we overtook the three riders and a dozen or so of Buffalo Bill's cowboys who had come to escort us in.

"Let's pull around 'em!" said Bill.

We did so. The cowboys from the show gave a rousing cheer as Dunnie and I tore out on the last stretch. "Tore" isn't just the word. We were making two miles to the others' one, but neither Bill nor I knew how much reserve power those other horses might have. They might not be nearly as tired as they looked. We had been assured that the big black was a thoroughbred, and though he certainly seemed to be dead on his feet, I knew you never could tell just how much last-minute power a really good horse might have. There was no question as to Dunnie's being in the best condition of any of the horses, but if I let this Coaly horse get too close, could he in a last-quarter drive beat me? Blood, I knew, will tell. In consequence, I decided to go at a saddle gait and put just as much distance as possible between us.

Three of the cowboys from the show rode along with Bill and me. At eleven-fifteen they sent word to the fair grounds that we would soon be in, as we had only three more miles to go. Just about then, Bill, yelled at me:

"Here they come, Jack. Look out!"

I took a quick look over my shoulder. We were now inside the city limits. Although it was late, the town was lighted up and was almost as bright as day. The sidewalks were lined with people, and the crowds got denser, the yells louder, the nearer we came to the finish line. In my quick look back I saw the thoroughbred, Coaly, come pounding up from behind. He passed me and took the lead.

"Don't race him!" Bill yelled excitedly. "Push him at a good gallop, but keep just behind. He'll come back to you in a mile."

And pretty soon one of the cowboys said, "There's only a mile more to go, buddy."

Away we hammered. People shouted and waved hats and handkerchiefs. Dunnie, being the smaller horse, got more 'n his share of the cheering— "Come on, you little buckskin!" But Coaly, though he looked to be gutted, was a wonder and got plenty of the yells too—"Come on, you black!" Once when the big horse stumbled, I thought sure he would fall. But with a thoroughbred's great grit, he recovered himself and kept on. Hornet and Ranger were left blocks behind. Bill threw the leather into his galloping mules and kept pace with me.

Inch by inch, Dunnie edged up on the big black. Now we were abreast of him. I could see that he was really dead on his feet. But he was trained to be a race horse, and a race horse he was to the last, even when he was running on nothing but breeding and nerve. A great horse—greater than Johnnie Dun—but not as well taken care of during the long week of that race. I gave Dunnie the spurs in earnest for almost the first time in five hundred miles, and with a spurt of speed that the black simply couldn't match, we shot ahead and through the fairground gate, breaking the string that was stretched between the posts, two good lengths in the lead. That was all. Just two lengths in a five-hundred-mile race.

A wild, screaming mob pulled me out of the saddle and carried me to the judges' stand, right up to say "Howdy!" to Buffalo Bill himself—and to this day I don't know what he said to me, but the check he handed me said one thousand dollars!

Nät-ah'-ki's Ride

JAMES WILLARD SCHULTZ

As the summer wore on the question of food became very serious to the Piegans, and we heard that the more northern tribes of the Blackfeet were also suffering. The Piegan agent, in his annual report to the Department of the Interior, had deplored the barbarism of his charges, their heathenish worship of strange gods, but he told nothing of their physical needs. "I have nothing for you," he said to the chiefs. "Take your people to buffalo and follow the herds."

This was in August. They all moved down near our place, and while the hunters rode the plains after antelope, the chiefs conferred with Berry, planning for the winter. They finally decided to move to the Judith country, where the buffalo were thought to be still plentiful and where there were practically as many elk and deer, beaver and wolves as ever. In September we also trailed out, Berry, the Crow Woman, Nät-ah'-ki and I, and in a week or more went into camp on the Judith River, only a mile or two above the mouth of Warm Spring Creek.

We were located in the heart of an extensive cottonwood grove, sheltered from the northern winds, and right beside us ran the river, then fairly alive with big, fat trout. According to agreement, the Piegans came and pitched their lodges near us, and a part of the Blood tribe moved down from the north and mixed with them.

Nät-ah'-ki and I went once after buffalo, camping with Red Bird's Tail, a genial man of thirty-five or forty. There were few lodges, but many people, and we traveled as light as possible. We found buffalo toward the close of the first day out, but went on until noon of the next, and camped on the head of Armells Creek. From a little butte nearby we could see that the prairie was black with them clear to the breaks of the Missouri, and to the eastward where the buttes of Big Crooked Creek and the Musselshell loomed in the distance. The Moccasin Mountains shut off the view of the south, but westward there were also buffalo.

"Ha!" exclaimed Red Bird's Tail, who had ridden up beside me. "Who says the buffalo are about gone? Why, it is as it has always been; the land is dark with them. Never have I seen them more plentiful."

"Remember that we have come far to find them," I told him; "that the plains to the west, and away in the north, are barren of them."

"Ah, that is true, but it will not be for long; they must have all moved eastward for a time as our fathers tell us once happened before. They will go back again. Surely, the good Sun will not forget us."

I had not the heart to destroy his hopes, to tell him of the vast regions to the east and south of us, where there were no longer any buffalo, where the antelope, even, had been practically exterminated.

Red Bird's Tail was the leader of our party, and the hunters were subject to his orders. We had ridden out on to the butte very early, and after getting a view of the country and the position of the herds, he decided that a certain herd southwest of us should be chased, as they would run westward into the wind, and not disturb the larger ones. The lay of the land was favorable and we succeeded in riding right into the edge of the herd before they became alarmed, and then they ran, as Red Bird's Tail had predicted, into the wind and up a long slope, an outlying ridge of the mountains. That gave us an advantage, as the buffalo were not swift runners on an up-grade. On a downhill run, however, they could easily outstrip the swiftest horse. All their weight was forward; there was not enough strength in their small, low hindquarters to propel their abnormally deep chests, huge heads, and heavy hump with any noticeable speed when they went uphill.

Nät-ah'-ki was riding a gentle little mare which had been loaned her by one of our Blood friends for the trip. All the way from the Judith she kept plying her quirt and calling it sundry reproachful names, in order to keep it beside my more spirited mount. But the moment we came near the herd, and the hunters dashed into it, the animal suddenly reared up, pranced sideways with arching neck and twitching ears, and then, getting the bit firmly in its

teeth, it sprang out into the chase as madly as any other of the trained runners. Indeed, that is what it was, a well-trained buffalo horse, but the owner
had not thought to tell us so. It was even swifter than mine, and I felt no little anxiety as I saw it carry her into that sea of madly running, shaggy-backed
animals. In vain I urged my horse; I could not overtake her, and my warning
shouts were lost in the thunder and rattle of a thousand hoofs. I soon saw that
she was not trying to hold in the animal, but was quirting it instead, and once
she looked back at me and laughed, her eyes shining with excitement. On we
went, up the slope for a mile or more, and then the scattering herd drew away
from us and went flying down the other side of the ridge.

"What made you do it?" I asked as we checked up our sweating, panting horses. "Why did you do it? I was so afraid you would get a fall, perhaps
be hooked by some of the wounded."

"Well," she replied, "at first I was scared, too, but it was such fun, riding after them. Just think of it, I struck four of them with my quirt! I just
wanted to keep on, and I never thought of badger holes, or falling, or anything else. And once a great big cow looked up at me and snorted so hard
that I felt her warm breath. Tell me, how many did you kill!"

"Not one," I replied. I hadn't fired a shot; I had noticed nothing, seen
nothing but her as she rode in the thick of it all, and I was more than glad
when the run ended. We looked back down the slope and saw the hunters
and their women already at work on the carcasses of their kill, which dotted
the snow. But we—we were meatless. It would never do for us to return to
camp without some, so we rode on for a mile or two in the direction the herd
had gone, and then turned off into the mountains. Up among the pines
there were deer, both kinds, and here and there were groups of elk feeding
or lying down in the open parks. While Nät-ah'-ki held my horse I approached some of the elk, and by good luck killed a fat, dry cow. We built a
fire and roasted some of the liver and a piece of tripe, and, after a hasty meal,
rode back to camp with all the meat our horses could conveniently pack.

We made another run the next day. The sun shone bright and warm, there
was a big herd of buffalo nearby, everyone rode out from camp in the best
of spirits. I had changed horses with Nät-ah'-ki; while mine liked to run as
well as hers, it had a tender mouth, and she could easily control it. Once into
the herd, I paid no attention to anyone else, but did my best to single out
the fat cows, overtake and kill them. I did not need the meat nor robes, but

there were those with us who had poor mounts, and what I killed I intended to give them. So I urged the little mare on, and managed to kill, seven head.

When I stopped at last, no one was near me; looking back I saw the people gathered in two groups, and from the largest and nearest one arose the distressing wailing of the women for the dead. I soon learned the cause of it all; Young Arrow Maker had been killed, his horse disemboweled; Two Bows had been thrown and his leg was broken. A huge old bull, wounded and mad with pain, had lunged into Arrow Maker's horse, tearing out its flank and knocking the rider off on to the backs of its close-pursuing mates, and he had been trampled to death by the frantic-running herd.

Two Bows' horse had stepped into a badger hole and he had been hurled to the ground, his right leg broken above the knee. Some of the women's horses were dragging travois, and we laid the dead and the injured on them and they were taken to camp by their relatives. We hurried to skin the dead buffalo, some of the hunters taking no more of the meat than the tongue and boss ribs, and then we also went back to the lodges, silently and quietly. There was no feasting and singing that night.

Thoroughbreds on the Hoot Owl Trail

GRANT MACEWAN

When Tom Lynch whisked a small group of impounded race horses out of Calgary at a midnight hour and headed for a scheduled foothills trail to Montana, he had no thought of making Thoroughbred history. He was merely trying to help a horseman who found himself the victim of despairing circumstances. But the fact was that in this little herd being snatched from under the nose of the Calgary sheriff was a mare destined through her daughter, May W, to bring fame to the breed. Just about everybody in the racing world at a later date knew about May W, said by the late James Speers to be "the greatest thoroughbred raised in Canada."

High River's Tom Lynch was a fearless fellow—also a foxy fellow with some Robin Hood qualities. In conducting long and dangerous drives with cattle or horses, nobody could compare with him. For years he spent more time on the dusty trails bringing foundation stock for Canadian ranches than on his own place beside the Highwood.

Some of the Lynch undertakings were big like the North West Cattle Company drive from Idaho in 1882. All of them called for courage and skill. And this one involving the debt-ridden Thoroughbreds, though small, possessed the essentials for a good mystery story. Fortunately, William Henry who went to High River in 1885 and retained a good memory for the many miles he rode with Lynch, was able to recall the circumstances.

166

Lynch loved a race horse—loved any good horse—and was always ready to place one of his own fast nags in a contest. Hence he knew all the horsemen who indulged in the sport, knew the Montana man, Reynolds, who brought a string of aristocratic Thoroughbreds to Calgary for some holiday racing in the summer of 1889. Calgarians, even at that period, were ever eager for a race, ready to drop their work at any hour to watch one on the main avenue or on a piece of level ground beside the Elbow River.

But Reynolds had under-estimated the calibre of the Calgary runners. Tom Lynch's Grey Eagle, driven from Oregon with stock for the High River Horse Ranch two years before, was there and too fast for the entries from Montana. Reynolds was not only losing races but he was losing bets and buying horse feed for which he was unable to pay. Sad to say, it was an experience not uncommon among horsemen; debt was mounting steadily, alarmingly. Then, as he might have feared, the local sheriff, with all the brusqueness of the law, seized the string of Thoroughbreds and announced a sale to satisfy the creditors.

Ruing the day he crossed the International Boundary to come to Calgary, Reynolds wished there was a means by which he could steal his beloved Thoroughbreds from the Canadian sheriff and drive them over some little-used trails to Montana and home. A man threatened with the loss of horses to which he was devotedly attached could be pardoned for such alien thoughts. Evidently the idea was shared with an understanding friend who advised in a whisper, "Talk to Tom Lynch. He's your man if you want to move horses—or move anything on its own legs."

In desperation the Montana man sought the tall, grizzled "King of the Cattle Trails" and found him ready to listen. Lynch was a law-biding citizen but in this instance he believed there had been some injustice. Reynolds, he was convinced, was really a decent fellow experiencing a bit of bad luck. He shouldn't be blamed if some of the sharp horsemen about town had contrived to fleece him. Sympathy for people in need was a characteristic by which Billy Henry and other pioneers remembered Tom Lynch.

Whether or not there was any promise of payment for services rendered is not known and never will be known. But Lynch, after listening to the fellow-horseman's story, nodded his willingness to help.

"We better move fast," Tom said. "Start after midnight tonight. If we can get 'em out of town, we'll be all right, I figure. Moonlight these nights.

I'll be ready. You be down there at the corral so we'll be sure to get the right horses. It would be hell if we got 'em into Montana and then found we had the wrong ones."

While Calgary was wrapped in the stillness of a foothills night and only a few of Peter Prince's newly-installed arc lights on short poles broke the darkness, a padlock was pried from a corral gate beside Atlantic Avenue and two men moved inside the enclosure.

"We might have trouble getting them across the river at night," Lynch said to Reynolds. "They're Thoroughbreds, you know. You better lead one until we are on the other side of the Elbow, and then I can take care of everything. It won't be long till sunup. All right, let's go."

As morning rays began to show on the eastern sky, Tom Lynch mounted on a favorite big gelding and guiding the uneasy Thoroughbreds, was crossing Fish Creek, a few miles west of Samuel Shaw's woolen mill beside the Macleod Trail. Now he could relax; nothing short of a bloodhound could overtake him from this point on in the sparsely settled country to the southwest. There in the shelter of the cottonwoods of the creek-bed he let the horses graze and rest awhile before moving toward Sheep Creek. He wondered how Reynolds would fare when the sheriff learned what had happened during the night. Perhaps, with a horseman's sagacity, he too was at that moment travelling south on the Macleod Trail at a fast pace.

At first the Thoroughbreds were difficult to drive. They wanted to turn back to Calgary, but now in the daylight a homing sense seemed to possess them, and they moved with fresh eagerness toward Montana.

Tom Lynch drove his little herd across Sheep Creek at a point close to the Quorn Ranch headquarters and there halted for the night. As the sun was setting, he talked with John Ware, a black cowboy who was in charge of the Quorn horses and inspected the imported Thoroughbred stallions heading the most ambitious horse breeding enterprise in the West. Together, the two great horsemen then studied each of the animals in the transient band and agreed that a little chestnut mare which Reynolds called Sangaroo was the pick of the lot. She had fine bone, excellent withers and an expressive face. Good breeding was plainly visible.

"She's sho' nice," John Ware said; "Ah think yo'd get somethin' awfu' good from that lady an' ma ol' Plume," referring to the Quorn stallion, Eagle Plume.

Tom Lynch continued on his way westward from the Quorn ranch and then south through foothill country rarely visited by any except Indians. Somebody called it the Hoot Owl Trail. Actually, there was no trail. Nor was there fenced field or corral into which the horses could be placed for security at night. But Lynch, from long experience, had learned how to wrap himself in a blanket and sleep with one eye open to watch his stock.

Though armed with the trusty revolver carried over thousands of trail miles, he didn't have any reason to use it on the trip; this country where foothills met the mountains, he had entirely to himself. Even the International Boundary presented no problems because there was neither an officer nor anything else to mark the place.

After six or seven days of circuitous travel, Lynch and the Thoroughbreds were at a designated point in Montana—near Flathead Lake. Reynolds had not yet arrived but Lynch delivered the horses, and with no more ceremony than would be expected from a grocer delivering prunes, the man from High River mounted and turned his horse toward home.

It was just one more in a long list of trailing expeditions for Tom Lynch but in this instance he was merely trying to help another horseman. Perhaps reward for these long days in the saddle and short nights sleeping on the ground had not entered his mind but recompense did come.

Weeks later, rancher Charlie Knox who lived in the hills southwest of High River, found a stranger sleeping in his stable at an early morning hour. In adjacent stalls were two horses, the man's saddle horse and a strikingly refined chestnut mare. Upon being questioned, the stranger admitted he had ridden from Montana to deliver the mare and was instructed to take a backcountry route.

It was quite evident that the stranger was guarding his answers with care but when leaving the Knox place, he had a question: "How would I get to Tom Lynch from here?"

The mare brought back in this one-horse drive and delivered to Tom Lynch as a reward for his professional and unselfish assistance was Sangaroo, the little chestnut John Ware had admired and Lynch considered the best of the lot. It was a gift the High River man thoroughly appreciated and in due course the mare was branded TL and turned out with the rest of the Lynch horses. Now and then she was brought in and saddled for a race and always she demonstrated her gameness and Thoroughbred mettle.

Tom Lynch loved Sangaroo but he was a horseman and, like others of the strain, was ready at any time to sell or trade. The mare was acquired by Duncan Cameron of Calgary and her name became Froila. Perhaps it was necessary, owing to the strange circumstances of her entry into Canada to have a new name. Anyway, when in Cameron's possession, she was bred to the Quorn horse, Eagle Plume, one of the greatest Thoroughbred sires ever to be brought to the West. It was the mating about which John Ware had speculated and in fulfillment of the hope expressed came a bay filly to be named May W.

Tom Lynch died in 1892 and did not see the foal but those who saw her recognized inherited quality, and some thought they could see the promise of speed and greatness. The filly was trained by George Wentworth and when Cameron's racing entries were moved to the United States, May W began to win fame. She loved a race, just like Tom Lynch loved a race, and could be counted upon to give all the effort she possessed. At the end of her first season, May W was proclaimed the outstanding two-year-old of the year.

But for May W as for her story-book mother, life was eventful. From a racing stable at Butte, Montana, she was stolen at night and recovered days later at Havre. She figured in a train wreck and emerged unscratched.

Then, Duncan Cameron died and his horses were sold by auction—May W among them. Her purchaser shipped her to England, home of the breed where none but the best were appreciated. There the Alberta-bred bay added steadily to her laurels. There she raced successfully and produced some outstanding offspring. She came to the end of a spectacular Thoroughbred trail at the age of twenty-one years, to be remembered as one of the greatest of her breed in Canada, the United States and England.

It was too bad that Tom Lynch whose skill with horses and cattle—and eagerness to help anybody in trouble—created the dramatic background for the story of May W, did not live to witness the climax.

Memories of "Amigo"

J. N. SWANSON

After World War II, my brother Reed and I headed north and, with the help of the GI Bill, started a small wilderness ranch in Oregon. In those days the country was still wide open. Everyone was eager to get on with their lives; they worked hard and were tough. Logging mills were stuck here and there in the woods and supplied a job for anyone who could fit in. Felling trees was done with a double-bitted axe and a two-man crosscut saw.

Good-natured fights and wrestling matches were common—just working off energy, not necessarily mad—no lawyers to intervene. Reed had been a Navy pilot and was more civilized than I. He frowned at me as he handed me a cold cloth for my black eyes and bruised cheek. I think he was also biting his lip to keep from smiling. No one had a better brother.

We cut logs and pulled them down with a saddle horse, built breaking corrals and soon had all the horses we needed to ride for local ranchers.

I've had so many good horses, but some stand out in my memory "larger than life." Such are my feelings for a certain sleek brown stud I called "Amigo." Maybe because it was a time of my youth, a time when adventure was at its height, when I was young and the whole world lay ahead of me, a time when my wants were simple, uncomplicated and full of hope—and everything was new and magnified in importance.

There wasn't a lot of knowledge about Quarter Horses or their backgrounds in the 1940s. I'd heard of Quarter Horses. Also vaguely termed "Steel Dust Horses," Quarter Horses ran short races. A good Texas cow horse often could beat a Thoroughbred in a short race and was called, as a general term, a Quarter Horse.

These Quarter Horses arrived in Oregon in the early '40s, generally trailered up from Oklahoma or Texas, where the horses had been bred for years and the breed was starting to be recognized. Some were registered with the American Quarter Horse Association and some with the National Quarter Horse Breeders Association before they fully merged. Amigo was "National."

Back then, everyone wanted papers to prove their horses were registered. I had a cowboy friend who sold a mustang stud off the desert to a fellow who had a hard time spelling his name, but definitely wanted papers on his stud.

My friend Ron rummaged around in his pickup and found a guarantee for a Sears Roebuck refrigerator and gave it to the buyer, telling him the horse was named Sears. "See, just like the papers say, S-E-A-R-S."

So, it seems, there were AQHA, National and Sears Quarter Horses. I was on the lookout for a Quarter Horse, but decided against a Sears Quarter Horse.

We slopped through the mud on a rainy Oregon winter day in 1947, the ranch owner with rubber boots—me in my high-heeled riding boots. The ranch lay on top of a pine-clad hill in Oregon, and it was an extra-rainy winter.

I wasn't expecting to see much—the two-year-old Quarter Horses standing in the stalls in the murky light of an old horse barn. I stopped to adjust my eyes as we entered the barn. When I could see better, I focused on the seal brown, sleek hindquarters of a young stallion, hip-shot and standing quietly, surveying us with turned head and inquisitive eyes. I went no farther and asked the owner to please lead him out in the light.

The owner quickly untied the stud and, as I got out of his way, led him to the muddy corral. The horse's hindquarters were ridged with muscle, and the trapezius muscle extended along his back in sharp definition folded into his shoulders. He had a head with old wisdom in the eyes, small ears and large nostrils.

These horses were the very early foundation breeding of Peter McCue and the like and, to my mind, the old early breeding hasn't been improved on to any great extent, particularly for brains. I asked the old rancher his price on the brown stud, and I reached in my wallet and gave him half down, the rest due in a week.

I was working in a small wildcat logging mill, ripping railroad ties from peeler logs—logs left from peeling plywood veneer—and was making a steady $1 an hour, so was rich beyond belief. Breaking and shoeing horses gave me weekend jobs.

When I got my brown stud home and hosed him off I found one front hoof grown crooked and facing inward. I started shaping the hoof, rasping off the inside edge. I went to the local slaughterhouse and picked out a gunnysack full of suet fat, then went home and started a fire between two trees in the orchard. In a tin garbage can lid, I boiled the suet to a nice, hot liquid. Then I crosstied the colt with both front feet standing in the lid, soaking up the hot lard. He soon came to enjoy that, and I'd sit with him to keep him from stepping out of the oil. After several months of regular treatments, his hooves became like hard rubber—sleek, shiny, healthy—and straight.

On that ranch I started riding colts in a large barn stall, to keep out of the rain, and then later rode into the corral. Few colts bucked with a roof over their heads, and they were easy to control, with no distractions. Because I rode with nothing but a rope halter, their heads were practically free, and they didn't panic because nothing hurt them, as a rawhide bosal or snaffle might.

Amigo and I became acquainted as we turned around and around the stall, first one way and then the other. With access to an out-of-sight bucket of grain that I could reach as we went by, we soon became friends as I handed him a tidbit while riding.

Riding into the corral was the same—free rein and easy pulls with the halter reins to turn. When the goose was gone from a horse, I introduced him to a rawhide bosal, pulled his head to my knees and suppled his neck on both sides, then trotted around the corral, stopping as I turned him into the fence. He learned to back with a gate pulled against him and me saying "back" every time, until he became acquainted with that word and backed away from the gate.

After his foot became straight with regular rubdowns and wrapping his pasterns, Amigo traveled straight and comfortably. He broke out exceptionally easy after a long, hard bucking session across an open field. He just couldn't help himself after a band of broodmares bunched up and ran ahead of him.

Amigo's interest in cows was bred in, and working cattle in the corrals was something he enjoyed and looked forward to. But one day I bought a stop-watch and paced out 220 yards to see what kind of Quarter Horse I had. Amigo wasn't far off the early record of 12.3 seconds for the furlong, and I knew I could have some fun at the county fairs.

But about that same time a newspaper notice said that after a certain date veterans could no longer take advantage of the GI Bill for education. My poor grades prohibited veterinary school, so one beautiful spring day I loaded my fine young stallion in a homemade trailer and with a horseshoer sign on my '32 V-8 Ford (Model B), my bedroll and saddle strapped on, I headed for the great College of Arts & Crafts in Oakland, California. They looked me over with a jaundiced eye and, sure enough, I was a veteran, so they let me sign up to start classes immediately.

I located some land in the open hills above Oakland, staked out my horse and threw down my bedroll. The great rage in those days was "non-objective" art. My horses had no place in the teaching stratagem of several of my classes. I did my best to fit in, until a big athletic teacher in his tweed suit jerked my drawing out from under my pencil and held it up to the class to illustrate what a "poor, misguided soul" I was, one, "who would never do well in the art world." Fortunately, he turned down my invitation to step outside and con-tinue the conversation. His "F" grade ended my first try to become an artist.

Amigo was fat and eager to get going, and since art school wasn't clamoring for my presence, my stud and I started on the county-fair circuit. I went to a harness shop with measurements of Amigo's heart-girth and had a heavy canvas surcingle made, with pads for each side of the withers and rings to hang leather loops for my toes. With a saddle blanket and the surcingle, I rode him, stripped down to my T-shirt and boot socks. My racing colors were T-shirt white and Levi blue. And because a 220-yard race isn't much affected by weight, Amigo didn't know my 150 pounds was on him.

Amigo soon found out if he made a slow start, he was bombarded with clods from the front-running horses. From then on his 20-foot jump at the first stride always put him in front. I had to put a strap around his neck to hang onto, along with the reins. A young jockey laughed when I told him how to ride Amigo and was left on his back in the dirt. That's the only time Amigo lost a race.

In no time at all, he was considered the horse to beat. I made gunnysack blankets to put over him and disguised him the best I could. There were always a few old-time, county-fair farmers with their fast horses around to check out a new horse: "How's he bred, sonny?" "How about a little breeze in the back stretch in the morning?"

Amigo's great conformation and hip and leg muscles would give him away. He was a horse I could jump on and ride with a string around his neck, winning first a race and then a stock-horse contest.

These early county-fair races had what they call lap-and-tap starts—the horses walking up to a line on the track and then starting, generally with a blank pistol shot. However, New Mexico, Arizona and Texas had regular starting gates in those early days.

Amigo and I were pretty square with each other. I never hogged the best part of the stall. I'd throw my bedroll along the back wall and lay there listening to the comfortable sound of him munching hay. He'd come over, checking my bedroll from head to foot, the slowly lie down alongside, being sure he didn't step on me. He put his head where he knew I could scratch his ears. In the morning he got up just as carefully and nickered that he needed breakfast. It was a pretty good relationship—better than most.

In Stockton, California, Amigo pulled up lame while I was again thinking of art school. This time, though, I needed an accredited school that was located on the ocean so I could work my horse in salt water. The old-time county-fair horse doctors had recommended working Amigo in the surf.

The art-school list showed only Carmel Art Institute, so one blustery and beautiful day I pulled into the quaint, small village of Carmel and looked for a place to put my horse and live, so I could start school and work my horse in the ocean every morning. I counted my assets—they amounted to $30, one lame horse and my saddle. Not bad—I was in good shape.

I soon found a dilapidated old stable near the ocean and the Carmel Mission. I made a deal with the owner to ride his colts for him, then threw my bedroll in an empty stall and put Amigo in an adjoining corral. I laid back and looked through the stall roof up to the open sky and said "How lucky can a guy get? Seventy-eight dollars a month, GI Bill, school and a nice place to live."

I washed my clothes in the water trough and prepared to go to my first day in school. The teacher greeted me with open arms, and my artist career was started.

Amigo wholeheartedly agreed that we were doing the right thing, and enjoyed the early morning gallops in the surf on the Carmel beach and an occasional match race with local cowboys, who figured they had fast horses.

Amigo being lame at Stockton due to a hard track was the reason for starting art school again—the fork in the trail that ended the footloose life I led and concentrated my energies on my career as an artist. I owe a lot to that great horse I called Amigo.

Coursing Rabbits on the Plains

FREDERIC REMINGTON

"Look here boys, what do you say to running 'jacks' to-morrow?" said Jim, as he brought his chair down from its canted back position against the wall of the room, and, by way of an emphasizer, striking the table a blow with his fist which made the little kerosene lamp dance a jig.

I seconded the motion immediately, but Bob, the owner of the ranch, sat back and reflectively sucked his big pipe, as he thought of the things, which ought to be done. The broken fence to the corral down by the creek, dredging the watering holes, the possibilities of trading horses down at Plum Grove and various other thrifty plans weighed upon his mind; but Jim continued—"It's nice fall weather now, dry and cold; why, a hoss will jest run hisself to death for fun; that old Bob mule scampered like a four year ole colt all the way to Hoyt's grocery with me today, and besides, there hain't nothing to do, and the 'jacks' is thicker 'n tumbleweeds on the prairie."

The sporting blood began to mount to Robert's great, contemplative eyes as the arguments went home; so removing his pipe he blew the smoke upwards as sedately as Irving's Dutchmen, shook off his Van Twiller doubts and declared he was an enthusiast, as indeed he was when he had made up his mind.

"That settles it," gleefully shouted Jim, "old Push-Bob (his horse) can have the bit to-morrow. Come here, Peggy, old son." Out from the corner behind the stove sneaked a dog and approached Jim in a delighted, sidelong, apologetic way, which gave the cue to his cur blood.

"I say, Jim, you hain't agoin' to make Peg-Leg run hisself to death over these yar prairies, be you?" came from Phip, the cook, as he put away the supper dishes. "Ha-ha," he laughed; "poor old Peg-Leg: he never seed a jack-rabbit 'cept the rabbit were a' disappearin' down the horizon like a fallin' star. Peg's a right smart good dog to run these yar land turtles with, but Peg hain't much account a' runnin' of jacks."

"Never you mind," replied the chivalric James, whose large nature always went out to the inferior and oppressed, "Peg ain't no sprint-runner fer a fact, but if them spider-dogs (meaning the greyhounds) misses bunny, old Peg gets him before the sun goes down," and patting Peg-Leg encouragingly, "We get there just the same. Well, go lay down and rest yerself; that's a good dog." And Peg-Leg sneaked back to the obscurity of the cook-stove. Peg-Leg was not a greyhound, nor indeed was he a fox-hound, although he was called such by persons not accurate on dog matters. He had lost the symmetry of one forward leg at some time during puphood and had been christened after the Indian fashion from his peculiarity, Peg-Leg. Peg was not a good coursing dog, but after the fashion of his breed, he always caught his rabbit. He ran at a limping gallop, but his nose was a most sensitive organ, and when on a trail he had a tenacity of purpose, which was nearly canine insanity. He was, besides, on personal friendly relations with all us boys, and attended our hunts from what I suppose was a sense of duty, as he certainly could not have enjoyed them, considering that he was a long tailing behind the fast hounds and bounding horses; but should the rabbit make a sharp crook and get away in some bad bit of country, we only had to wait until Peg-Leg came up and showed us the way he had gone. The jack-rabbit does not run far at one time, although his break away is indescribable except as a disappearing shadow, but Peg would manage to rout him out again.

The next preliminary was to enlist John S. in the scheme, for he owned the greyhounds, so I was deputized to go and see Johnnie as I rode on the way to my home down the creek.

"Hark! didn't I hear horses?" ejaculated Phip, as he stopped at the open door after discharging a pan of dish-water into the outer darkness. "Yes, and comin' like mad."

We all went to the door and listened a moment, when James retired to his chair and began to roll a fresh cigarette with the remark, "It's that crazy

Englishman; no one but a — fool would ride like that on a dark night." Jim's language was merely figurative, however; for when the clatter, clatter of the horse's hoofs stopped in front of the house and a big red face was thrust into the room with the greeting, "'Ello, bies," one could immediately see that Charlie B. was not as Jim had described him.

"Come in, Charlie; tie yer hoss to the corral and come in," was Bob's return greeting, whereat Charlie disappeared.

"That chap 'ill go hunting," said the practical Phip, sententiously, as he chuckled away, and poked at the fire; "it's a cold day when that Englishman won't go hunting, or anywhere else where there hain't no work ter do." We realized the force of this, and Charlie verified it by declaring that he was delighted with the prospect when he had come in from outside.

Charlie B. was your typical country Englishman, and the only thing about him American was the broncho he rode. He was the best fellow in the world, cheery, hearty and ready for a lark at any time of the day or night. He owned a horse ranch seven miles down the creek, and found visiting his neighbors involved considerable riding; but Charlie was a sociable soul, and did not appear to mind that, and he would spend half the night riding over the lonely prairies to drop in on a friend in some neighboring ranch, in consequence of which Charlie's visits were not always timely; but he seemed never to realize that a chap was not in as good condition to visit when awakened from his blanket at three o'clock in the morning as in the twilight hour.

"'Ose going, Bob," he asked.

"Well, let's see;" and Bob surveyed the company. "There's Jim and Fred, and you and myself and Johnnie S.; and Bill Carr will want to go, won't he, Fred?"

"Yes. Bill will want to give old Prince a whirl, and Prince will want to be whirled; for do you know that that old, grey, sleepy plug never wakes up and acts like a horse unless he sees a 'jack' in front of him;" and by way of peroration I added, "He never saw a horse there."

As I had expected, this stirred up the horse question, which commanded all the intellect, the interest, the finer feelings and the subtle jealousies of the cow-camps. The exact running qualities of the horses were debatable, and every new horse that came into the White-water bottoms had to cost its owner a couple of snug bets in order to find out that Prince and Push-Bob could beat him. But whether Prince or Push-Bob was the best was an active subject of conjecture, and one which we never tired of. Jim immediately indulged in some sage doubts on my reflections on Prince, and we all laughed as James began to nerve up for a storm.

"Don't stir up that yar horse question or you'll have Jim a bettin' more money in this ole shanty than the Santa Fé road could put up," came from Phip, who was one of your intellectual horsemen, not given to betting, but taking a more sensible view; "still," he continued, "that 'ar Prince is as good as anybody's horse 'cept fer that heavy for'd leg, but then Push he's a right smart sort of a plug hisself—"

"Hold on, Phip, thought you didn't want the horse question," came from another corner, and Phip laughed, subsided and poked the fire in silence.

"What are you going to ride, Charlie?" was asked.

"The blue mare—the big un's gone lame in 'is stifle of late; think the bloody mules must 'ave landed 'im one on 'is joint; but the little blue mare's a good 'n, she's a good 'oss. I'll show ye fellows a fine pair of 'ind 'oofs to-morrow;" and Charlie slapped his boots with his whip and smiled triumphantly.

"I suppose the little yaller gal will have to take it to-morrow," said Jim, as he gazed humorously at my 180 pounds avoirdupois.

"Yes," I replied; "Terra-Cotta and I'll try and keep up with the procession."

"Bob, there, 'e'll ride that black vagabond of 'is; 'e'll go in partnership with what's 'is name 'ere—Peg-Leg," bantered Charlie.

Bob allowed that if old Jane felt like it, he would distinguish himself, but he added: "I expect she'll get located out there on the prairie and I'll have to send in to the ranch for a pair of mules," referring to a propensity of his favorite mare to balk; "but if she don't, I am not hunting sympathy, fer I won't need it."

So the evening passed pleasantly amid boyish banter, and the horse talk so dear to the stockman's heart. Presently, finding the hour to be late, B. and I bade the boys on Bob's ranch good night, went out, bestrode our horses and rode off down the creek to our homes. Passing Johnnie S.'s ranch, we pounded a *reveille* on the door, which presently brought the owner to it, rubbing his eyes and inquiring what the — we wanted in the middle of the night? "Oh! it's you, is it, B.? Well, I might know. Say, B., what's the matter with the daytime for calling on a fellow?"

We explained that our visit would be short, disclosed our plans, and expatiated on the joys of "jack" running, and finally Johnnie concluded that the interests of his cows required that he run "jacks" on the morrow; so we rode off and left him to his slumbers. Johnnie was an important adjunct, as he owned the greyhounds, but now that his co-operation was assured, everything was ready for the sport. At last I was snug in bed, and B. was presumably in his somewhat later, though it mattered little as to that, considering his personal habits. Poor B.! later on, his remittances from the old country stopped, and the last I heard of that lump of generous nature he was working for the man who owned his ranch, and keeping better hours in the interest of his employer.

I mention these preliminaries to allow the reader to become interested in the horses which were to do the running, as "jack" coursing is a succession of sharp quarter or half mile dashes, generally run in a clump, and well adapted to the spry little broncho horses, who would cut a sorry figure in a long English fox chase; and then this neat little sport is generally practiced by the ranchmen and farmers of the West, and while not exactly an event in our lives, yet it was a day spent apart from the usual duties, and therefore interesting.

I ate a light breakfast, and indeed the ranch larder helped me to do that; and after a feed of oats, rubbed Terra-Cotta down, and then put a light saddle on in place of my heavy stock saddle weighing some thirty-five pounds. Terra-Cotta was a nervous little half-breed Texas and thoroughbred, of a beautiful light gold-dust color, with a Naples yellow color mane and tail. She always knew that the light saddle meant a sharp run, and her fiery little thoroughbred nature asserted itself. In a moment she was in a te-he, and could scarcely wait for me to mount, but was off in a gallop before I was fully seated. Bill, my ranch-hand, followed me on old Prince, and the gallop across the prairie to Bob's was glorious. A light haze hung over the plains, not yet dissipated by the rising sun. Terra-Cotta's stride was steel springs under me as she swept along, brushing the dew from the grass of the range and taking the bit smartly in her teeth as though to say, "Come on, let's have a run," but I pulled gently and coaxed her to save herself for a later hour. Off to the right we saw another figure going toward Bob's, and in a few moments, by converging, found Johnnie S. mounted on his big bay and leading one greyhound.

"Good morning, Johnnie, where is the other dog?"

"She thought she would stay at home to-day—you see, the old lady has expectations, and—well, it's good judgment on her part. But here's Daddy, and he's good for all the jack-rabbits on the range."

Later on we came up with Charlie B. on the blue mare, and rigged out in full English hunting tog, all except a red coat, which is an addition not generally appreciated in the western country.

On over the smiling reach of grass, grown dry and sere in the August suns and hot winds, we galloped four abreast. The boys had on light saddles and snaffle bits, and while Mr. B. sported a hunting stock, the rest contented themselves with light poles some six feet long, which were to be used as lances, with which to touch the rabbit, a feat most difficult and improbable. We had all discarded our *chaparajos*, and the horses were lightly blanketed. The rise and fall of the perfect lope peculiar to the American broncho was observable in all its ease and beauty. The blue mare looked blue indeed. She was one of those freaks of color which one sees occasionally on the plains. Johnnie's bay horse was a powerful animal, and a pleasant horse to get along with. Johnnie and he had a perfect understanding, and never seemed to clash. It made no difference to the horse on which part of his back Johnnie was, he attended strictly to his own business. Terra is already known, but now glance at Prince. You would not think him a quarter-horse, for he looks like a clumsy, sleepy old plug. Iron grey, with no flesh and big bones, he moves powerfully, steadily, but "where is the snap?" you will say. Oh, it's there, somewhere, and always comes out on occasion. Many a man associates wealth that is gone with the name of Prince, and many a quarter-horse has found his Waterloo as he has followed old Prince over the scratch; still he is not much of a horse to look at, and that is a strong point, because the other fellows always went their last dollar on appearances.

After a few moments' ride we drew rein in Bob C.'s corral and went into the house, where the boys were eating their breakfasts.

"Do you know, old Phip has got waked up, and thinks he wants to run jacks, so he's going to lower his dignity and take a spurt on Bob," explained Jim.

We all laughed, for we knew Phip was an eminently practical person, who had rarely spared time for trivial things, and had neglected to learn in his studious career to ride a horse. Furthermore, we knew "Bob." "Bob" was a mule, somewhat advanced in years, but with his character as yet unformed, as it were. At least, those who were charitable toward the mule said this, but I think he was bad and malicious. Of course he had spells of goodness, but even a mule must rest from crime; in the main, though, he was sulky, was known to bite, was believed capable of kicking, was grossly given to bucking, and perfectly certain to balk; and the only thing he would not do was to run away, and that is a virtue in a hunting horse. "Bob" had at various times elevated some of the best riders in that part of the country toward the stars, but Phip was incredulous, and had evolved a theory that the base of Bob's character was good, and that all he needed was intelligent handling, etc., all of which will appear later on.

"Jim, do you want to gaunt Peg-Leg for a race, or will you give him his ration?" grinned Phip, as he held up the remains of breakfast on a plate, which Peg-Leg was regarding with fixed and intelligent gaze.

"Oh, give him his grub—he don't exercise violently when he runs; if he don't start on a full stomach he'll starve to death before he can catch a 'jack'." This brought breakfast and contentment to Peg-Leg.

The horses were saddled, and all being mounted, Phip included, the cavalcade moved out of the corral, across the creek, up the bluffs and on over the range.

"I'm going to watch Push-Bob and Prince to-day to see where the money is," whispered Johnnie to me as we rode ahead. The horses were all fretful and uneasy, except old Prince, whose great good sense always told him when the hour had come. Even old Jane, Bob's mare, condescended to take an interest and manifest a disposition to pound sod, which was exceedingly gratifying to Robert, inasmuch as the condition of Jane's feelings were to be considered as to whether she would go or not. Jane was not a plug, be it understood, but a good American mare, with all the saddle gaits, but she was in the years of discretion, and had multiplied her race in various instances.

"Say, Jim, do you know—"

"There's a jack—take him, Daddy," came a quick cry from Johnnie, and the next moment Johnnie's big bay was off. There goes the rabbit, the dog flies after. "Go on, Terra," I shouted, loosing on the bit, hitting her lightly with a spur, and away we went, all in a ruck. Old Prince was shouldering heavily away on my right, Push-Bob on my quarter, Jane off to the left, and Phip at a stately gallop behind—the blue mare being left at the post as it were.

The horses tore along, blowing great lung-fulls of fresh morning air out in snorts. Our sombreros blew up in front from the rush of air, and our blood leaped with excitement. Away scurried the jack, with his great ears sticking up like two antique bedposts, with Daddy closing the distance rapidly, and our outfit thundering along some eight rods in the rear. Down into a slew of long grass into which the rabbit and dog disappeared we went, with the grass snapping and swishing about the legs of our horses. A dark mass on my left heaves up, and "ho—there goes Bob head over heels." On we go.

"Hope Bob isn't hurt—must have put his foot into a water-hole," are my excited reflections. We are out of the slew, but where is the rabbit and dog?

"Here they go," comes from Phip, who is standing on the edge of the slew, farther down toward the bluffs of the bottoms, where he has gotten as the result of a short cut across.

Phip digs his spurs into the mule, sticks out his elbows and manifests other frantic desires to get there, all of it reminding one strongly of the style of one Ichabod Crane, but as we rush by, it is evident that the mule is debating the question with that assurance born of the consciousness that when the thing is brought to a vote he has a majority in the house. Poor Phip, now for your theories!

Up a rise in the "draw" onto the plain we go helter-skelter, over some stony land and then a nice level, with Mr. Jack-rabbit twenty rods in the lead and Daddy skimming along in his wake. It is no use running now, he has too much of a start; so I pull in the impetuous Terra and I cut across to the left, hoping bunny will dodge that way, and of course, in the event that he does not, I am out of the race. "Ah, just as I had expected, bunny has dodged," and Daddy whizzed by some two rods before he could feel his rudder and come about. The jack was bearing nearly on to me, with Daddy flying quite far behind. Terra sees it, I think, as I turn her head, shake the rein and whisper, "Go on, girl," and we are off. "Now go on, Terra; what are you good for?" I yelled, lifting her forward. I leaned over and extended my stick, but the jack is by two feet too far. A couple of jumps and—"There, I missed him. Whoa, Terra, you little fool; do you want to run all over the prairie for nothing?"

The rabbit made back for the "draw" or ravine, considering the broken country as better than "a fair field and no favor." He kept doubling and throwing the dog off, for he was evidently old game. The "draw" was rough, stony, and the bed of the dry stream was filled with a thick growth of willows. By some good maneuvering, James got right on to him, and was going straight for the willows. The rabbit and dog shot through, and Jim gallantly followed on Push-Bob, for I verily believe that the horse would have charged a stone wall. As they struck the thick brush, Jim was swept from his seat like a fly from a sugar-bowl, and the horse went on.

After more running about, doubling and twisting, Charlie B. and Bill C. started in together, and as I stood in the "draw" dismounted, the rabbit, dog, Charlie and Bill swept over a little hill and full at me, with a regular, reckless "cannon-to-the-right-of-them" swing. I leaped into the saddle as they came. Crash through the willows they went, and there came disaster. The bank was worn away on the other side by a cattle-path just wide enough for one. They were neck and neck, both ambitious to use the narrow path; so at it they rushed, and any philosopher will anticipate what befell them. They bunted rudely together, upsetting each horse and rider, while I galloped up the path between them with a cheer, leaving them rolling in a cloud of dust, and blaming each other. As accidents seemed to be the rule of the run, I helped out the rule in this wise: The bluffs which overlooked the White-water bottoms lay off to the left some forty rods, and toward them went the dog and rabbit, with me following after pell-mell. I have since explained how it happened in some dozen odd ways, but at this distant day I do not seem to concur in any of my own explanations, so I have ceased laying the blame on Terra-Cotta, and taken upon my own shoulders the responsibility of riding full tilt over the bluffs. When we arrived at the bluff, Terra-Cotta could not be stopped. The incline was about 50° and well sodded, though lumpy, and Terra's knees bent under her at the first step downward, and others have said that we made the descent sandwich fashion, though the details are somewhat obscured. I lay on the ground for a moment, expecting to find a bone on a strike, or some blood running, but did not, and so arose to find I was not hurt in the least. Terra got on her feet, shook herself and looked foolish. I took her by the bridle, saying, "Are you hurt, old girl?" As though to say, "Not a bit," she turned about, and every muscle and bone answered its summons. The rabbit got away, and he had almost avenged his race in the ordeal, for upon assembling, Mr. Robert C. presented himself in a guise which I can only compare to a sketch in plaster. Old Jane had put both forward legs into a slew-hole, and Mr. Robert was dumped in the mud. When we met he still carried a nice coating of slime and blue clay on his person, while old Jane was gradually growing white as the clay dried in the cool air that was blowing. She looked as though she thought her matronly dignity had been trifled with. We did not take these calamities to heart, but thought it a good opening for a day's sport.

Peg-Leg came up and sat down on his haunches near our group, and looked sulkily at the far horizon as much as to say, "That's a nice way to hunt."

"Well, let's try it again! Come along up the 'draw.' Come, Peggy, old boy," said Jim, as he led off at a fox trot. Johnnie had caught the greyhound, and we were ready for another view. We drew up our girths and made up our minds that we would not let the next jack get such a start on us. We kept a sharp lookout, when suddenly Peggy barks and goes limping off across the prairie on what will evidently be a lone hunt, as it is only a trail and no rabbit in sight.

"That's good day for Peg-Leg," laughs Jim. "Peg-Leg is abused, and I'll be hanged if I blame him for bein' disgusted—but he's got a hunt all to hisself now, so good luck to him."

We rode up the "draw" about a quarter of a mile and stopped for Johnnie to fix a *cincha*. He was long about it, and we sat on our horses and chatted. Off to the right about a third of a mile was Peg-Leg, nosing along with an occasional bark. We watched him when he gradually turned toward us.

"Peg's coming this way and I wouldn't wonder if there was a jack somewhere in the grass, as it's long enough to hide one," remarked one.

"Jest mind your eye; I wouldn't wonder if Peg would start one, so look out," went on another, and the words were hardly out of his mouth before a jack of enormous size sprang up from right under Peg's nose, and like a rubber ball came bounding toward us.

"Hi, Johnnie, give Daddy the sight," we yelled.

Daddy got it and was off—we after. The rabbit was evidently only thinking of Peg-Leg, and was running right into the jaws of Daddy.

"There, he got him," we shouted, but "no," for the jack had passed seemingly right under Daddy's body, was among our horses' feet the next moment, and gone in our rear before we could stop.

Phip, who was galloping in our rear, had his golden opportunity now, and got out his stick to deal the champion stroke, when the mule spying the rabbit coming toward him, shied violently and left Phip sprawling about on the grass. We had swept about with a wheel to the right and left, and were again on the trail. As we passed Phip, he was using some of the strongest parts of the Saxon language with very telling effect. We all laughed and passed on.

After a sharp run, Bill got near enough to the rabbit to deal a violent blow, which started the dust in a shower and broke his stick, but Charlie caught the rabbit on the turn, and with a backhand stroke he knocked what little life was left out of bunny, and Daddy finished him.

Phip caught his mule and came up. He insisted that the mule was perverse beyond all rule and precedent, and passed without discussion some ironical remarks about "riding a horse" which were made by Robert, who was in duty bound to champion his own mule. Peg-Leg was far more disgusted than Phip, and grew melancholy as he reflected on the unfairness of our methods. After being jeered and laughed at a few moments, he started off for the bottoms in a sulk to have a hunt all alone, with no one to gobble his hard-earned glory and meat at the finish.

We proceeded on our way, hoping to find another jack soon, but no jack appeared. Jim's prophecy of the night before fell flat, but still we hoped with the true heroism of the hunter, who should never be discouraged in his search for game. In some respects I consider the hunting field a very good place to test character.

"Do these — jack-rabbits think we'll 'unt hall day?" queried Charlie, with his rising inflection. We were silent, as we had our doubts as to the jacks having any thoughts in the matter. We were some ten miles from home when we started a jack at last, and took after him, horse, dog and man. Charlie B. was in the lead, and the rabbit was going toward the ranch and corrals of one John Mitchner, a new arrival in those parts, from somewhere in the Indian Territory. The rabbit made straight for a corral and shot through a wire fence, the dog with a graceful bound went over, and the blue mare seemed to be going through, though Charlie succeeded in stopping her, thus saving himself a good scraping. We lost the rabbit, as it got under a hay-rick and Peg was not about to help us out of our difficulty, he having left in a tiff.

Old John came out of his house smoking a corn-cob pipe, and extended his compliments with a graceful "how-de, boys."

"Hello, John! Come out and hunt rabbits; you have nothing else to do," was the reply.

"Well I reckon as how I'm gettin too ole to be chasing them nasty little rabbits over these yar prairies, but this yar a runnin' of horses kinder gets me. If I only had that cow-skin horse now what I used ter own back in old Missouri, I'd show—"

"Oh, come off, John; that old cow-skin business is played out," broke in Jim, who had heard old John discourse on the cow-skin racer until he was sick of it. "You will get the world to moving backwards if you keep dinging away about that old hoss. Why, I met a chap from Missouri the other day what allowed as he knew the cow-skin hoss, and he says he's beat him with a mule once back thar in Missouri," went on Jim.

We realized that Jim had evolved this last fabrication on the spot, with no basis of truth, but were content to see old John's cow-skin ghost of discussion annihilated at once.

Old John removed his pipe, his eyes glistened and he replied vehemently, pointing a long, bony finger at Jim—"That feller's a liar, do ye understan'?

That feller's a d— liar, and it's ole John Mitchner as will fill his lyin' hide full of holes ef ye'll jest show him up, do ye understan'? Fer I don't allow no Missouri liar to come browsin' about these parts a sayin' as how the cow-skin hoss was ever beat by any critter as wears har—do ye understan', Mr. Jim C.?"

"Oh, yes; I understan', Uncle John. I thought he was a liar at the time, but I did not tell him so, 'cause he had red eyes and was loaded with guns," replied Jim in a conciliatory manner.

"I don't care a peg if he were a man-of-war; you jest allow as I say. I'll make a mineral lead of his carcus if I get a sight on him," added Uncle John, as he grew more resigned, seeming to think the cow-skin stories vindicated by this reckless harangue. "Come, dismount and come in; it's near time fer dinner," said John, as he walked back to the house.

We tied our horses to the fence and followed. "I tell you, boys, if that cow-skin horse ever existed a better horse could have broke old John pretty bad. We'll have to put up a job on old John's sporting blood to-day. You go in, Jim, and run a bluff on him," said Bill to us in a whisper, as we stepped into John's cabin.

We sat about and smoked while old John's boy got a dinner of bacon and eggs. The conversation turned on horses, and with old John in the company, horse talk was a synonym for cow-skin horse talk. At last Jim spoke up, saying, "Say, Uncle John, I don't think you ever owned but one good horse in your life. You hain't any horse in yer corral as could beat a Mexican sheep fer a quarter."

Old John gazed at the stove a few moments and then awoke and began: "Wall, my hoss stock ain't nothin' to brag on now, because I hain't got the money that you fellers down in the creek has got fer to buy 'em with, but I've got a little mare down thar in the corral as I've got a notion ken run some shakes."

"How fast, Uncle John?" queried Jim.

"Well, tol'able fast. I reckon as how she's a smarter horse than is hitched to the fence on the outside of the corral."

"Ha! Ha! You don't mean it, Uncle John. Why, my bay Push-Bob or grey Prince would shovel sand into her eyes in great shape at a quarter," provokingly retorted Jim.

"Ye've got a great notion of them 'ar horses of yourn. I'm an old man, and I've got done a racin' of horses, but if your hoss can beat mine you can have the mare," replied John Mitchner, fixedly eyeing Jim.

"It's a go—hoss agin horse," spoke up Jim, rising. "I'll ride mine and you ride yourn."

"Come on," said John, putting on his hat. We all arose and went out. The boy left the bacon and eggs to burn to a cinder on the cook-stove and followed.

"I'll bet Prince can beat either of you," said Bill, at this stage of the proceedings. "I'll ride him, and we'll all three run, the winner to take both— this yer is going to be a horse race, and it's a good time to see whether Prince or Push-Bob is the better horse."

The offer was accepted, and with this understanding the men began to strip their horses and to remove all their own superfluous clothes, for the quarter-races on the plains are all ridden bareback, and nearly naked. We began to get excited, and finally I provoked old John into betting with me. He wagered a fine mare and colt, which he pointed out in the corral with the remark, "agin yer yaller nag," and continuing, "This yar is a horse race, and I'm a bettin' man when I race horses, which is something I hain't done this ten years." At the last moment, as we had the track paced off on the level prairie, Bob bet his mare against four head of cattle, to be picked from John's herd. The Englishman wanted a hand, and staked the blue mare against a three-year old, said to belong to John Mitchner's boy, and Phip mounted the mule and regarded the proceedings as ominous in an extreme.

"Ye'll get beat sure," he whispered to me; but I sneered, "What, that grey mare beat Push-Bob? Why, Phip, what are you thinking of? She's an old brood mare, and looks as though she had come through in the spring instead of off the grass in the fall."

I was to fire the starting shot with old John's musket, and Charlie and Bob were to judge at the other end along with Mitchner's boy.

The three racers came up to the scratch, Bill and Jim sitting their sleek steeds like centaurs. Old Prince had bristled up and moved with great vim and power. Push-Bob swerved about and stretched his neck on the bit. The boys were bare-footed, with their sleeves rolled up and a handkerchief tied around their heads. Old John came prancing out, stripped to the waist, on his mare, which indeed looked more game when mounted than running loose in the corral. The old man's grey, thin locks were blowing loose in the wind, and he worked his horse up to the scratch in a very knowing way. We all regarded the race as a foregone conclusion and had really begun to pity old John's impoverishment, but still there was the interest in the bout between Prince and

Push-Bob. This was the first time the victors of the White-water bottoms had met, and was altogether the greatest race which that country had seen in years. How the boys from the surrounding ranches would have gathered could they have known it, but it is just as well that they did not; for as I fired the gun and the horses scratched away from the mark, Old John went to the front and stayed there to the end, winning by several lengths, while Prince and Push-Bob ran what was called a dead heat, although there was considerable discussion over it for a long time afterwards. There was my dear little Terra gone to the hand of the spoilsman, and the very thought almost broke my heart, as I loved that mare as I shall never love another animal. I went back to the corral, sat down and began to whittle a stick. It took Bob and Charlie a half an hour to walk the quarter of a mile back to the ranch. Bill and John said nothing kept them from flying the country to save their horses but the fact that they had no saddles.

Old John rode up, threw himself from his broncho and drawled out: "Thar now; I've been a layin' fer you fellers ever since I came inter these yar parts and I recon as how I've sort of got ye. If ye'd had more horses with ye, I'd a hade a right smart horse herd arter this race;" and then turning to Jim he added, "Mr. Jim, ye'r a pretty smart feller, don't ye? P'raps ye'l hev more faith in the cow-skin horse stories now, seein' as how this yer grey mare is known back in parts of Missouri as the cow-skin horse, all along of a circumstance the particulars of which I allow p'raps yer don't keer to hear now," whereat he turned his mare into the corral, went and untied Terra-Cotta, the black mare, the brown horse and the blue mare, which he also turned loose in his horse corral along with a half-dozen head of his own stock.

"Mr. Jim, will yer be so good as to jest turn that alleged race-horse inter this yar corral, seein' as yer don't own him no more?"

Mr. Jim and Mr. Bill, as old John insisted in calling them in his chilling discourse, did as requested, whereat old John invited us to dinner and turned on his heel. But no one manifested a disposition to dine. We stood leaning over the corral fence, regarding intently the cow-skin horse, as John called her, and wondering at the deceitfulness of appearances. Some one suggested that it was a right good distance home but the walking was good.

"Let's borrow the 'osses," suggested the Englishman.

"I'd walk from here to old Mexico before I'd ask old John fer a horse," replied Bill, and we all declined to solicit John's charity in the matter. So the walk began, and a long, solemn tramp it was over the dry plain. Phip rode the mule, as he was a rather old man and not in shape to walk an odd ten miles, and carried the saddles, and the rest of us trudged along beside.

As we neared home, or Bob's ranch, we began to feel gaunt, and Phip cheered us by assurances of some tid-bits in the shape of a can of white pears and a cold roast goose which Jim had shot some days previous. As we descended into the bottoms, Peg-Leg greeted us, and as he gazed at our solemn procession, it seems that I could detect a smile of comfort on his canine countenance. The boys on the ranch regarded us curiously and seriously, but it gradually dawned upon them, after numerous questions and evasive answers, what had happened, and they retired to the barn, where I thought I heard discordant sounds for an hour after. Phip set up the can of pears and we picked the goose clean from a sense of duty.

"Every man in this country will know this inside of two days," regretfully sighed Bob.

"If there war any brush hereabouts I'd take to it," asserted Bill, "but there ain't, and we'll have to go down to Hoyt's grocery to-morrow and face the music—and say, gentlemen, it will be pizen."

Phip was dying to work the "I told you so" business, but he was suppressed by ominous threats of dire resort.

We procured horses of Bob and saddled up to go our various ways. As we started, Jim said—

"Well, boys, how do you like running jacks?"

We all laughed and parted as goodhumoredly as the circumstances would allow.

That night, Bill and I rode down to Hoyt's grocery and post-office to purchase some necessaries, but through the window in the light of the store we could see old John Mitchner perched on a barrel of sugar and a crowd of the boys around him all convulsed with laughter.

"Bill, let's go home," I remarked, and we trotted off up the road into the darkness.

Mares
&
Foals

Sonata for Horses

LINDA HASSELSTROM

'd been dreaming of horses for so long that I expected to find one waiting in the barn when I woke up on my first morning on the ranch. I'd already heard tales of horsemanship from my father and his older brother, Harold. Proudly, Harold said that if the Hasselstrom boys couldn't handle a horse, nobody could. I longed to join a clan with such a reputation. My father said, "Save your money. One of these days I'll find you a horse to buy." I was disappointed but too busy following him around, listening to his stories, to mope.

Though most of our neighbors had tractors, my father used a team of workhorses to mow and rake hay the first few years. I went to the barn with him and watched as he seemed to weave the net of harness over the horses' broad backs. He wouldn't let me help. "Bud and Beauty aren't used to kids," he said. "If one of them stepped on you by mistake, it'd break your leg." When he saddled Zarro, he made me stay on the other side of the fence until he'd finished and tied the gelding in the corral, explaining, "He's so spooky he's liable to kick your head off."

So I dreamed of riding a black stallion and made secret plans. For doing my chores—gathering eggs, taking out the garbage—I earned fifty cents a week. I gave up candy and stowed every cent I made in my checking account, where Mother made me put the cash distant relatives sent on birthdays and Christmas.

At the county fair in August, I watched horses sprint past carrying kids half my age—four or five years old—while I ate dust stumbling along afoot. Determined to alter my greenhorn status, I'd already pilfered my checkbook from Mother's dresser drawer and stuffed it between my spine and the waistband of my jeans. Then as my folks examined every apron and potholder in the women's building, I escaped and bolted toward the horse stalls, shoving the checkbook in my back pocket, muttering, "I'll buy my own damn horse." The balance was nearly a hundred dollars.

That sweltering morning, I went to the horse barn and immediately spotted a "Horses for Sale" sign. I spent the next several hours dickering with the skinny man who told me to call him Mote. He kept squinting at me and blinking sweat out of his eyes.

"You're Johnny Hasselstrom's daughter?" he said when I introduced myself. "Hell, I mean heck, honey, I didn't even know he was married. Sure, you can look at my horses."

He leaned silently against the fence, elbows hooked over the top plank, while I walked to the first stall and began to stare at the horses, trying to remember what I should look for. I asked him the history, name, and price of every horse. Before I'd studied more than three, he sauntered over to the water tank, filled his hat with water and dumped it over his head. He shook, swept his hair back, and replaced the hat, sighing.

I studied the horses intently, but Blaze was the only one I could afford. White hairs dappled her muzzle, but she nudged my arm sociably, and I needed all the friends I could get. While I stared at her, Mote yawned and sighed and said he'd trade the mare's rope halter and bridle for a beer.

"But Mote—Mr. Mote," I stammered, "I'm not old enough to buy you a beer." Laughing, he wiped his forehead with a black silk neckerchief, declared me a hard bargainer, and said he'd throw in the halter and bridle.

While he led the mare out, I wrote a check for eighty dollars, contemplating the attractions of a career as a horse dealer. Mote was already hurrying away when I grabbed the mare's mane to pull myself onto her back. Wrapping my legs around her well-padded ribs, I rode toward the grandstand.

Behind the sheep sheds, I met Aunt Josephine. As practice for telling my folks, I tucked a thumb in my belt and announced my news. She whooped and slapped her knee when she heard the horse trader's name. Years elapsed before I understood half the remarks Jo mumbled about him while she lifted the mare's hooves and pried her mouth open. By the time she straightened up, I knew what to look for the next time I bought a horse.

Jo slapped the mare on the neck and said, "Now you can ride in the parade. I'll be lining them up in about ten minutes." She strode away, chuckling to herself, her hips jiggling in her tight pants.

My father rolled his eyes when I met him in the parking lot. As he inspected the mare, I babbled about my deal. At the big finish—that the horse trader already had my check—he shook his head and patted my shoulder. "I guess you've bought yourself a horse. We'll see about a saddle when you can stay on her." He turned toward the grandstand. I knew then that I had officially joined the scions of other ranching families, traveling properly on four legs among the wretched women and kids walking.

Next I saw my mother, wearing a thin cotton dress and high heels, buying a cold drink at the shack behind the grandstand. I clucked to the mare and was waiting when Mother turned, wobbling a bit on the uneven ground. "Hey Mom! Look at my horse!"

She snapped her white handbag shut and looked up at me. Her blue eyes widened, and then she frowned and shook her head. "No. I told you not to ride any strange horses. Get off this instant!"

"She's mine, Mother. I just bought her. With my own money." I nudged the mare with my heel, hoping she'd prance a bit. "Her name is Blaze."

"Oh, my God," Mother said. Backing away, she looked down to check her footing. "Oh! My shoes! Damn." The white heels were stained green with manure. "You'll fall off and kill yourself." As she tottered toward the grandstand, I heard the loudspeaker announce that it was time to line up for the parade. I could already hear my Aunt Jo yelling at people over by the loading chutes at the railroad tracks.

Blaze broke into a shambling trot, joining a tumult of horses carrying kids. Anyone who wanted to ride in the parade waited until Josephine, wearing a gleaming white hat and shirt with red polyester pants, motioned him or her into line. Watching as her twitchy thoroughbred mare pirouetted, I envied her graceful balance. She'd stand in the stirrups to bawl at some slowpoke. A moment later she'd flip the lines, her mare spinning away toward another knot in the parade line. For an hour, Jo was limber and willowy. At the end of the parade, she rode past the grandstand, her broad red face beaming as people applauded.

Blaze was at least fifteen years old and round as a loaf of homemade bread, her sides slick as gumbo. My father insisted I learn to ride bareback so I could learn to anticipate the horse's moves directly, through the muscles in my thighs. Mother predicted I'd be killed in several gruesome ways until Father pointed out that without stirrups, I wouldn't get my foot caught and be dragged to death. I could slide off the horse anywhere. Remounting was a problem, however. It wasn't hard at the fairgrounds, where I could lead her into a stall when no one was looking. But if I slipped or fell off in the pasture, I had to find a fence or rock—sometimes a long hike.

At the ranch, I mounted from the edge of the water tank until the time Blaze slid me off into the mud as she lay down to roll. When I was ready, I'd tap her ribs gently with my heels. She'd flip one ear and turn her great square head, rolling one eye back toward me. "Giddy up!" I'd shout, kicking her a little harder, whereupon she'd turn her head and gaze at me from the other brown eye, flapping her lips. "Move, Blaze!" I'd demand, pounding my heels against her slick barrel. Yawning, she grunted, raising her tail to eliminate excess weight in a steaming pile. Then she inhaled, spreading my thighs another six inches apart.

Meanwhile, my father would open the gate, lead Zarro out of the corral, and wait. "Hit her with the reins," he'd advise. I'd slap her hindquarters, kicking as hard as I could with both heels. As soon as her haunches cleared the gate, she would stop, and my father would have to shove her out of the way to close it.

Among the prairie swells, learning to ride from the horse's natural rhythms, I watched my father, pared to bone and sinew, leaning with every move his horse made. He stood in the stirrups when Zarro trotted, knees flexing with each jolt, spine straight and head raised. As soon as I stood so my bottom cleared the saddle, I could feel the shock of each hoof beat travel from the soles of my feet up through my thighs and hips. Instinctively, I flexed my knees and centered myself over the horse's spine, brimming with a sense of power and freedom.

While we rode, Father constantly scanned the grassland around us. A flicker at the edge of vision might draw his eye to a coyote pausing with his head and tail low before slipping out of sight. He'd gesture so I wouldn't miss the sight. Antelope made lean, racy-looking silhouettes on hilltops. Instead of running away, they dithered, stamping their front feet and whistling at us.

The first time Blaze scraped my leg on a barbed-wire fence, ripping my jeans and slashing my thigh open, I wailed until my father rode over to look. "You'd better keep her away from the wire," he said, handing me his handkerchief. "Tie that around it. We've got work to do." The next time I got hurt, I kept silent. I discovered I could keep my face immobile by setting my jaws, but my stomach always hurt at night. "If it hurts, hide it" was a rule familiar to me long before Michael Martin Murphey sang the phrase in "Cowboy Logic."

After a year or two of making fun of Blaze, trying to shame my father into buying me a better horse, Uncle Harold and Aunt Josephine gave me a yearling filly. "Better take the mare, too," Harold said, shrugging. "She's too wild to keep in the corral, so I don't want her around my thoroughbreds." The mare, Donna, was carrying another colt, so in one day I acquired three new horses.

I named the little mare Rebel and started petting and gentling her at once, frustrated because my father said she wouldn't be big enough to carry my weight for at least another year. Every day I worked with Rebel—catching her, haltering and bridling her, leading her around the corrals. Murmuring endearments, I picked up each of her feet and brushed her until she was used to feeling my hands everywhere on her body. Repeatedly I tossed an old cloth feed sack on her back and dragged it off to imitate putting on a saddle. Finally I dragged a broken saddle out of the barn and began putting it on her back a dozen times a day. Sometimes I tied the stirrups together under her belly and left her tied in the corral for an hour or two.

While I worked at training Rebel, I began to compare her to Blaze. Rebel noticed every sound and movement, flicking her ears and rolling her eyes until I reassured her, and she learned to trust my voice. Blaze seemed to pay little attention to me, dozing even when I was riding her. Rebel not only responded to my voice and hand signals but also sometimes seemed to anticipate what I'd want her to do. The more time I spent with Rebel, the more boring poor Blaze seemed to me. When the old mare heaved herself into a plodding lope, I felt every ponderous step at the back of my head. The first time I galloped Rebel, her gait was so smooth I expected to see wings rippling behind the saddle. After months of jolting around on Blaze's broad belly, I felt light, as if I absorbed Rebel's grace by sitting on her.

By the time Rebel was two years old, my father said she was "green broke" and ready to be trained to ride. He wanted to hire a man to train her, but I argued until he nodded and said I was a natural rider. After that, when we headed over east, my father drove the pickup slowly with Blaze tied on behind. I rode Rebel to "wear her down," as father said, and get her used to the way we worked. At first, I used Blaze when I moved among the cattle, sorting some into a different pasture. If we trailed some home, for sale or treatment, I'd use Rebel and let Blaze rest, tied to the pickup as she plodded home. Before long, Rebel learned to watch the cattle more alertly than Blaze ever did. She seemed to anticipate their moves and if a cow veered out of the herd, the horse sometimes turned so abruptly I had to grab the saddle horn to stay on.

I rode the little mare everywhere, getting her used to a variety of situations. One day I was riding with Uncle Harold to check on cows and calves in one of his pastures. His horse splashed a gully filled with runoff from spring snows, but Rebel balked at the edge.

"What's the matter," he bawled. "Don't she like water?"

"I've never been able to get her into it," I said, kicking her in the flanks and whispering to her to quit embarrassing me.

Harold rode back and caught the reins close to Rebel's bit, gathering them into his massive hand. Then he turned his horse toward the stream again. His bulky arm stretched and bulged. Rebel leaned back and rolled her eyes, but Harold never let go. Rebel's hooves left four furrows in the mud as she slid down the bank and into the water. Then she snorted and tried to lunge to the right and left before giving up and following the pull of that big arm. Grinning over his shoulder at me, Harold hauled her twenty feet up the bank. Then he told me to turn her around and ride her back across the stream. When she balked again, he dragged her once more.

Riding on, we found the cattle Harold wanted to look over, loafing by a stock dam. Harold leaned back in the saddle, folded his hands on the horn and said, "Now ride her in there and let's see what she does." Rebel tossed her head and walked steadily into mud and water up to my stirrups.

Harold guffawed. "If there's anything else she don't like," he said, "just let me know and I'll drag her through that!" She never again refused to go where I wanted her to.

I think it was about that time that Mother gave me a tiny set of manicure tools in a zippered case of imitation leather. She made me sit still while she showed me how to push back my cuticles and file my fingernails. When I had a hangnail, either I couldn't find the blasted kit or I was on horseback. So I chewed my nails until they bled or whacked them short with my pocketknife.

About the time Rebel settled down, her wild red mother bore a red "horse colt"—my father's euphemism for a male. I named him Yankee. He bucked the first few times I rode him as a yearling, so my father hired a young cowboy who lived in the Badlands to break him. When I got the horse back a year later, he was terrified of everything, especially men. He bit my father and any other man who turned his back. Before Yankee quieted enough for me to bridle him alone, the young cowboy who'd ridden him was killed when a horse went over backwards, landing on top of him.

After a few summers, my father put Zarro out to pasture and began driving the pickup to the summer pasture. I followed on Rebel who responded to my lightest message through the reins, or my slight lean in the direction I wanted her to go. Yankee spent most of his time in the pasture with old Zarro until father decided he was getting too fat. To keep "that old broomtail nag" worn down enough so he'd be quiet if we needed him, he'd tie Yankee to the back bumper of the pickup. Often, the horse simply trotted over east and back, like a dog on a leash. If we brought cattle back, I drove them with Rebel until she got tired or we ran into the neighbor's herd. Then I rode Yankee, who was fresh and ready to run.

Once as Father raced up a long hill ahead of me to open the gate, I realized I couldn't see the gelding. Dust tumbled in the pickup's wake. Yankee had fallen and Father was dragging him up the hill. I yelled and waved but couldn't get his attention, so I kicked Rebel into a run and caught the pickup just past a rocky stretch. The dust settled over Yankee, lying still.

"You've killed my horse!" I howled.

"Well, he was never much good," Father said, getting out to stand with his thumbs in his belt looking down. Yankee groaned. Father kicked him in the belly. "Get up! C'mon, get on your feet. Next time maybe you won't pull back, by God."

"You mean you knew he was down?"

"Sure. He kept pulling back, trying to break the halter or the rope. I got tired of it. The workhorses used to do that in the barn. Pull back so hard they sweenied themselves—pulled a haunch muscle."

Yankee extended his bloody front legs and tried to heave himself upright, then fell back. Dust caked both eyes. Dismounting, I tried to brush it off. Unable to see me, he jerked his head away.

"We can't have him pulling every time we tie him. Ropes are expensive," Father said behind me, "and he might get away on you when you need him."

Yankee lunged ahead, getting his back legs under him, then stood up and shook himself. Patches of hair dangled from his ribs, scraped raw.

"Teach him a lesson once, he won't forget it," Father said, getting into the truck. He grinned at me as he shut the door. "Horses are just like kids. Got to get their attention."

Nothing But Trouble Since the Day He Was Born

JANA HARRIS

There is no other way to describe Byron. Everything about him was wrong. When he was unloaded from the horse van on a cloudy October Monday, he was the ugliest weanling I'd ever seen. The color of wet cement, scrawny, hammerheaded, with marble frog eyes too narrowly spaced. No wonder his dam kicked him in the head. There had been a wild ice gale the night before, so violent that falling trees had killed several pigeons roosting in the haymow. Recalling the terrible cracking noise the Alaska blue spruce near the barn made as it split apart, I imagined that that might have been the sound of Byron's jawbones breaking.

Byron had been sent to my farm in the foothills of the Cascade Mountains from a Thoroughbred breeder near the Canadian border to recover from his fracture and to be a pasture mate to my gray six-month-old foal, Colette. I'd had no other foals that year, and horses mature better mentally and physically if they have the opportunity to romp with youngsters their own age. In the jargon of the industry, this is called "laying down bone."

Byron? Wherever did he get that name, I wondered as I lead him to his box next to Colette's roomy double-size nursery stall. Colette had a sweet temper, a lovely dish face, and enormous soulful walnut eyes. She put her head over the stall door, sniffed noses with Byron, then pinned her ears, turning her butt to the door. In equine body language, this maneuver read: Go home, ugly.

Horses have a keen sense of smell, and I chalked Colette's adverse reaction to her new best friend as her sensory ability to ferret out the odor of surgery that lingered on Byron's recently wired-together lower and upper mandibles.

An hour later, while on the phone to the barn manager at Magic Meadow Racing Stable getting Byron's feed and medication instructions, I asked how he got his name. Default, the manager told me. When Philipa's Magic took offense at the gray colt's familiarity with her new foal, Philipa's Pride, and whacked him in the head, the grooms had started calling him Beaver-eater. When his mother divvied out the same punishment a day later, the name stuck. The Jockey Club, however, takes a dim view of sexually explicit expressions, so Beaver, etc., evolved into Byron's Song.

Static crackled on the telephone line, followed by a long pause wherein I should have asked, "And this is what you sent to me as a companion to my already sick foal?" Colette wasn't a Thoroughbred bound for the racetrack, she was a Warmblood, a sort of cross between a racehorse and a workhorse, bound for a riding discipline called dressage that has been likened to ballet on horseback. Her bones had grown more rapidly than her tendons and she was relegated to a special diet of low-protein hay and muscle relaxers.

I had hoped to house both foals in the large nursery stall, but within ten seconds of leading Byron into Colette's roomy indoor run, the hair started to fly. For the first time in her life, my little gray filly planted her hind hooves into the stall wall, knocking out several two-by-sixes. Byron was quickly removed and stalled two boxes away, which didn't seem to be far enough for Colette.

Turning the new pasture mates out together in a grassy paddock the following day met with a little less friction, at least for the first five minutes while the two were distracted by pigeon calls. The cries of birds for their lost mates even cut into the barn cat Yoda's heart.

Colette had a large round behind, a short back, and a neck attached at the top of her withers, effecting the posture of a sea horse. Half her size, Byron resembled something between a charred chicken bone and one of the fallen tree limbs that littered the back pasture. After the pigeons reorganized themselves on the barn roof, things seemed uneventful for the length of time it took Colette to pick a corner of the corral and position herself with her rear end aimed at the center of the turnout and one hind foot cocked. She resembled a loaded cannon. Byron danced around her, eager to light her fuse. Two steps forward, one step back, I thought, securing a lead rope to Byron's halter, then moving him into an adjacent paddock.

The other horses eyed the newcomer suspiciously. When none would even so much as play "touch nose" with him through the fence rails, Byron began to fly around in his turnout like an electron. Between bites of grass the yearlings, Miss Piggy and Kermit, stared at him sidelong. Mom, Colette's dam, stared transfixed for several seconds, then galloped to the far corner of the pasture as if Byron were a space alien. Before fleeing, Mom turned so quickly that she pulled both front shoes off her hooves and they flew through the air as though she'd thrown them at the little gray colt. Not even the two older riding geldings could be induced into running the fence line. I watched Byron try to entice Willie Africa into a biting match between the lowest rail and the ground, imagining that the baby racehorse compared his saucer-size feet to Willie's dinner-platter hooves.

We spent the day cleaning up after the storm, collecting fallen limbs, repairing broken fence rails and downed gutters. During barn check that night, Byron's stall looked as if the hundred-mile-an-hour gusts of the day before had blasted through it. He'd torn his grain bucket off the wall, stepped on his salt block, defecated in his water bucket, and pawed a hole in the floor. His half-eaten hay rations had been trod upon. Watching Byron eat made me wince. What few milk teeth remained in his mouth hit in a nerve-jarring clap-clap sound. Though cracked corn and rolled oats dribbled out of his mouth, no expression of discomfort crossed his face. I'd give him one thing: He had the devil's willingness to thrive.

During morning feeding two days later, I noticed a lone pigeon roosting in the rafters of Byron's stall. He (with a ruff like that the bird had to be male) was there again that night. One of the birds that lost his spouse in the storm, I thought. Since pigeons in my neck of the woods mate for life, I felt a pang of sadness for the little gray bird that gleamed green in the early winter sun, then remembered that messy pigeons were hardly welcome guests. When Byron, who had by now earned the barn name Nothing But Trouble (shortened to Nothing But), lay down, Pij swooped out of the rafters and began eating the water-and-molasses-soaked grain that had fallen from the weanling's mouth.

Was it loneliness or Pij's fog-colored feathers and the foal's mousy coat that bound them? In the weeks following, Pij moved from the barn beams to the plank of the stall divider, gliding down to peck the manger floor free of corn right alongside Byron as the weanling ate his dinner rations. During daytime turnout, the nurse mare continued to pin her ears at the newcomer, eyeing him as if he were a green fly. Colette kept as far away from his paddock fence as possible. Once, I carried Byron's noon hay rations to him in the turnout pen, and the weanling decided that I was someone to rear and run with. Never, before or since, have I come so close to getting kicked in the head by a horse. In his stall that night, however, Byron was sweetness and light as he and Pij ate grain together from the manger. I watched the foal gently butt the bird aside with his teacup-size muzzle, then stand protectively over Pij, shielding him from Yoda's lustful feline eyes.

The first morning of November was a day so clear that the glaciers on the side of White Horse Mountain glowed pink in the rising sun. Leading Byron to his paddock, I noticed that Pij followed, perching on a gatepost. Then—I could not believe my eyes—Pij flew the fence line as Byron galloped after him, up and back. Colette's head turned, her stunned stare mirroring mine. A pigeon exercising a race colt? As Pij circled overhead, Byron began running circuits around the rectangular-shaped corral. His spidery legs blurred as he galloped into the corner, across the diagonal, around the far turn, down the home stretch, faster, fast enough to out-fly a bird to the pole-like water-bucket-of-a-finish-line near the gate.

After Thanksgiving, I began turning the weanling out in the wooded back pasture, and then the pond pasture. Each time the bird followed Byron from his stall. Always Pij began to fly around the fence line. Always Byron ignored the lush year-round grass and ran after the bird, ringing the racecourse that had been bred into his genes. And always foal trailed bird, finally overtaking the gray-green wingspan. On New Year's Day, according to the Jockey Club rules, Byron officially became a yearling. His chest had broadened and the muscles in his upper forelegs had gained definition. The horn of his hooves grew straight and dark and strong. As horse and bird bolted into their morning workout, the flair of Byron's nostrils widened, turning the rose hue of a mountain sunrise.

By February, Byron's jaw had healed without scar or disfigurement, and it was almost certain that by the time he turned two he'd be able to tolerate a snaffle bit in his mouth and begin his first thirty days of training. On the Saturday after Valentine's Day, a sleek silver tractor-trailer pulled into my driveway. We loaded Byron onto the ten-horse van that would whisk him up the Interstate, across the border, and back to the farm in the Kootenai where he'd been born.

The day Byron left, Pij vanished. I never saw either of them again. I like to think of Byron's Song running the grassy turf of British Columbia race-courses, a lithe grindstone-colored gelding leading the field as he chases a ruff-necked bird eight furlongs across the finish line into history.

Mares

ANN DAUM

Shortly after the turn of the century, just before the western Dakota plains were carved apart and fenced for settlers, Tom Jones drove a herd of horses from Colorado to South Dakota. Tom Jones was no farmer. He dreamed of running a thousand head of steers and horses on a spread of his own someday. In fact, he would settle down to run steers and horses on the cedar breaks and grassy plains between the White and Bad Rivers, and to become one of the most powerful cattlemen in the region. Then, though, he was just a hand hired to trail broom tails north and east.

The horses were a rough lot, too, mostly unbroken, a mixture of mares and geldings and proud-cut colts. Tom was paid a dollar a head to break them. These broke horses were sold to ranchers along the way for whatever they would bring, which wasn't much. The rest of the herd milled and grazed along the way. When Ann Yokley wrote about Tom Jones in her book, *Grass and Water*, the story of the first cattlemen to settle Midland, South Dakota, she said he was a horseman, first and last. He lived with those horses in every way, knew each one by its nature if not by name.

When Tom reached the prairie between the White and Bad Rivers he stopped his horse and looked around at the rolling hills and hock-high prairie grasses. I think it must have been that time of early evening when all the world glows; when after the glaring light of day, it becomes possible to dream again. He said in all his thousand miles of travel, over mountains and prairie, he had never seen such grass as this. This land, Tom Jones swore, was made for grazing horses. And he promised to come back.

As night begins to fall I like to sit out by the horse barn and watch the sun set behind the cottonwoods. The chores are done, the horses still lined up at buckets spaced along the fence, chewing thoughtfully as they gaze off into space. All is quiet except for the rattling of buckets, the occasional restless pawing from inside the barn, or the indignant squeal as one yearling shoves another from her feed.

Every evening at about this time two great horned owls begin to hoot from two dead cottonwoods just outside the horses' paddocks. They perch, two silhouettes, always in the same two trees. They make the same conversation, at the same time, every night. All that is needed are rocking chairs and a front porch to complete the image. I hoot back at them almost every night.

Dusks are best in early spring, when there is so much to come. I watch the mares' bellies grow with a sort of awe. They are my future.

As the spring grows warmer, my hopes begin to coalesce into dreams, dreams in which I wake up knowing about a newborn foal, all bright clover smell and hot white newborn strength. I can breathe in that smell for hours after waking.

Usually these dreams aren't just of foals in general, but specific foals. Meg's colt Atlas came to me in a dream early last spring—I saw him take his first steps on pasture and, though I'd bred her to a wildly spotted pinto, saw that he was a chunky, solid bay. Meg foaled early, and with no warning, in May of 1999, while she was still on pasture. She had a solid bright bay colt.

This winter, while I was in Budapest visiting friends, I had a disturbing dream of Meg just having foaled. Her flanks were steaming, sharply concave. A tiny rope of gleaming white umbilical cord swung from her vulva, but there was no foal. I searched for hours in my dream and never found it. When I arrived home in March, Meg's belly was sucked up to her flank. She had been confirmed in foal the fall before, and by Christmas had grown a lovely rounded padding in her flank. Now she's trim and lean as her four-year-old daughter, Mina, and there's a quiet, a look of expectation missing from her eye.

The few friends I've told about these dreams are no longer skeptical. I am rarely wrong. The mares must be dreaming, too, as they knit the foals together. Sometimes I wake with the sense that we're dreaming the foals alive, the two of us, in that very instant. Weaving bone and fuzzy coat and curled-in ears from the weightlessness of dreams.

I wonder if Tom Jones ever dreamed about the foals. The herd reached the prairie east of Rapid City in May, the time for a mare to find a silent draw or hollow, on the darkest night she could, to birth her foal. Tom Jones must have expected these foals. Few mares, even when they're fit and lean, can hide a full-term foal. With the first pangs of dawn, or over coffee, he and the other wranglers must have noticed a mare off by herself.

Newborn foals would slow the herd down, most likely starve along the way. Death of starvation or exhaustion isn't kind, and slowing down the herd was not an option either, for it was spring, the time of year for selling horses farther east.

Tom Jones loved horses. Probably dreamed horses at night. That is why he got the job of shooting all the newborn foals.

Nature is not often kind. Growing up, I watched as cows battered and killed their own calves. At the age of six, I held a pet goat poisoned by chokecherry leaves and stroked her on my lap while she died. I saw my father's hired hands shoot coyotes and badgers and broken-legged cows. I grew up in the middle of it all, this spinning cycle of birth and death, and thought I could imagine what it meant to be a horseman. But I could not imagine shooting newborn foals.

Summit already looks hugely pregnant, though she's not due until the end of June. I watch her with a worried eye, knowing she tends to foal early, sometimes very early. But so far she's still gloriously pregnant, her blood-bay coat toned with jeweled red, a hint of dapples beginning to stand out on her quarters. I smile as I watch her eat, head tipped sideways, grain spilling in a foaming mash from her flapping lips. Every year I ask the vet to file her teeth, hoping the comfort of smooth molars will convince her to eat more gracefully. But she seems to like to eat this way. Now I've noticed her three-year-old son dutifully chewing his grain with flapping lips, spilling half of every mouthful. So far, no dreams of Summit's foal.

Theory always looks her best pregnant, and she is glowing with it this spring. A golden bay with four socks and a blaze, substantially built but not tall, she can look coarse coming in from a summer at grass. But now, with her belly curving and her coat thick and glossy, she looks statuesque—"a leg in every corner," the old-timers used to say. I've dreamed of her foal already this year—a pinto filly, white, splashed with chestnut, or the lightest honey bay. This morning as I fed her, I watched her flanks jump, her belly twist and heave. I stepped inside the paddock to put my hands on her belly, felt the life inside. I wonder if Theory knows this foal already, will recognize its milky eyes and peach-fuzz muzzle, its newborn scent that will be unlike any other in her world.

Nightshade holds my eye longer than any other. She was the first filly from my favorite mare, Pine Song, and has grown up to be uncanny in her intelligence and sheer naughtiness—so far her three foals have inherited those traits as well. They look like her, too, which is a good thing. Her lines are graceful and curving, her head is small and clever, like that of a keen black fox. She herds the mares in her pen away from their buckets with a single shake of her heavy black mane, then settles down to eat their share with her forelock hiding her dancing eyes. The Trakehner stallion she's bred to this year is a noble-headed bay, tall and kind, though the stallion I choose doesn't really seem to matter with Nightshade—the foal will be a naughty black or dark bay with dancing eyes and a talent for opening latches and untying lead ropes with its clever little mouth.

Busy may be carrying her final foal, and we talk of this softly in the evenings as I rub her white-streaked face. I've had to separate her from the herd, which she doesn't understand, so she can eat a processed feed instead of hay, which makes her wheeze. Busy heaves, which is a bit like having asthma. Any dust or tiny specks of mold will start her coughing, straining the muscles along her belly and flank as she forces out each breath, and will perhaps cause her to lose her foal. Once the grass comes in, Busy will be the first to move to pasture, but for now she has to wait it out alone. I explain this as I groom her, and she drops her head and sighs. When the big herd of mares gallops down into the trees, Busy stands at the end of her run and stares with longing. She is graceful in her every move, even now as she approaches seventeen. Her foals, which she and I equally adore, are long-legged, graceful things with eyes like does'. I am praying for a filly—one that will grow to replace her mother in my herd. Busy, so far, has given me no clue.

Once the grass is up, all these mares will go to pasture, and then my evenings spread to include walking over prairie to inspect udders for any sign of milk or waxing. I love walking out to check the mares. In a wet year the prairie will be alive with frogs and locusts, nighthawks and meadowlarks. The grass stretches as far as I can see; farther. The mares move across the hills, even with their pregnant bellies, with the grace of wild things.

In the midst of springtime's joy and expectation there is also fear, the knowledge of coming sorrow. I know that to love is a risky thing, whether one loves horses or humans.

My love for the mares and their coming foals has a dark center. Just as our land is far from hospitals, it is far from veterinary clinics, too. No vets make farm calls for foaling mares in this part of the state, even if something goes terribly, tragically wrong. I am afraid that one day my hands will not be enough to turn an upside-down foal, to coax a wet muzzle and two bony forelegs out of the birth canal in time. And there is so little time.

Once a mare's water breaks, the clock starts ticking. The mare has between thirty and forty minutes to birth her foal alive. This speed makes sense when you know that mares are prey animals, and birth smells like dinner to her many enemies. She wants to be on her feet again as soon as possible. But when you are behind a straining mare, looking up at the clock on the wall and waiting for two hooves and a muzzle, thirty minutes can seem impossibly short, or unbearably long.

Usually nothing goes wrong. I try to be there when my mares foal, though, just in case. This means waking up every hour, sometimes for several nights in a row, and eventually just stretching out on straw bales outside the stall. Because it doesn't take long to be too late.

Two years ago, in April of 1998, Meg foaled an immense dark brown colt. She was restless and dripping milk for three days before active labor began. I made hourly foaling checks two nights in a row; then, exhausted, I asked our foreman, Ben Seaman, to watch her for the third. I got the call at 2 A.M.

"Mare's foaling," the voice on the phone said. Ben was not one to waste words. I was instantly awake, pushing back the sheet and reaching for my boots in one movement.

I'd been worried about this mare for the last few days. Mares, unlike heifers, usually don't experience distocia, or difficulty birthing, due to the size of the foal. But my gut instinct, along with a hazy dream two months before of a mouse-colored colt with three socks and a massive, raw-boned frame, told me Meg was carrying a huge foal. She'd been bred eleven months ago to a big-boned, 17.2 hand Hanoverian stallion, and while she's not a small mare herself at 16.3 hands and twelve hundred pounds, I was worried for her. In the past, whenever my mares moved from a yellowish, waxy milk discharge to thick white colostrum, the birth wasn't far behind. But Meg had been milking nearly three days now.

When I arrived Meg was lying flat already. Her water had broken when Ben called, so I was more than ten minutes into my thirty already. I stopped to wash, slip on a glove, and slather lubricant up to my elbow before cupping my hand and reaching inside Meg. I felt a hoof immediately, and panic started tingling in my stomach. The hoof was huge—bigger than my wrist and forearm. I reached farther in and found the second hoof but no muzzle. Farther. Then back. I realized the two front feet I was feeling were flexing upward, sole to the sky. The foal was upside down.

I didn't panic, exactly. Foals often begin their descent through the birth canal upside down, twisting into the swan-dive position once the head has cleared the rim of the pelvis. But this foal's sheer size was obviously causing Meg some problems. I suspected her side-to-side contractions weren't strong enough to twist him over. I turned to Ben.

"Call Brenda and Deanna right away. I think I need some help."

By the mercy of God, or some stroke of good fortune, both my sister and my friend Deanna, whose husband, Greg, used to work for my father, were visiting for the week. While neither was a vet, at least my sister was a doctor. She'd delivered both upside-down calves and babies—foals must be somewhere in between. In ten minutes I would know.

Meg made little progress as I waited in the shadows. I wanted to let her do this on her own, if she could. Too much interference can be as dangerous as too little, sometimes, causing damage to the mare's reproductive tract or difficulties bonding once the foal is on the ground.

Meg was breathing harder now, grunting with each contraction. I saw her lip curl into the straw, one slim black foreleg paw absently into the air. I looked down at my watch. Twenty-two minutes had passed. The tingling in my stomach was rising.

I heard the pickup before catching the reflection of headlights. It took a very long time between the soft click of door and hearing Brenda whisper, "What's up?"

"The foal is huge," I whispered back. "And upside down." My voice shook. I couldn't help it. Brenda just nodded and started getting into a glove. I moved toward Meg again, talking to her softly all the time.

By now the forelegs, gleaming white inside their drape of amnion, were outside the mare, soles still pointing up. Brenda ran her hand beneath them and found the muzzle. Meg didn't seem to notice the activity around her tail. Her eyes had moved into that other place mares go inside of labor. She groaned and rolled with the next contraction. The slippery white hooves didn't move.

"Let's help her turn him," Brenda said. I'd been thinking that, too, and knelt to tear away the amnion from the two front feet.

Gently, we crossed the forelegs, careful to leave one slightly behind the other, and pulled across and down. Nothing. With each contraction we crossed and pulled, gently, always gently. From the shadows, I saw Deanna step forward and tap the face of her watch.

"When did she start?" she asked. I looked down to where I'd buckled my watch to the belt loop of my pants. "Thirty minutes," I said. Deanna's face was grim.

Brenda and I upped the tension on the forelegs. Ben had stepped inside the stall. "He's turning," he said. We crossed and pulled one more time with Meg's next push and felt something shift. Ben was right. The foal's soles were pointing sideways now, and a white-striped muzzle lay between them.

Suddenly, with the next contraction, the foal's head was out past the ears. I stripped white sac from his eyes and ears, pressed thumb and forefinger down the length of his nose to clear his nostrils. Meg stopped to rest, then suddenly she was rolling again and Brenda had to jump back from one big black hock.

We started pulling again, over and down, one foreleg ahead of the other. But there was no give.

"Shoulders stuck," I grunted. We pulled one front foot and then the other. The colt's eyes were shut, ears plastered back along his neck. His tongue curled from his mouth, still pink, which was good.

Finally, with an effort that I could feel through the stall floor, through my grip on slippery gray-black legs, Meg pushed the foal's shoulders out onto the straw. She stopped for a moment, then groaned again. Now every minute counted double, because in this position the umbilical cord was surely pinched off on Meg's pelvic girdle, and this quivering wet foal was getting little or no oxygen.

I shifted the colt's shoulders downward, toward Meg's hocks. She groaned and pushed, Brenda and I pulled. Nothing happened. Again. Nothing. The foal's tongue was turning blue.

"Forty minutes," someone said. I barely heard. My hands were shaking now. If the foal's hips were locked in Meg's pelvic opening, we'd have to shift him left and right, slowly, to walk him through. He was so big, though, this would take both of us.

Brenda helped pick up the colt's front end and we pulled him down and to the left with the next contraction. Then down and right. A little slip farther out. Left. Right. Nothing. Meg panted, no longer pushing. I slipped my hand in along the colt's ribs, hoping to stimulate her into pushing again. With one final grunt, Meg tried again, and all at once the whole foal was out, wet and alive and in my lap. He sneezed and took a breath, ears flopping back and down, hind feet resting inside the mare. I was panting, laughing, shaking, all at the same time. It was a colt, mousy brown with three white feet and a blaze, big as a newborn Simmental bull calf and with twice the leg. He arched his neck up against the palm of my hand as I moved away and I felt a strength that awed me. He was so beautiful. I thought I would call him Granite, for his strength and beauty and stubbornness of stone.

After a foaling it is easy to have eyes for only the foal. A new life, drawing first breath. Fear dissolves to joy.

I felt Meg's convulsions before I saw them, turned just in time to see her eyes roll back into her head. All four legs jerked, rustling straw. I ran, slow motion, to her head, and lay my hands upon her neck.

"Meg," I whispered, "come back." She shook and shook, and then I wasn't whispering anymore. "Come back!"

Somehow, I don't know how much later, the shaking stopped. Her eyes became her own again, and she lay flat in the matted straw, breathing like a horse that has won a race. I was breathing hard, too, and for a moment I couldn't see. I blinked and stepped away.

It seemed a long time before Meg tried to stand. Perhaps little Granite helped by kicking at the sack still wrapped around his hind feet. I was ready with iodine when the umbilical cord broke, and from there everything went normally, if a little slowly, for this exhausted mare and foal.

There is fear mixed with awe and expectation when I look at my pregnant mares now. I imagine the fragile strength curled inside them, the coming breath, and all that could conspire to snuff it out. In life there are few pure joys that do not come with risk, sometimes with pain. I walk the line between joy and suffering with my mares, careful to pick my way between.

In the evenings sometimes, when I am musing in the company of owls and mares and sunset, I look across the hills to the west. My gaze lingers on the cedar breaks above our valley, trying to find my way to the place between the White River and the Bad, to the place where newborn foal bones melted into grass.

Ann Yokley wrote that Tom Jones loved horses. Knew horses. Made a living from their sweat and speed and breath. He must have loved those foals, the way any horseman would. Foals are all whiskered curiosity and wobbly-legged wonder. They snuffle toward danger the first few hours of life, blinking soft blue-tinged eyes. His would have been the toughest kind of love.

Tom Jones was probably the best shot, the surest hand with a nervous new mother. I imagine it all and wince with every imagined crack of rifle and crumpling of legs. See the mare standing, head down, over her dead foal, nuzzling hip and withers and silent, silken-whiskered muzzle. What could it have done to a horse lover to have to shoot a foal? Ten foals? Fifty, or a hundred? I hope I never have to know.

Most days, and almost every evening, I would not trade my life, this world of grass on horses' breath and the joy of coming foals, for anything. There are times, in the hours before dawn when I am sick with fear over a laboring mare or searching frantically for reasons to explain the death of a foal, however, when I think I could. I give up on joy and anguish both. But then morning comes, and another crimson evening. I watch a mare stand over her sleeping foal, run my hand along an expectant mother's flank at feeding time and feel the flutterings inside. And I am sure again.

The mares graze, peaceful, as I think on these things. They tear up grass that has been nourished by the bones of those who've gone before. In the darkest hour of the night they sleep, three legs solid and one hind cocked. The foals inside their bellies lie quiet in their warm, suspended sleep. I sleep, too. Together we dream of possibilities and the warmth of newborn breath. We dream the future into life, one foal at a time.

The Pinto Horse

CHARLES ELLIOTT PERKINS

In the spring of '88, "Patch" was running a band of Oregon mares in the Bull Mountains of Southern Montana. The Bull Mountains are a range of high and broken hills, sparsely covered with jack pine, and heavily grassed in the open parks, with springs at the coulee heads; an ideal winter range for horses. On the south, the country falls away in lessening grassy ridges twenty miles to the Yellowstone. To the north, it drops more steeply to the Mussel Shell Flats.

In those days, the country north of the Yellowstone had not been re-stocked after the terrible winter of '86, the range was all open to the Canadian Line, and the native grass grew in its natural abundance.

From May to November the mares were divided into two bands; one which ranged south to the Yellowstone; the other, to the north of the Bull Mountain hills. Each spring, the Honorable William Spencer Fitzhenry Wantage, third son of the Earl of Palmadime, brought up from his ranch on Powder River the thoroughbred stallions that were to run with the mares; each November he came for them. In the meantime, all Patch had to do was to ride each morning from his cabin in the foot-hills, locate his mares, count them, and once a week cross over to the other side of the hills to see that his assistant, Mr. "Slippery Bill" Weston, and the mares that he looked after were in good order. It was a pleasant life; twice a week the Billings stage left the mail in a tin box on the Yellowstone Trail, and once a month Patch

217

hooked up his mule team and drove into Billings for supplies. That trip took three days, and always Patch came back strapped, but happy.

In the Autumn, when the stallions had gone back to Powder River, the horses of both bands were brought together to the corrals at the head of Big Coulee, the weanlings branded, the geldings that were to be broken, cut out and turned into the saddle-horse pasture, and the balance of the herd turned loose again to winter in the hills.

Range horses know the seasons as well as man, and they know their range as no man ever knows it. They know the pockets where the Northers never strike; they know where the warm springs are that never freeze, and they know which ridges are exposed to the Chinooks—warm winds that melt the snow. The range horse loves its native range as no other animal loves its home, and will return to it hundreds of miles, if it has the chance. Especially is this true of mares, which never forget the range where their first foal is dropped. Once a mare has foaled, she will spend the rest of her life within a radius of a few miles, if there is enough feed and water.

The first autumn and winter that Patch had the Oregon mares, he spent all the days and many freezing nights riding to turn them back in their drift toward the West.

When Patch and the Hon. Wm. Spencer Fitzhenry Wantage, who owned a half interest in the horses, were bringing the mares from Oregon, their regular pack horse went lame and they caught what seemed a quiet mare to pack in its place. They haltered the mare and tied her to a tree, packed on her their bedding and cook outfit, and then, as she seemed frightened by the pack sheet, the Honorable, thinking to get her used to it, tied one end to the front of the pack saddle, and with a corner of the other end in each hand, stood behind her and gave it a flap. The result was electric. The mare broke away and dashed down the road, the loose sheet flying and flapping above her like a cloud. The first thing she struck was the band of mares, which scattered far and wide; the next thing she ran into was a herd of beef being driven to the railroad; these stampeded like the mares. There were two drummers driving out from town, with a pair, in a top buggy. The flying mare met them head on. The team jack-knifed, broke the pole and a drummer's leg, and disappeared like the beef steers and the mares, while she pursued her unhallowed course into town, wrecked a mounted pageant of the Knights of Columbus, threw the Grand Knight through the plate glass window of the Masonic Hall, and finally fell down herself in the public square.

Patch and the Honorable Wm. Spencer Fitzhenry Wantage spent the next two days rounding up all of the scattered mares that they could find. Twelve they never got, and of these, nine eventually found their way back from Montana to the range in Oregon where they were foaled, *eight hundred miles away*, swimming the Snake River to get there.

So Patch was looking after the band of mares on the Bull Mountain range, when one morning in June, he rode out to locate them, and to see if Stowaway, the thoroughbred stallion which had begun his first season on the range a month before, was all right. Over the grassy ridges he jogged, whistling "Garryowen," while the larks, out of sight above, poured down a stream of song. He had found the band the day before and knew, if nothing had disturbed them, he would find them again a few miles further on toward the Yellowstone. Sure enough, when he was still two miles away, he saw them feeding on a little flat along the Cottonwood. But before he reached them, crossing a dry wash, he came upon Stowaway, covered with blood and carrying all the marks of battle, too lame and sore to climb out of the shallow gully into which he had staggered.

Patch knew it meant that some range stallion had found the band, nearly killed Stowaway, and taken them for himself. That must be seen to. He kicked his pony into a gallop, but before he had come within one hundred yards of the grazing mares, a black and white spotted stallion came snorting out to meet him. Indian, thought Patch, escaped from some band of Crows off their reservation south of the Yellowstone, or else a wanderer driven from some herd of Crow horses which had smelled the mares from miles across the river and come over to get a harem of his own. On came the pinto stallion, ears back, mouth open, until within twenty yards, Patch untied his slicker and swung it around his head. The wild horse slid to a stop, stamped, snorted and trotted back to the mares.

It was lucky for him that the cowboy feared Indians might be camped nearby, or a bullet from his forty-five would have ended the career of that spotted Don Juan there and then, for thoroughbred stallions were scarcer on the Montana Range than feathered frogs, and Patch was mad; it would take Stowaway weeks to get over his beating. What was to be done? He could not shoot the pinto. For, though the Indians were peaceful enough at home, they did not leave their reservation unless they were up to some mischief; and in killing a lone cowboy, and stealing his horse and guns there would be no great risk of discovery, in that unsettled country. There was nothing for it but to start the mares quietly up the creek toward the corrals, twelve miles away at the winter camp at the head of Big Coulee; the wild stallion would go with them, and once started Patch knew that they would head straight for the corrals where they were regularly salted. So, with one eye over his shoulder in case of an Indian surprise, he worked his way to the lower side of the herd, careful to keep below the rim of the encircling hills.

The Indian stallion dashed to and fro, snorting, always between Patch and the mares, but the flying slicker kept him from attacking the saddle horse, and gradually the cowboy got near enough to turn one grazing mare and then another, until he had the whole band slowly walking up the creek. For a mile they strolled on, feeding as they went, and then, as they got far enough away so that the dust would not be noticed, Patch crowded the last ones until they began to jog and then to gallop. After another mile he knew he had them fully roused, and that they would not stop or turn until they got to the corrals.

Then Patch pulled up and watched them out of sight—the wild stallion turning to snort and stamp once more before he disappeared after the mares. The cowboy loped back down the creek, and cutting across to where Stowaway was still standing in the dry wash, dropped his rope over the stallion's head and started with him to the home camp; but the battered horse went slowly, and it was mid-afternoon when Patch left him in the shade of some alders half a mile from the corrals. There, as he hoped, he found the mares, some licking salt, some rolling in the dust, the pinto stallion just inside the gate. Patch knew that the only way to get rid of him was to scare him so badly that he would go back to his own range, and to do that he would have to catch him. He could not keep the mares in the corral; there was no feed, and if the stallion were not badly scared he would stay in the broken country nearby, and wait until the mares came out. Patch slipped off his horse and crept nearer; the stallion did not wind him, and he got within ten yards, screened by some chokecherry bushes.

Then with a yell he started. The wild horse saw him the fraction of a second too late, and the heavy gate slammed in his face as he reared against it. The rest was simple; the pinto was roped, thrown, and hog-tied, and a lard pail full of stones, the top wired on, tied to his tail. The mares were penned in the second corral, the gate thrown open, the tie-ropes loosed, and the terrified stallion crashed off down the draw, the lard pail banging at his hocks.

That night, thirty miles to the south, the sleeping Indians on the Little Horn clutched each other in terror, and their frightened ponies scattered to the hills.

One May morning, when Patch was counting the mares, a year after he had tied the lard pail to the painted stallion, he missed Bald Stockings, a thoroughbred English mare that the Honorable Wantage had turned on the range with Stowaway. Patch did not try to find her, but a week later as he went to get his saddle horse in the morning, he found her in the corral licking salt, and beside her a wobbly-legged pinto foal. Bald Stockings snorted and trotted to the far end of the corral as Patch shut the gate. For half an hour he could not get near her, but he knew horses; so for the first few minutes he sat on the fence and whistled, and gradually as the mare quieted, he strolled nearer, until he could rub her nose, and then her neck; then he left her and went about his day's work.

Late that afternoon he tried again, and this time with little trouble he haltered her, and soon the foal, too, would allow him to scratch its back. For a week, Patch kept the mare in the hay corral, and by that time the foal would follow him about and lick his hand for sugar. The pinto colt started life with confidence in man, and Hinton knew that some day that confidence would save him much trouble. Later, the mare joined the band, and each day when Patch counted them, he gave the foal some sugar. Before the end of the summer it would leave the band and trot to meet him when he whistled the first few bars of "The Spanish Cavalier."

Bald Stockings was a good mother; the colt grew fast, and as the summer drifted by he learned the lessons of the range: how to stick close to his mother's side, so as not to be stepped on or knocked down when the band of mares was galloping; how to give Stowaway a wide berth; how to keep one eye always on the watch for prairie dog holes; and also about wolves—that was a terrifying experience. One hot noon, Pinto lay stretched out asleep on a hill-side; Bald Stockings gradually had grazed on fifty yards down the swale. The foal never knew exactly what happened. There was a snarling rush, which knocked him over as he scrambled to his feet. He heard his mother squeal, and the next thing he knew she was striking and biting at a gray thing that writhed on the grass, while another gray streak vanished over the ridge. It was over in a minute, and the mare, with nostrils flaring and a red light in her great wild eye, was nuzzling the still dazed foal. The gray thing on the grass was still; but before they trotted off to join the band the big mare shook it like a rag, while the foal huddled against her. And ever afterwards, when he smelt the wolf smell, he remembered; and when he was older, he would follow it to kill, sometimes with success, until no wolf of that range would come near any band of horses that the pinto ran with.

September came and went; the long strings of wild geese went honking overhead, and the quaking aspen had yellowed in the gulches, when one morning two men, strange to Pinto, helped Patch drive the band of horses to the big corrals. There Pinto was whistled from the band, and there was much talk that he did not understand. Then he and Bald Stockings were driven into a smaller corral where they waited, snorting, while the dust went up in clouds in the main corral, and the smell of burning flesh and hair added terror to the shouts of men, the wild calls of the mares, and the squeals of branded foals. Pinto did not know until long after that Patch had bought the Hon. Wantage's half interest in him, and had declared he should never be disfigured with a brand.

Late that afternoon, with the first winter storm breaking overhead, when the band of mares was turned out and driven into the foot-hills to their winter range, Bald Stockings and Pinto were turned into the saddle-horse pasture with the geldings, and there Pinto spent his first winter, feeding on the buffalo grass, when the Chinooks swept the ridges clear, warm and snug in the hay corral when a wild Norther roared down from the Canadas. And always he kept learning; for every few days Patch whistled him from the others to give him a bite of sugar or a piece of bread, so that he never had the range-horse's fear of man.

From the wise old geldings, he learned to find the least windy spots along the wind-swept hill-sides; he learned how to paw through the crust and get the sweet grass underneath, when the strongest bull would have starved, for no member of the cow family has learned to break the crust with its feet, and so, when it cannot push through the snow with its nose, it dies, where a range horse fattens. He learned something, too, of the tactics of war; for the veteran geldings would fight like wolves for a warm pocket in which to feed, or a specially sheltered nook near the hay stacks, on the bitter winter nights when the sky over the Mussel Shell shivered with the Northern Lights. Once there was an attack of wolves, but the geldings, without excitement, almost with indifference, headed in a circle, in the center of which were Bald Stockings and

Pinto, presenting an unbroken battery of heels, which only one rash wolf dared venture, only to be hurled back, a broken thing, and torn to pieces by his ravening friends. Bald Stockings was for breaking out into open attack, but the sour old geldings knew better and met her with flattened ears and clicking teeth, and the wolves, half fed on their foolish companion, slunk away.

And so the winter passed, until one morning, while snow still lay in the deeper gulches, Bald Stockings and Pinto again found themselves in the small corral from which they had neighed good-bye to the brood mare band the autumn before. Again came the two strangers, leading Stowaway; again, the big corral was filled with dust and squeals, but this time there was no smell of burning, and the squeals held a different note. That afternoon when the band was turned out, Bald Stockings and Pinto went with them, while Stowaway, like a king, trotted here and there, nipping a careless yearling that crossed his path, courted by some mares, but met by Bald Stockings with a swish of her thin tail and a warning snap of her white teeth.

In a few days, the life of the last summer was resumed, but not until Pinto had, in the meantime, established his standing with the colts and fillies of his own age. He was the only pinto among them, and half a hand taller than the biggest—the good blue-stem hay eaten through the winter, plus an inheritance from his tall English mother, accounted for that. For the first day, the other yearlings, all intimate friends from their long winter together, amused themselves by chasing Pinto in wide circles around the band of feeding mares, and, for a time, this seemed to Pinto good sport, for he found he could easily out-gallop them, but at last, getting out of wind—they had chased him in relays—he stopped and faced them.

A woolly brown colt, the leader, with a head like Stowaway's, walked out to fight him. Pinto stretched out his neck for a friendly touching of noses, and received, to his surprise, a cruel slash across the throat. He screamed, and instinctively looked around for his mother's help. Bald Stockings, feeding only a few yards off, looked up and then went on grazing. Then something moved inside of Pinto that he had never felt before; his ears went back along his head, and he went for that woolly yearling like a painted wild-cat. It was not in vain he had watched the vicious old geldings fight for a warm spot on the windy side-hills, or for those snug corners near the hay-stacks in the bitter winter nights. Squealing, biting, striking, he hurled himself at the other colt. The latter, trying to turn and run for it, was knocked flat, screaming, while the painted devil, his fore-feet beating like flails, tore at the brown throat. It was going too far. The brown colt's mother raced up with squealing fury, only to be met by Bald Stockings, a demon now herself. Another battle was started, when Stowaway rushed the mares apart and drove Pinto cowering to his mother, a bleeding wound in his rump.

A range stallion is absolute king of his band, until some other stallion beats him in open fight; and from then on he is never allowed to approach it. That fight, however, established Pinto as the yearlings' leader. He would lead them to the top of some grassy ridge, and then pretending to be frightened, he would turn and come racing back ahead of them to the herd. He had tremendous fake fights with the other colts, rearing, striking, biting and whirling to kick, all in rough play, while the fillies stood about admiring. And then one night, while he was asleep, Bald Stockings vanished. For a day and a night, the homesick colt walked the ridges, calling; going as far as he dared, alone, from the band. But no answer came, and when Patch rode up the second morning, Pinto followed him on his day's round. That night the cowboy fed the tired yearling in the corral, and next day, turned him with his old friends, the saddle-horses. Most men would have tried to drive him back to the herd, but Hinton was that rarest of men, a cowboy, and a really fine horseman, who understood horses in all their phases. He knew what would happen, and not for anything would he have risked losing the pinto's confidence.

Sure enough, a few mornings later, Bald Stockings was again licking salt in the big corral; but this time with a brown foal instead of a pinto, by her side. When Pinto was let in from the saddle-horse pasture, he ran to her whinnying with delight, but the big mare kept between him and the foal, and when Pinto, in his curiosity to investigate the strange wobbly brown thing, tried to push past her, he was met with a gleam of teeth that he understood meant "no crowding," and gradually, as they joined the herd, his jealous disappointment vanished, and he was soon leading the other yearlings, as before; but now he was more independent of his mother, although he always lay down near her, and when the band was moving, always kept where he could see her.

By mid-summer, Pinto was as big as the average well-bred two-year-old, and, except for his coloring, bore no trace of the painted Indian stallion that two years before had wrecked the peace of a June night and frightened the Plains animals from the Big Coulee to the Little Horn. The lean, game head; the great, brown eyes, with a touch of wildness; the thin, tapering, mobile ears; the deep chest; the shoulders raking far back; the powerful, arched loins; the thin, high-set tail; and broad quarters, heavily muscled to the hocks, were all an inheritance of his English ancestors. While the brain, that was developing behind that thin-skinned bony forehead, was that of a courageous and intelligent thoroughbred horse, combined with the alert and instinctive cunning of a wild animal, ever ready to meet the emergency which always comes to the wild things. Patch Hinton realized that so perfect an animal, driven by such a brain, would, if wisely handled, develop into a horse matchless in the cow country, from California to the Missouri, from Alberta to the Gulf.

Red Mare, Red Foal

JENNIFER OLDS

After our night at Raptor Rock, Tucker drove carefully through the sudden fog, turning frequently to search my face, his eyes softened and full of wonder. I stared back, smiled hesitantly. Tucker beamed in response.

"The red mare is going to foal," he said. "I've never seen a baby anything born."

"Oh. Is she waxing?" I pictured the milky beads of wax forming on the mare's teats, an indication that she was almost ready to give birth.

"A little," he replied.

When we pulled in front of Alice's barn, the fog was flowing around us in deep drifts. It made an isolated pocket of warmth of the interior of the Jeep.

"The light's on," I said. "Let's check Scarlet."

Alice shushed us as we entered the barn, taking in our disheveled appearance with a raised eyebrow, then motioning us closer to the foaling stall. The foaling stall was twice the size of the other stalls in the barn and opened to a private paddock and "creep." (A creep is a feeding area that only the foal can "creep" into so that the greedy mare can't eat the baby's oats and vitamins.) It overflowed with rich, golden straw. We tiptoed forward, stopping to pet Barnabus—Alice's Irish wolfhound—then stood in wonder. Scarlet lay stretched on her side, sweat darkening her liver chestnut body. Her tail was braided and wrapped. It arched away from her body as she strained through a contraction so intense it was visible to the naked eye, rippling around her abdomen in a tight band. Milk squirted from her teats as she grunted, eyes closed.

Alice moved out of the doorway and crouched near the mare, easing a reassuring hand on her damp flank. "Here we go, Scarlet girl. It's time."

Tucker and I watched in awe as the foal pushed into the world. A sharp contraction sent out two white forelegs, a tiny head nestled tight against them, ears pinned back aerodynamically. Alice folded the birthing sac back over the small creature's head. Her hands were kind as she cleared both nostrils and ears. Another push revealed reddish fawn shoulders and midsection. Scarlet rocked slightly forward, curling her forelegs in front of her so that she could crane her neck around to see her child. Her ears pricked forward, eyes glowing with love. She blew a welcome through her nostrils, a low breathy greeting.

"One more time, darlin'," Alice whispered.

The tiny foal squealed in indignation as the last rippling contraction sent her sprawling into Alice's lap. "Hey," she seemed to be saying, "take it easy, Mom," and "I'm wet, I'm hungry, where's the grub?"

"Come and help," Alice said, motioning Tucker into the straw. I nodded. I had already been and done this particular thing many times. I wanted to give it to Tucker, the best gift I could think of. "Like this," Alice said. She gave Tucker a small, dry towel and showed him how to buff the wriggling filly, rub in gentle circles all over her body.

Scarlet watched in agreement, talking to everyone, proud of herself. She wrenched suddenly to her feet and turned to join the humans.

"What's that? Is she all right?" Tucker asked, catching a glimpse of the bloody sac hanging from the mare's vulva.

"It's the afterbirth. Pay it no mind," Alice told him.

The mare nuzzled Tucker's shoulder, then shoved him aside so that she could reach her foal. Tucker sprawled in the damp straw, baffled.

He said, "But it's all bloody and it's just hanging there."

"Better if she passes it natural," Alice assured him, "then we'll put it in the bucket and give it to the vet to check." She nodded toward a tall, covered bucket in the corner of the stall.

"Yuck," he said, scrambling back into a crouch. "Look, he's trying to stand."

"She," Alice corrected. "It's a little chestnut filly. Congratulations, Papa," she grinned at him. "Your new polo pony has arrived."

That explained Tucker's interest in Scarlet, although she was interesting enough on her own. At 24, she would probably only be bred once or twice more, depending on her strength. As her dam, a racing mare with many wins to her credit, had lived to the ripe old age of 32, Alice had great hopes for Scarlet's longevity.

"Best mare I ever knew, bar her momma," Alice told Tucker. "Her momma could spin on a dime and leave a nickel change."

"She's beautiful," Tucker said, full of magic. "I'll keep her forever."

"Or she comes back to me," Alice said. "Promise."

"I do," Tucker whispered. "Little Miss Ruby," he said, "you're a spunky thing."

Ruby hefted herself to her feet, squealing with hunger, then sprawled headfirst into the straw. Mad as hell, she splayed her front legs out in a wide base and heaved again, this time succeeding in trembling upright. Scarlet cradled the little filly to her side, nudging her toward good, warm milk. As Ruby found the nipple and began to nurse, her tiny flaxen tail whisked back and forth. She grunted in contentment.

"Well, that's something I never get tired of seeing," Alice said, smiling.

"It was the most beautiful thing in the world," Tucker said.

I yawned, nodding in agreement. "I gotta go," I told Tucker. "I really need some sleep."

"Can I call you?" he asked, his shadow looming over me.

"Sure," I answered. "I mean, I guess so." I backed away, grateful for the hair swinging forward to cover my flaming cheeks. "See you later."

As I drove home, I wondered how to break off something that hadn't really started. We had had tender, breathless sex on the side of a mountain as a dense fog rolled in. What I didn't know, as I pulled into the parking lot outside my apartment, was that I would never be done with Tucker. Deep inside my womb a tiny egg had been found by an even tinier sperm and six years later, our son would settle himself comfortably on Ruby's red back.

Life has a funny way of giving us answers when we haven't even asked the questions.

Bloodlines

LINDA HUSSA

Something woke me. It's still dark. I push the window higher and listen. Our stallion and the gray mare mix their music of deep drums and squealing horns. I know their song will end in the breeding. Yesterday he sensed the approach of her foaling heat and stayed beside her—two sides of a coin to be spent before dawn. Her sorrel foal, light-stepping away from the confusion, holds its head high in a kind of worry. Now the mare stands, the stallion rears up, gripping her flanks with his front legs. No need to see; sounds draw their own pictures. She submits because her body must keep working in this way. Between his peaks she snatches at grass absentmindedly and he prowls, his neck arched tight, smooth as a swan's. Every throb of his in step with her for a few days until the band that holds them tapers to a break. They have no friendship made of seasons. She arrived a week ago in a trailer and will be led from his pasture once she passes by her next cycle. Eleven months and eleven days is the country measurement of a mare's gestation, nearly a year for the birth of the foal he just began in her. Their finest traits combine, a dominance is decided and weakness pressed further to the shadows.

I learned the basics of genetics at our kitchen table. Before breeding season Mom and Dad got out the stud books and papers and developed a theory together. Generations linked backward through the stack of royal blue volumes narrowed to a handful of foundation sires. Their research, their treasure map of a blind journey, told me nothing was left to chance. Blood always mattered. An individual surfaced now and then but the odds were with blood.

What I heard, knew was happening just beyond the fence was not the summation, merely a step on the path. The test would come after birth. Their interest was in conformation but not just for conformation's sake. They wanted no hothouse beauty queen but an athletic horse, a working horse. "No leg, no horse" was an absolute truth Dad took possession of. If a sacrifice was made it was never in the direction of sound structure. Training provided another split chance for success or failure. But if a concentration of genetic power dominated, breeding would be proven in performance. It was a long-range plan, a devotion, carrying them toward something of value. This wasn't a horse to be roped out of a bunch. They made this horse to order and it was as scientific as a kitchen table, a stack of stud books, and common sense can get. Their deliberate concentration made me wonder at the value of my own pedigree. I was the obvious product of whimsy.

At the end of a rain-rutted road nearly overgrown by blackberry vines a small barnyard opened between a gray clapboard house and a small dairy barn. A dog waited by the gate. I waited in the truck. Dad never met a dog he couldn't charm. I didn't know what he said to them but they'd look up as if he poured food into their dish every morning and night. When he was in his seventies I saw him stand his ground as two Doberman guard dogs galloped at him, slobbering, growling, thrilled to finally have someone to kill and eat from hat to bootheels. He ignored their charge and kept walking, going on about his business. They followed him around on their tiptoes awhile, growling up at him until they lost interest and went back to their mats by the door. I was in the truck that time too, with the windows rolled up. It's a recessive gene.

Anyway, at that little forty-cow dairy, an old man came out the back door. I had a child's sense that he was born in the long dirty beard, rubber boots, and sloppy overalls, and that he couldn't take them off any more than his dog could shake out of its matted orange hair. He led us to the low, dark barn, took a halter off a nail by the door, and handed it to Dad. In the back of the barn in a double stall we could barely make out a white horse in the hock-high muck and long hay pulled from the feed trough. There were no windows on the back wall. The only life beyond her own was a flurry of pigeons coming and going through a narrow door in the upper story of the haymow. It was anybody's guess how long she'd been in there. Ammonia burned the air. Dad said if her hooves weren't rotted off, he'd shoe her. The old guy was busy kicking the door open and didn't hear him.

I led her to the creek and let the current wash her legs while Dad pushed his tools around the back of the truck, his anger escaping in a whistling that was no song at all but a mad noise of bees swarming. I held her halter rope and watched her look around. I think she'd forgotten what the sun was, and trees and grass, even. She jumped when a meadow lark flicked overhead and trembled when I brushed my hand down her neck. By the time Dad nailed on the shoes, he had her bought. He probably paid more than we could afford but he couldn't leave her in that nasty place. I led her down the lane. She pranced alongside me like a butterfly. Dad tied her to a tree by the mail box and we went home for the trailer.

While we were gone her ears grew a foot longer. Or else she was a mule. Or else we were so upset at the condition of that barn we didn't look at her very carefully. Dad swore to Mom the old guy switched horses on him. It didn't matter. She walked into the trailer, he closed the door, and we took Heidi home.

The next morning Dad saddled her up. He pulled his hat down to the pegs of his ears and stepped aboard, ready for anything. He wasn't ready for Heidi. She untracked sweet as a kid's horse, picked up both leads, switched on a figure eight without missing a stride, stopped straight with that little *zzziiit* a stock horse man hungers for. By this time he'd uncorked his hat and was riding a Sunday morning smile. He asked her to turn. The rein barely touched her neck. His leg fell lightly against her side. She planted her pivot foot and came around like a top. Dad pitched his hat over the apple tree and hollered this was his lucky day.

Heidi was their show horse from then on, and until word got around, the "white mule" was their sleeper. She wasn't pretty but she won every stock horse class on the western Washington circuit that year. The next summer they decided to take her over the mountains to the Eastern Washington Fair at Yakima. Mom checked in at the office while Dad unloaded Heidi. He was saddling her when two other contestants rode by. "Hee-haw," one brayed. "D'ya bring yer plow, farmer boy?" Dad smiled.

There were twenty-five entries in the championship stock horses class. It was the toughest class Heidi had ever faced. Horse after horse stepped from the line to perform the pattern set by the judge. The pattern could be compared to the school figures of ice skaters. Individual movements are those required to work cattle properly in a practical ranch situation. Each contestant is scored against an ideal of perfection. When it was Heidi's turn she did her work, balanced, fast, and graceful as a dance. She won first place. No one laughed when Dad picked up the trophy. No one could deny she was the best working horse they'd ever seen, big ears and all.

Heidi won every class Dad or Mom showed her in. She gave her best effort every time. Not because a pedigree predicted success. Not because she was grateful to us for getting her out of that horrible barn, away from that old man. Animals aren't capable of that kind of thinking; anyone who knows anything about science knows that. Heidi was an individual occurrence, a spark that would burn a theory to char. It was her bit of magic that gave me hope.

Legendary
&
Supernatural Horses

The Woman and the Horse

ALFRED A. KROEBER / ASSINIBOINE

The people sent out two young men to look for buffalo. They killed one and were butchering it. Then one of them said, "I will go to that hill and look around; do you continue to butcher." He went on the hill, and his companion went on with the butchering. The one on the hill looked about him with field-glasses. At Many-Lakes he saw a large herd of wild horses. He continued to look at them. Then he saw a person among them. Then he saw something streaming behind the person. He thought it was a loose breech-cloth. He called his companion, and said to him, "Look!" Then they went nearer. They saw that it was indeed a person. They thought that it was something unnatural (*kaxtawuu*). Therefore they did not try to disturb the person, but went back. They asked the people, "Did you ever miss a person?" An old man said, "Yes. A man once lost his wife as the camp moved. She was not found." Thereupon the young men told what they had seen. The people thought this must be this woman. The whole camp went there. All the people mounted their best horses in order to catch her. When they approached the place, they surrounded the whole country. All of them had mirrors. When they had gone all around, they turned the mirrors and reflected with them, signaling that the circle was complete. Then they drew together. The four that were mounted on the fastest horses started toward the herd. The wild horses ran, but, wherever they went, they saw people. The person in the herd was always in the lead. The people continued to close up

on the horses. When they got them into a small space, they began to rope
them. Six of the horses and the woman escaped. She was exceedingly swift.
The people headed them off, and at last drove them into an enclosure. With
much trouble they at last succeeded in fastening one rope on her leg and one
on her arm. Then they picketed her at the camp like a horse. *Pubis svæ crines
equi caudæ similes facti erant.* At night a young man went out. He lay down
on the ground near her, looking at her. Then the woman spoke: "Listen,
young man. I will tell you something. You must do what I tell you. It is the
truth. Long ago the camp was moving. I was far behind. I saw a large black
stallion come. He had a rope on him. I jumped off my horse and caught him,
thinking he belonged to someone in camp. When I had hold of the rope, he
spoke to me. He said, 'Jump on my back.' Then I climbed on him. He is the
one that took me away. He is my husband. I have seven children by him,
seven young horses. There is one, that gray one; there another one, that
spotted one; there a black painted one; there a black one." She showed him
all her children. "That is my husband," she said of a black horse that was tied
nearby. "I cannot go back to the tribe now. I have become a horse. Let me
go. Let us all go. Tie a bell on a horse of such a color, then you will be lucky
in getting horses. If you will let me loose, I will give you forty persons (you
will kill forty enemies). If you do not loose me, many of the tribe will die."
Then the young man went to his father and told what the woman had said.
The old man went outside and cried it out to the people. Then they freed
her and the horses. They ran amid flying dust, the woman far in the lead.

The Grandfather Horse

RAY GONZALEZ

The grandfather horse was last seen galloping across the *llano* when Francisco was five years old. That morning, his father, Antonio, came running into the house. He yelled to Miranda, Francisco's mother, to come look at the grandfather horse running in their fields. She set the morning dishes on the table and followed him outside. Francisco jumped from the table and ran to join his parents. He caught sight of the ugliest yet proudest animal he had ever seen. The grandfather horse reared up on its hind legs and let out one of the most disturbing neighs Francisco had ever heard. Old scars and wounds were visible on its gray hide—the identifying mark of the grandfather horse. It turned in tight circles and kicked dirt into the air. Antonio hesitated before approaching the horse. He wanted to open the gate to the corral, hoping it would run in. The previous time the grandfather horse had appeared, many things had happened. Francisco's grandmother Lucha had died, and his brother Mario was drafted into the army. When Mario returned from his service, he was killed in a car wreck outside of town, two of his drunk friends dying with him. Now, the grandfather horse ran into the corral. Antonio shut the gate and watched the wild animal as it snorted and galloped in defiant circles, its heavy legs kicking mud and grass into the air. Francisco ran to the fence and looked in. When the grandfather horse sensed the boy, it suddenly stopped running and stood in the middle of the corral, its chest heaving, huge nostrils flaring as it tried to

237

catch its breath. The horse looked in Francisco's direction and calmed down. His father noticed and turned to look at his son without saying a word. They watched the horse, and the animal watched them. Later, Francisco's parents were quiet at the dinner table. He asked his father what he was going to do with the horse, but his father shook his head and told him to eat his dinner. That night, Francisco woke to the neighing of the horse and went to the window, expecting to see his father at the corral, but all he saw was the horse prancing inside. When he realized his parents were asleep in the other room, Francisco dressed and went outside. The horse stopped and waited. At the fence, Francisco reached into his pocket and took out an apple he had grabbed from the kitchen. The horse ate it from his hand, its ancient eyes looking beyond the boy. Francisco tried to pet it through the fence, but it reared up. The boy pulled back and heard his father come outside. He turned to find him on the porch with his rifle cocked in his arms. Francisco ran to him, hooves pounding the earth behind him. He wanted to yell "No!" as Antonio aimed the rifle at the horse. Before his father could fire, the loud splintering of wood shattered his concentration. Francisco grabbed his father by the waist, and together they watched the grandfather horse leap over the broken corral, its mane a stream of fire. The horse galloped across the dark fields, its fiery neck a torch lighting the way for something Francisco and his father lost that night. For days afterward, father and son did not speak to each other. When Miranda asked about the horse, her husband refused to answer. Over the next twenty years, Francisco's parents passed away and he went to college and became a successful agricultural businessman. One summer, while visiting the farm he had inherited, he met with the foreman who oversaw Francisco's cotton fields. The foreman took him to a shed and showed him what the workers had recently uncovered. He said most of the bones were gone, but he opened a large cardboard box that held the huge petrified skull of a horse. Francisco never would have known what the bleached thing was if the foreman hadn't told him. As they held the box in their hands, the foreman pointed to the petrified teeth and told him to look closer. Francisco bent down and saw the stem of an apple core embedded between the teeth of stone, the stem as fresh and moist as the ones on the apple trees that grew abundantly on his land.

How Morning Star Made the First Horse

CECILE CREE MEDICINE / JOHN C. EWERS

Before the Piegan had horses they had dogs. Then everything was flint. There was no iron.

One night a Piegan invited all the chiefs to his lodge. He told his wife, "You sit outside with the baby." Her sister saw her sitting there and asked her what she was doing outside alone. She replied, "My husband does not want me to be in the lodge with the chiefs." She was very unhappy. Later she looked into the sky and saw the bright morning star. She said, "I wish I could be married to that pretty star up there."

Next morning she went to pick up buffalo chips for fuel. She saw a young man approaching her. He said, "Now I have come for you." But she replied, "I will have nothing to do with you. Why do you want me to go away with you? I'm married." Then the young man reminded her, "Last night when you were sitting outside your lodge you said you wanted to marry me, the bright star. I heard you and now I have come for you." She replied, "Yes, that's right. Let's go."

The young man said, "Take hold of my back. Follow me, but keep your eyes shut." She did as she was told. After a time the young man told her to open her eyes. When she did she saw that the country was strange to her. Young Morning Star then asked her into his lodge where an old man was sitting. He was Sun, Morning Star's father. Sun said, "My son, why did you bring this girl here?" The young man answered, "It was the girl's wish. So I went after her."

After a time Morning Star and this woman had a little boy. Old grandfather Sun said, "I shall give the boy something to play with." He gave him a crooked tree which was every bit the shape of a little horse, and said, "Now, my boy, play with this." When Morning Star saw his son playing with the wooden toy he said to his wife, "Wouldn't it look better if this plaything had fur like a deer?" She agreed. So they put fur on it. Then Morning Star said, "Another thing it should have is a tail." So he put a black tail on it and added some ears as well. Then he said, "Now let's take some black dirt and rub its hoofs so they will shine." So it was done.

Then his wife said to the Morning Star, "Now you are finished. Are you satisfied?" "No," replied Morning Star, "Put the boy on the animal's back. Let him ride it." When the boy was astride the toy, Morning Star said, "Now I shall make it go. I shall call sh-sh-sh-sh four times. The fourth time it will start like an animal." The first time Morning Star called, the horse began to move its legs. The second time, the horse began to move its tail. The third time it moved its ears. When he called sh-sh-sh-sh the fourth time the horse shied. Then Morning Star called "ka-ka-ka-ka," and the horse stood still. Morning Star cut a piece of rawhide for a bridle. The boy had great fun with his little horse.

Later, when the boy's brothers and sisters went to dig wild turnips, his mother asked Morning Star, "Why can't I do that?" He told her she might go with the others, but she must not dig the turnip with the big leaves. So she joined the party. She saw the big-leafed turnip and began to dig around it. At last she dug it up. Dust came up through the hole. When the dust cleared away she looked into the hole and way below she saw her own camp and her parents. She began to cry.

When she returned to Morning Star's lodge he saw her swollen eyes and knew what had happened. He asked her, "Why are you crying?" She told him that she was lonesome for her parents. Morning Star then told her she could return to them. He instructed his people to cut rawhide rope. They made a great pile of it. Then he told his wife, "I'll take you down the rope first. Then I'll take the horse down by my own power." He wrapped his wife and son in buffalo robes, tied them to the rope, and lowered them through the turnip hole.

Two young fellows lying on their backs near the camp of the woman's parents saw a strange object descending from the sky. They were frightened and started to run away when the bundle reached the earth. But the woman called to them, "Untie me." They untied her and went to camp to tell the woman's husband that she was back. When her husband saw the little boy he told his wife, "I don't want him here. Don't feed that boy. Don't give him any bedding. Let him sleep by the door." The woman was watched so closely she couldn't help her son. A half-brother took pity on the little boy. He hid some of his own food and gave it to the little boy to keep him from starving.

Morning Star saw how badly his son was treated on earth. One day when the half-brother took the boy into the brush hunting they saw a strange man. They were afraid and started to run when the man called, "Stop!" They halted and sat down beside the man. He told the little boy, "You are my son. I know your brother loves you and has fed you. But I have come after you because you have been abused." The little boy began to cry. "No, I want to stay with my brother." Then Morning Star explained, "Three of us cannot go. I can only take you. But I promise you I'll give your brother some great power here on earth."

Before he departed Morning Star told the older boy, "Go to that lake yonder. Sleep beside it for four nights. I'll give you power. The man in that lake will help you too. But I warn you that before sunrise, while you are sleeping, animals like I gave your little brother will come out of the lake. When you wake, pay no attention to the other horses. Just try to catch the little, shaggy buckskin colt. If you catch that colt all of the other horses will stop beside him. If you don't catch him, all will run back into the water."

The morning after the older brother's first night by the lake he tried to catch one of the pretty colts rather than the ugly little buckskin Morning Star had told him to get. All of the horses ran back into the lake. The second morning the older brother tried again and failed. The third morning all of the horses got away once more. During the fourth night Morning Star came to the boy in his dream and said, "Now, my boy, I told you to catch that shaggy buckskin colt. If you don't catch him tomorrow you will not have my power."

Next morning, when the boy awoke he saw the horses again. This time he singled out the little colt and roped him with a rawhide line. All the other horses stampeded toward the lake. As the leading ones reached the shore the little buckskin whinnied. They all turned and ran back toward him. On the fifth night Morning Star again appeared to the boy in his dream, saying, "Now, my boy, when you return home with those horses give everyone but your father a horse. Because he abused you, he shouldn't have any."

When the boy returned to camp and distributed the horses, his father became very angry. "Why didn't you give me one of them?" he raved. The boy, with Morning Star's power, struck his father and killed him.

Morning Star then told the boy, "From now on your people will have horses. You will no longer need to use dogs. In time you will have many horses. Your horses will never disappear. You need never walk any more."

The principal chief of the camp sent word to the boy that he wanted him for a son-in-law. He gave the boy his two daughters and offered him his place as head chief.

The Mescal-Drinking Horse

JOVITA GONZÁLEZ DE MIRELES

The thick brush country of the Rio Grande saw his birth. His mother, a scrub mare, famous for her ability to smell and dodge the law, had saved Juan José, her smuggler master, from a prison fate. *El Viento*, she had been called, for she raced with the fleetness of the Gulf winds as they blow over the prairie, defying the thick mesquite thorns, and the screw-like spikes of the *granjeno* and the flexible but tough cactus needles. His father was a powerful stallion of Arabian blood that had wandered away from the stables of his rich master.

And so it was that El Conejo came into existence. An awkward creature since birth, he had been a contradiction of everything a horse should be. "He looks like a rabbit," his master had said, laughing uproariously, seeing the trembling creature with his mother's short, stubby hind legs and the powerful front legs of his Arabian father. So he was called El Conejo (the rabbit). He grew, a gentle, good-natured pony. Juan José's children made him their pet, spoiled him, and he in turn bore them from their home hidden in the thick *chaparral* to the *camino real*, where he and the children peeped with curiosity at the outside world.

One never-to-be-forgotten day, his placid life of easy-going contentment came to an abrupt end. Juan José, doubly drunk—drunk both with success

243

of his latest exploit and with a quart of *Pajaro Azul mescal*—opened a new and vicious world to him.

"Come here, Conejo," Juan José called to him, waving a newly opened bottle of *mescal.* "I don't like your looks," he laughed. "A horse like a rabbit is neither a horse nor a rabbit. I know you don't like your appearance, either. Come here to me; this will make you forget." And, saying this, he poured the quart of *mescal* into a tin wash basin.

Conejo approached the basin and, without even the faintest sniff, took a deep draught. He looked up, surprised at the fire that burned him, gave a snort and a kick, circled the pan gingerly, sniffed at the contents this time, and without hesitation quaffed the *mescal* to the last drop. He looked up. If ponies can smile, Conejo did so now, and foolishly too, rolled his eyes and wiggled his ears at the same time. Then, as if stung by a wasp, he bolted, kicked the air and ran away to the nearest brush. All day long he was heard running and snorting. At dusk he returned slowly, a sober horse, his colthood days behind him.

Next day, Juan José, seeing the sadness in his eyes, and knowing how it felt to have a *cruda* (hangover), offered him the bottle he always carried in his hip pocket.

"You need it, Conejo," he told the horse, "but just a little this time—two drinks—three drinks—and plenty of cold water." The horse, seeming to understand what his master was telling him, drank two swigs—three swigs—and then swallowed enough water to float his own body.

From that day on Conejo took his daily drink of *mescal,* and he was none the worse for it. In fact, it made him a horse of reputation. Other smugglers came to see him drink, and all admired him. "He should be called *El Pájaro Azul*," suggested one of the smugglers, noticing his fondness for that particular brand of *mescal.* And so *El Pájaro* he became now, little knowing that the name so glibly given would become a by-word among the people of the borderland.

A new relationship developed between El Pájaro and Juan José, one of respect and mutual admiration. But there was something he missed, the close contact with man, which only comes to a horse when he is ridden by his master. The children were no longer allowed to ride him; Juan José still laughed at his queer shape and thought him unworthy of riding. Every day, after his customary drink, he ran off like a flash of lightning to the brush, where he remained—unmolested—until the effects of the *mescal* left him.

Time passed for master and horse in this manner, and then on the feast day of Santiago, the patron saint of horses, Juan José, feeling unusually gay after their daily drink, said to El Pájaro, "Pájaro, I am going to ride you; you are to be my horse." And without more ado, he jumped on the unsuspecting horse. The struggle that followed was one of endurance—Pájaro trying to throw his master down, Juan José to hold on. At last, each recognizing the stubbornness and tenacity of the other, both stopped from sheer exhaustion.

The following day word came that a load of tobacco leaf and *mescal* was ready to be brought across the river. Calling his men together, Juan José planned the expedition for the first night after the last quarter of the moon, which would be four days hence.

El Pájaro was made ready for the expedition. He did not mind the saddle at all; and the bridle merely gave him a ticklish sensation in his mouth. Under cover of darkness Juan José and his men met at the river.

"*Vamos, Pájaro! Adentro,*" the rider whispered in his ear. Horse and rider plunged into the stream and swam to the other side. The hidden load of smuggled goods was found; the mules were packed, and the smugglers again plunged into the river. Land was reached in safety. Juan José was whispering commands in his horse's ear, but Pájaro was sniffing the air.

"*Ya, ya, Pájaro,*" whispered Juan José. "Keep quiet, steady."

Unheeding his master's words and caresses, Pájaro reared on his powerful, short hind legs and without warning fled to the chaparral. Hardly had he brought his master to the safety of the brush when the Rangers fell upon the smugglers, wounding some and taking the rest under their custody.

Because of this incident, Pájaro's fame as a "Ranger sniffler" spread over the borderland. Fleet as a rabbit, with the intelligence of his Arabian father and the endurance of his plebeian mother, he was the envy of all the *rancheros*. Fabulous sums of money were offered for this mescal-drinking horse, but Juan José would not sell him. He was too valuable to the smuggler; with his aid, Juan José and his men became unconquerable.

However, with the development of the lower Rio Grande Valley, swift changes came to the border. Smuggling became unprofitable. No longer did it pay the smugglers to bring in fresh supplies of tobacco leaf. Bull Durham and brown paper was taking the place of the corn shuck *cigarillos*. No longer was it spectacular to swim the river under the very nose of the Texas Rangers. For these officers, seeing the demand for tobacco diminish, directed their activities to more active sources. And without the thrill of persecution, smuggling lost all zest and glamor. Juan José, who always liked to occupy the center of the stage, did a dramatic thing then. Repenting of his sinful life, he acquired religion and decided to lead the life of a saint. It was then that he sold El Pájaro, the wonder horse. A rich ranchero, Don Manuel de Guevara, became his new master. Juan José wept over his horse at parting, begging Don Manuel not to give him any more *mescal*.

"He is part of my very soul," Juan José explained. "With my repentance came his too. He is as much of a Christian as I am."

But with the new master and the new life, El Pájaro lost spirit. His eyes lost luster, he refused to eat, and when saddled merely stood still. His new master cursed and swore, saying he had been cheated in the bargain. Then like a flash a thought came into his mind. The horse needed *mescal*. And he was right. A quart of the fiery liquid restored the horse to his former manner. El Pájaro pitched and snorted as of old. He became so spirited that no one, except the ranchero, could ride him. A man in his early forties, Don Manuel was the typical ranchero of his time. A good *jinete*, he bragged that no horse could throw him and no rider could outride him. And to a certain extent the boast was true. Except when he was "in the grape," the polite border way of saying he was drunk, he could ride any horse. He used to boast that if Pegasus himself, the fabulous winged horse, were placed before him, he could ride him—wings and all. El Pájaro had met his match.

In those days, at the turn of the nineteenth century, there was no better-known figure than Father José María. A native of France, he had come to the border country as a young man of twenty-five, forty years before. Because of his excellent horsemanship, he was lovingly known as the "Cowboy Priest." Now as an aging man of sixty-five, he still rode all over the lower border administering the sacraments and preaching the gospel. Loved and respected by all, his word was law among a people who had very little liking and less respect for American law.

One evening, just at sunset, Father José María, riding his white mule, arrived at Don Manuel's ranch. Hearing the cries of a woman, the hoarse swearing of a man, and the weeping of children, he entered the yard of the ranch house without announcing himself. The sight that met his eyes did not surprise him at all, for he knew Don Manuel only too well.

The ranchero was much "in grape" and so was El Pájaro. Don Manuel could hardly stand on his feet; yet he was trying to ride the snorting and pitching horse. His wife stood on the porch wringing her hands and weeping.

The children were adding their wails and tears to hers, and the two peons standing against the house were paralyzed with fear. Don Manuel would surely be killed if he succeeded in getting on El Pájaro.

Father José María took in the scene at a glance. Dismounting from his mule, he came to where Manuel struggled with El Pájaro. "*Hola, Padre,*" the ranchero called out, "watch me ride this devil of a horse."

"Stop a moment, Manuelito," answered the priest. "I'll make a bet with you."

Manuel stopped, for if there was a thing he loved more than *mescal* and horses, it was to make and win an honest bet.

"A bet, Padre, did you say?"

"Yes, I bet I can ride El Pájaro."

"All right, Padre. I take your bet. If you ride this demon of a horse, he is yours. Agreed?"

"Agreed," the priest answered.

With slow steps the priest approached the horse—caressed him gently, patting his mane and rubbing his nose. In less time than any one realized, Father José María was riding El Pájaro. The *mescal*-drinking horse and the *mescal*-drinking ranchero had been defeated.

From that time on El Pájaro was the priest's property. Years passed. The black-robed, white haired priest, learned in Latin, and the gentle, queer-shaped horse, Stella Matutina now, *alias* El Conejo, *alias* El Pájaro, traversed the borderland, bringing consolation to the sick and afflicted. Whenever the good priest talked to some impertinent sinner, he would often comment, "My horse, Morning Star, is a good example of what religion can do for a man. Imitate him. He has left his evil ways."

The Ghost Horse

BUFFALO CHILD LONG LANCE

With the first touch of spring we broke camp and headed southwest across the big bend of the upper Columbia, toward the
plateau between the Rockies and the Cascades. It was on this
lofty plateau that the world's largest herd of wild horses roamed during the
last hundred and fifty years. Several hundred head of them are still there,
where every summer efforts are being made to exterminate them by the
provincial government of British Columbia. It was these horses that we were
after, to replace the herd which the storm had driven away from our camp.

We struck the herd in the season of the year when it was weakest; early
spring, after the horses had got their first good feed of green grass and their
speed had been slowed by dysentery. Since these wild creatures can run to
death any horse raised in captivity, it is doubly a hard job to try to ensnare
them on foot. But, like wolves, wild horses are very curious animals; they will
follow a person for miles out of mere curiosity. And, when chased, they will
invariably turn back on their trails to see what it is all about; what their pursuers look like; what they are up to.

They always traveled ahead of us, but they had a way of turning back on
their own trails and coming upon us from the side or the rear, to keep watch
on us. It was this never-satisfied curiosity of the wild horse that enabled our
braves to capture them on foot.

·

The method of our warriors was to locate a herd and then follow it unconcernedly for hours, and maybe for days, before making any attempt to round it up. This was to get the horses used to us and to show them that we would not harm them.

We had been trailing fresh manure for five days before we finally located our first herd away up on the expansive Couteau Plateau of central British Columbia. There they were: a herd of about five hundred animals grazing away over on the side of a craggy little mountain on top of the plateau. Their quick, alert movements, more like those of a deer than those of a horse, showed they were high-strung beings that would dash off into space like a flock of wild birds on the slightest cause for excitement. There was one big, steel-dust stallion who grazed away from the rest and made frequent trips along the edge of the herd. It was obvious to our braves that this iron-colored fellow with the silver mane was the stallion who ruled the herd, and our warriors directed all of their attention to him, knowing that the movements of the entire herd depended on what he did.

When we had approached to within about five hundred yards of the herd, our braves began to make little noises, so that the horses could see us in the distance and would not be taken by surprise and frightened into a stampede at seeing us suddenly at closer range.

"Hoh! Hoh!" our braves grunted softly. The steel-dust stallion uttered a low whinny, and all the herd raised their heads high into the air and, standing perfectly still as though charmed, looked intently over at us with their big, nervous nostrils wide open. They stood that way for moments, without moving a muscle, looking hard at us. Then, as we came too near, the burly stallion tried to put fear into us by dashing straight at us with a deep, rasping roar.

Others followed him, and on they came like a yelling war party, their heads swinging wildly, their racing legs wide apart, and their long tails lashing the ground like faggots of steel wire. But before they reached us, the speeding animals stiffened their legs and came to a sudden halt in a cloud of dust. While they were close they took one more good look at us, and then turned and scampered away with the rest of the herd, which had already begun to retreat over the brow of the mountain.

But the big steel-dust stood his ground alone for a moment and openly defied us. He dug his front feet into the dirt far out in front of him, wagged his head furiously, and then stopped long enough to look and see what effect his mad antics were having upon us. Around and around he jumped gracefully into the air, swapping ends like a dog chasing its tail. Then again he raised his head as high as his superb stature would carry him, and with his long silver tail lying over his back, he blazed fire at us through the whites of his turbulent flint-colored eyes. Having displayed to us his courage, his defiance, and his remarkable leadership, he now turned and pranced off, with heels flying so high and so lightly that one could almost imagine he was treading air.

Our braves laughed and said: "Ah, *ponokamita*, vain elkdog, you are a brave warrior. But trot along and have patience. We shall yet ride you against the Crows."

For five days we chased this huge herd of horses, traveling along leisurely behind them, knowing that they would not wander afar; that they would watch us like wolves, as long as we were in the vicinity.

By the fifth day they had become so used to us that they merely moved along slowly when we approached them, nibbling grass as they walked. All during this time our braves had been taming them by their subtle method. At first they just grunted at them. But now they were dancing and shouting at them. This was to let the horses know that although man could make a lot of noise and act fiercely, he would not harm them; that no injury could come to them through closer contact with man.

On the tenth night of our chase our warriors made their final preparations to capture the herd. They had maneuvered the horses into the vicinity of a huge half-natural, half-artificial corral, which they had built of logs against the two sides of a rock-bound gulch. From the entrance of this corral they had built two long fences, forming a runway, which gradually widened as it left the gate of the corral. This funnel-shaped entrance fanned out onto the plateau for more than a half mile, and it was covered over with evergreens to disguise its artificiality. It was a replica of the old buffalo corral, which we used to build to round up the buffaloes when they were plentiful on the plains.

The mouth at the outer end of this runway was about one hundred yards wide. From this point on, the runway was further extended and opened up by placing big tree tops, stones and logs along the ground for several hundred yards. This was to direct the herd slowly into the mouth of the fenced part of the runway, where, once wedged inside, they could neither get out nor turn around and retrace their steps. They would be trapped; and the only thing left for them to do would be to keep on going toward the corral gate.

Subdued excitement reigned in our hidden camp on this tenth night of our chase; for it was the big night, the night that we were going to "blow in" the great, stubborn herd of wild horses. No one went to bed that night. Shortly before nightfall more than half of our braves, comprising all of our fastest-traveling scouts and young men, quietly slipped out of our camp and disappeared. According to prearranged directions, they fanned out to the right and left in a northerly route and crept noiselessly toward the place where the herd had disappeared that afternoon. All during the early night we heard wolves calling to one another; arctic owls, night hawks, and panthers crying out mournfully in the mystic darkness of the rugged plateau. They were the signals of our men, informing one another of their movements.

Then, about midnight, everything became deathly quiet. We knew that they had located the herd and surrounded it; and that they were now lying on their bellies, awaiting the first streaks of dawn and the signal to start the drive.

One of our subchiefs, Chief Mountain Elk, now went through our camp, quietly giving instructions for all hands to line themselves along the great runway to "beat in" the herd. Every woman, old person, and child in the camp was called up to take part in this particular phase of the drive. We children and the women crept over to the runway and sprawled ourselves along the outside of the fence, while the men went beyond the fenced part of the runway and concealed themselves behind the brush and logs—where it was a little more dangerous.

Thus we crouched on the ground and shivered quietly for an hour or more before we heard a distant "Ho-h! . . . Ho-h!" It was the muffled driving cry of our warriors, the cry which for ten days they had been uttering to the horses to let them know that no harm could come to them from this sound. Thus, the horses did not stampede, as they would have done had they not recognized this noise in the darkness.

We youngsters lay breathless in expectancy. We had all picked out our favorite mounts in this beautiful herd of wild animals, and to us as we lay there it was like the white boy lying in bed waiting for Santa Claus. Our fathers had all promised us that we could have the ponies that we had picked, and we could hardly wait to get our hands on them. My favorite was a beautiful calico pony, a roan, white and red pinto—three different colors all splashed on his shoulders and flanks like a crazy-quilt of exquisite design. He had a red star on his forehead between his eyes, and I had already named him *Nay-tukskie-Kukatos*, which in Blackfoot means One Star.

Presently we heard the distinct rumble of horses' hoofs—a dull booming which shook the ground on which we lay. Then "Yip-yip-yip, he-heeh-h-h," came the night call of the wolf from many different directions. It was our braves signaling to one another to keep the herd on the right path. From out of this medley of odd sounds we could hear the mares going, "*Wheeeeeh-hagh-hagh-hagh*"—calling their little long-legged sons to their sides that they might not become lost in the darkness and confusion.

Our boyish hearts began to beat fast when we heard the first loud "Yah! Yah! Yah!" We knew that the herd had now entered the brush portion of the runway and that our warriors were jumping up from their hiding-places and showing themselves with fierce noises, in order to stampede the horses and send them racing headlong into our trap.

Immediately there was a loud thunder of pattering hoofs—horses crying and yelling everywhere, like convulsive human beings in monster confusion. Above this din of bellowing throats and hammering feet we heard one loud, full, deep-chested roar, which we all recognized, and it gave us boys a slight thrill of fear. It sounded like a cross between the roar of a lion and the bellow of an infuriated bull. It was the massive steel-dust stallion, furious king of the herd. In our imagination we could see his long silver tail thrown over his back, his legs lashing wide apart, and stark murder glistening from the whites of those terrible eyes. We wondered what he would do to us if he should call our bluff and crash through that fence into our midst.

But, now, here he came, leading his raging herd, and we had no further time to contemplate danger. Our job was to do as the others had done all along the line: to lie still and wait until the lead stallion had passed us, and then to jump to the top of the fence and yell and wave with all the ferocity that we could command. This was to keep the maddened herd from crashing the fence or trying to turn around, and to hasten their speed into our trap.

"*Therump, therump, therump.*" On came the storming herd. As we youngsters peeped through the brush-covered fence, we could see their sleek backs bobbing up and down in the star-lit darkness like great billows of raging water. The turbulent steel-dust stallion was leading them with front feet wide apart and his forehead sweeping the ground like a pendulum. His death-dealing heels were swinging alternating to the right and left with each savage leap of his mighty frame.

Once he stopped and tried to breast the oncoming herd, but these erstwhile slaves of his whims struck and knocked him forward with terrific force.

He rose from his knees, and like something that had gone insane, he shot his nostrils into the air and uttered a fearful bellow of defiance at any and everything. He seemed to curse the very stars themselves. Never before had he tasted defeat, utter helplessness. The loyal herd that had watched his very ears for their commands was now running wildly over him.

I believe that, if at that moment there had been a solid iron wall in front of that stallion, he would have dashed his brains out against it. I remember looking backward into the darkness for a convenient place to hop, if he should suddenly choose to rush headlong into the noise that was driving him wild with helpless rage. But, even as I looked back, I heard a whistling noise, and my eyes were jerked back to the runway just in time to see the steel-dust king stretching himself past us like a huge greyhound. With each incredible leap he panted a breath that shrieked like a whistle.

No one will ever know what was in his brain; why he had so suddenly broken himself away from his herd. But on he went, leaving the other horses behind like a deer leaving a bunch of coyotes. A few seconds later the rest of the herd came booming past us. As we went over the fence, shouting and gesticulating, we looked into a blinding fog of sweat and breath, which fairly stung our nostrils with its pungency.

I thought that herd would never stop passing us. I had never seen so many horses before, it seemed. We stuck to our posts until it was nearly daylight, and still they came straggling along; now mostly colts limping and whinnying for their mothers.

When we climbed down the fence and went down to the corral at daylight, the first thing we saw was four of our warriors lying on pallets, bleeding and unconscious. They were four of the best horsemen in our tribe: Circling Ghost, High Hunting Eagle, Wild Man, and Wolf Ribs. When our mothers asked what was the matter, someone pointed to the corral and said: "*Ponokomita—akai-mahkah-pay!*" ("That very bad horse!")

We looked and saw a dozen men trying to put leather on that wild steel-dust stallion, who, with his heavy moon-colored mane bristling belligerently over his bluish head and shoulders, looked now more like a lion than a horse. He was splotched here and there with his own blood, and his teeth were bared like a wolf's. Four men had tried to get down into the corral and throw rawhide around his neck. While the other wild horses had scurried away to the nethermost corners of the corral, this ferocious beast of a horse had plunged headlong into them and all but killed them before they could be dragged away.

He had proved to be one of the rarest specimens of horse known to man—a killer—a creature that kicked and bit and tore and crushed his victims until they were dead. One might live a hundred years among horses without ever seeing one of these hideous freaks of the horse world, so seldom are they produced. He had already killed two of his own herd, young stallions, right there in our corral. Little did we wonder, now, that he was the leader.

Our braves were taking no more chances with him. They were high up on top of the seven-foot corral fence, throwing their rawhide lariats in vain attempts to neck the murderous monstrosity. But this devil disguised as a horse had the reasoning of a human being. He would stand and watch the rawhide come twirling through the air, and then just as it was about to swirl over his head, he would duck his shaggy neck and remain standing on the spot with his front feet spread apart, in defiance of man and matter. None of our oldest men had ever seen anything like him.

It was finally decided to corner him with firebrands and throw a partition between him and the rest of the herd, so that our braves could get busy cutting out the best of the animals, before turning the rest loose. This was done, and by nightfall we had captured and hobbled two hundred of the best bottoms anywhere in the Northwest. The next day our braves began the arduous task of breaking the wild horses to the halter.

Four months later we were again back on our beloved plains in upper Montana. Our horses were the envy of every tribe who saw us that summer. They all wanted to know where we got them. Our chief told the story of this wild-horse hunt so many times that it has since become legend among the Indians of these prairies.

But at the end of the story our venerable leader would always look downcast, and in sadly measured words he would tell of the steel-dust stallion with the flowing moon-colored mane and tail, which he had picked out for himself. He would spend many minutes describing this superb horse; yet he would never finish the story, unless someone should ask him what became of the spectacular animal.

Then he would slowly tell how our band had worked all day trying to rope this beast, and how that night they had decided to leave him in the little fenced-off part of the corral, thinking that two or three days contact with them might take some of the devil out of him. But the next morning when they visited the corral he had vanished. The horse had literally climbed over more than seven feet of corral fence, which separated him from the main corral, and there, with room for a running start, he had attacked the heavy log fence and rammed his body clear through it. Nothing was left to tell the tale but a few patches of blood and hair and a wrecked fence.

That should have ended the story of the steel-dust beast, but it did not. On our way out of the camp on the wild-horse plateau we had come across the bodies of seven wild stallions and a mare, which this fiend of the plateau had mutilated in his wake. He had turned killer through and through, even unto the destruction of his own kind. Our old people said that he had been crazed by the fact that he had lost control of his herd in that terrible dash down the runway. This blow to his prowess and pride of leadership had been too much for him; it had turned him into a destructive demon, a roaming maniac of the wilds.

This horse became famous throughout the Northwest as a lone traveler of the night. He went down on to the plains of Montana and Alberta, and in the darkest hours of the night he would turn up at the most unexpected points in the wilderness of the prairies. Never a sound from him; he had lost his mighty bellow. He haunted the plains by night, and was never seen by day. His sinister purpose in life was to destroy every horse he came across.

This silent, lone traveler of the night was often seen silhouetted against the moon on a butte, with his head erect, his tail thrown over his back like a statue, his long moon-colored mane and tail flowing like silver beneath the light of the stars. Owing to his peculiar nocturnal habits and to the fact that his remarkable tail and mane gave off in the moonlight something like a phosphorescent glow, he became known throughout the Northwest as the *Shunka-tonka-Wakan*—the Ghost Horse. The steel-blue color of his body melted so completely into the inky blueness of the night that his tail and mane stood out in the moonlight like shimmering threads of lighted silver, giving him a halo, which had a truly ghostly aspect.

Casualties & Survivors

The Bluebird of Happiness

GRETEL EHRLICH

I bought Blue from a Mormon horse trader in 1978 for $400. "He's worth a little more than the others because he's got some cow in him," the trader told me. Meaning, lie liked to work cattle. "He probably knows a little more about cowboying than you do and that's good. You'll learn something from him if you keep your ears up." The trader supplied all the horses for the sheepherders on the 200,000-acre ranch where I had lived for two years.

Sheepherder horses are rarely things of beauty. They're usually old, hairy-legged, often white (an unpopular and impractical color). In other words, the horses, like the herders who rode them, were the unwanted ones in society.

Blue was long-headed, donkey-eared, hairy-legged, and had spots. He had been sired by a Government Remount stallion—now a thing of the past. These stud horses were taken around small communities and for a very nominal sum would breed a rancher's mares. It was the fast and economical way of increasing one's horse herd. The stallions were part of the original quarter-horse breed—big, stout, drafty, with just enough thoroughbred to get them moving and turning fast. And they had plenty of "cow." Which is why Blue looked the way he did and loved to sort cattle.

He arrived at the end of a very bad winter. I had suffered the loss of my fiancé and had been living alone in a one-room log cabin on a road out of

Cody, Wyoming, that wasn't always plowed. As soon as the snow melted and the winglike drifts gripping my house began to melt, Dave Cozzens arrived with Blue in the back of his red stock truck. There was no ramp or loading dock so Dave just jumped him out of the back. "He's a damned practical horse, if nothing else," he said.

We turned him out into a large pasture. The first night he was lonely so I sat on the fence in my long flannel nightgown and held his head in my arms until he quieted down. We were both bereaved and he was salve to my wounded mind.

When spring came I moved across the Big Horn Basin to a little town in the foothills of the Big Horn Mountains. The log house was bigger and Blue's pasture was luxuriant with early grass and a fast-running creek moving through. I rode him to the post office, then back the other way, past the pink house and the petroglyphs into the bug-ridden meadows that smelled of wild mint. Looking up, I could see the sunlit rock walls of a long canyon that cut all the way to the mountaintop.

That same week, an extraordinary woman, "Mike" Tisdale Hinckley, asked me to go cowboying with her. "I'll be there at 5 A.M. and you can take those damn sheepherder's pots and pans off your saddle," she said. Sheepherders are the brunt of everyone's jokes. When I loaded Blue into the trailer beside Mike's fancy quarter horse, we began laughing. "God, I should have come when it was still dark, so no one could see what I was hauling," she said. That summer we gathered and trailed cattle in the Big Horns and the Wolf Mountains in Montana. Everyone laughed at Blue—but that was an asset. When I laughed just as hard, everyone knew that at least I had a sense of humor—the first prerequisite on any ranch.

Blue was eight years old when I bought him. He was hard-mouthed and head-shy. He'd been beaten and abused and could be difficult. Once he almost dragged my friend Laura to death. She'd gotten a rope wrapped around her thigh and he spooked, not knowing she was attached to the line. Eventually he stopped and she survived—she had a lot of cuts and bruises, which I cleaned, nothing else.

On his good side, Blue traveled farther than any other horse and stayed at it for more hours. At the end of a fifty-mile circle gathering cattle, he still had enough juice to sort strays out of the herd and pair up mother cows and calves. All I had to do was let the reins loose and touch his withers. He'd do the rest.

Every year I rode hard all summer and fall, and when the snow flew Blue was turned out with the other horses until spring. In March or April I'd catch him, hold his big mule ears, and make my annual pact: "Are we going to get along this year, you old lunkhead, or am I going to have to sell you to the canners?" I'd ask sweetly. I could almost see him smile. Then he'd put in another seven or eight hundred miles, carrying me.

Sometimes in the autumn, when the ranch work slowed down, we'd take idyllic rides up into the mountains. I'd always let Blue pick his own trail. He loved to smell trees, bushes, and flowers. At eight thousand feet he'd stick his nose into the powdery yellow pollen flying off lodgepole pines and pucker his big lips around a flowering thistle. He sniffed every creek, every trickle of water, and let low tree branches brush the horseflies off his rump. One afternoon a sudden storm came in. Ground lightning swept down a meadow, up Blue's legs, through my feet, and a white ball bounced off the tops of our heads. Blue stood dazed and paralyzed. His eyes had rolled back and his big ears had lain down on either side of his head. I leaned down to look at his face. "Are you still alive?" I asked. Then he snorted, coughed, and continued on down the mountain.

One year we wintered in another town. Blue was pastured alone, which he hated, as do all horses, being extraordinarily sociable beings. The highway was being widened that year. And without my consent, they took the horse pasture fence down along the highway. When someone called and mentioned that my horse was loose along the highway, I ran out to find him. There he was, standing with his head resting against a telephone pole, so lonely, I imagined, that he was listening in on others' conversations. The fact that the fence was gone never fazed him.

Blue loved hanging out with people. If the kitchen door was left open, he'd come right in, helping himself to dog food, cookies, and apples. He was used to being fed from a sheepwagon's Dutch door. One night I came home and he was in the kitchen. My dog, Rusty, was gazing lovingly at Blue, who had just consumed a fifty-pound bag of kibbles.

Blue's sociability was ultimately his demise. One spring, he was turned out with a bunch of dude horses. One of them, Sticker, was "proud cut"— that is, he still thought he was a stallion. Apparently, he fought with Blue and Blue lost. He was found with his back leg hanging—a clean break just above the hock. There was nothing to be done.

We gave Blue a sky burial on the little knob at the southern edge of the ranch, just beyond the lake. He was facing east, toward the rising sun. For weeks I could smell his decomposing flesh. I wanted it that way. I wanted his death to sift into me just as his cranky, faithful, devilish life had seeped into my bones. After that, I bought better-looking, fancy-bred horses. But it's Blue who I miss, who I long for. No one else would have put up with him. The same has been said of me. That was our secret and the core of our annual spring pact: that if I tolerated him, he'd do the same for me.

The Horse in the Kitchen

RALPH M. FLORES

I was sitting in the backyard just fooling around when I heard Teresa shouting in front. I ran around the house to see what was happening. A cow had wandered into our front yard and was trying to get into the garden to browse. Teresa was shouting at it, waving her arms, while the cow stood undecidedly between fear of the little human and desire to munch on our corn. Olga and Mother came running out the front door, and the cow backed off, lowing as Mother flapped her apron in its face. Father came around the corner to see what the commotion was about.

"That's Filoberto's milk cow," he said. "I'd better take her back."

Filoberto had a large ranch next to our small piece of land and lived about a mile up the road. Father saddled his horse and then looped a rope around the cow's neck. He got on the horse and reached his hand down to me. "Get on," he said. I got on behind him and he handed me the rope. "Hold on to this."

We rode down the road with the cow following behind. As we approached Filoberto's house, the cow suddenly lurched forward and jerked the rope out of my hand. She headed toward the gate at a clumsy gallop, mooing loudly. Benito, Filoberto's son, came off the front porch and grabbed the rope around her neck. We could see Filoberto in one of the corrals off to the side of the house. He saw us, waved, and came toward us.

"*Ay compadre*," he said to Father. "You have come at a bad time."

"*¿Que pasa, hombre?*" replied my father. "You look troubled."

"My horse is very sick. He is suffering greatly and I have not been able to make him better. I was getting ready to shoot him when you rode up."

"Your roan?" asked Father. "Charro, your big roan?"

"Yes, Charro. He is like my child. I have waited as long as I can, but now I can wait no more and must put him out of his misery."

We had been riding toward the corral while they talked, and as we dismounted I could see the horse lying still on the ground. Father walked over and knelt beside it. He stroked it, talking to it in a low voice while his fingers ran over the horse's head. He leaned down and smelled the horse's breath.

Father stood up. "He is so beautiful. Are you sure he cannot be cured?"

"I am certain. We have tried everything for three days, but he won't eat and gets weaker and weaker. I just want to end his suffering."

"So you're going to shoot it?"

Filoberto had tears in his voice. "Yes."

"*Compadre*, will you let me take the horse and try to heal it? You're going to shoot him, and you will no longer have him, so why not let me take him? If I cure him I will keep him, but I promise you I will not let him suffer too much if I don't succeed."

"I don't think you can do anything for him, but if you want to try, go ahead."

"If I heal him, will he be mine?"

"Yes. If you give him back his life, he will be yours."

"Then I'll go home and come back with a wagon."

As we got back on the horse, Benito came and gave me the rope we had used to tie around the cow's neck. We left, promising to come right back for the horse.

"Do you really think you can heal the horse?" I asked. The possibility that Charro might be ours excited me greatly.

"I don't know for sure, but there is a chance. When I was a young man, I worked on a ranch with an old *vaquero* who knew more about horses than anyone I've ever met. He taught me things that most people don't know, even those who think of themselves as experts."

"He is so lovely. I hope he will be ours."

"*Sí.* One can tell at a glance that this horse is special. My compadre Filoberto is in a hard spot. He wants to end the horse's suffering, but he doesn't want to shoot him; he hopes I can heal the horse, but he also knows that if I do, he will lose the horse anyway. I guess he would rather have the horse alive with someone else than have him dead."

We were now turning off the main road into our front yard. We dismounted and I went to look for Antonio and Roberto while Father hitched the team of mules to the wagon. The four of us then headed back to Filoberto's ranch.

With Filoberto and Benito helping, we managed to get the sick horse on a pallet, then drag it up a ramp onto the back of the wagon. We went back home with Charro too sick and tired to raise his head.

As soon as we got back home, Father had Roberta and me go out and gather a wild shrub Mexicans call *hediondilla*. We came back with our arms loaded. Meanwhile Father had started a fire under a kettle. He stripped the leaves off the shrub and dropped them in the kettle to steep in the boiling water. After a few minutes he ladled out a pot of the mixture, then dipped a blanket into the kettle. He brought out the steaming blanket and draped it over the corral to cool. Finally, when the blanket had cooled sufficiently, he draped it over the horse's torso and had me hold up the horse's head while he forced some of the liquid down its throat.

After that he rolled back part of the blanket and began to massage Charro slowly and gently, talking to him softly all the while. Then he told Antonio, Roberto, and me to help him roll the horse over onto his other side. Father once again soaked the blanket in the liquid and let it cool, then repeated the massage process. After he was done, we left the horse lying there outside the corral.

The next morning Roberto and I had to go gather some more hediondilla, and the whole process was repeated. Toward sundown, we went through it again. The following morning, however, when I went outside I saw Father sitting on the ground by the horse. Charro had managed to lift his head, and Father was stroking it softly, talking to him lovingly. Once more we repeated the massage process. That afternoon Charro stood up and managed to eat a little. My dad was smiling. "I think he's going to be all right," he said.

Within ten days Charro was back to normal. Filoberto could not believe it. "You are a magician," he said to Father. "I swear I was certain that horse would be dead long before now." He hugged Charro's head, and then said, "Well, I gave you my word, and he's yours now. You deserve him."

Of course, that horse became my dad's special friend. Father was almost as careful and loving with him as he was with his family. Sometimes, when the horse was loose, he would follow Father around almost like a dog follows his master.

And then trouble came for Father and his beloved horse. A band of so-called revolutionaries rode into town to steal whatever they could. As always, their cloud of dust gave us advance warning. Immediately people in the village were running around hiding anything of value, no matter how small. As we always had during previous raids, Roberto and I went to get Charro to hide him in the kitchen, knowing that the bandits would not think of going into houses looking for what they prized most after money—horses. They had little hope of ever getting any money from villages like ours, but with luck they might stumble on a horse or two.

We ran into Father, who already had Charro and was walking him toward the house. Then Pamfilo Ortiz, one of the townspeople, called to him. "*Compadre!* Don't put your horse in the house. If they look in your house they are sure to find him. I have a special place in the hills where I keep my horse. They'll never find him there!"

I don't know why, but Father handed the reins to Pamfilo, who took the two horses off into the hills. A few minutes later the bandits arrived and spread out through the town, riding up and down streets, shouting at people to come out of their houses.

There was one horse in town that nobody claimed, a beat-up, sway-backed nag that ate whatever anyone fed it. It was barely strong enough to carry the smaller kids in town. When this horse saw the bandits riding in, it spooked and ran out the other end of town toward the foothills. Several members of the gang saw it and galloped after it. Of course, this nag led them directly to where Pamfilo had taken his horse and Father's. They rode back into town leading the two horses by a rope. They had not, of course, bothered with the old nag. The leader of the band took one look at Charro and claimed him as his own.

As a crowd of townspeople gathered, he dismounted his horse, put his saddle on Charro, and got on. The horse began to buck, trying desperately to dump the rider, but the bandit was an excellent horseman and would not be thrown off. Finally the roan gave up and stood exhausted in the middle of the street, panting hoarsely with sweat running off him, soaking the ground.

My father had been watching in the crowd silently, but I could tell what a struggle it was for him to see this stranger not only sitting on his horse, but actually taking it as his own. It was more than he could handle, and he stepped out of the crowd and faced the horseman. "That horse is mine," he said.

The bandit seemed surprised that anyone would question his right to the horse. He looked down on my father from his seat on the horse. Then he spoke: "The Revolution needs horses. Would you deny this horse to the Cause?"

The crowd was dead silent. I was aware that Father's life was in danger if he pressed the matter further, but I also knew that he would not stand quietly by while his beloved Charro was taken from him. Suddenly my mother came running up and placed herself between the bandit and her husband. She was standing there with her back to me, her hair pulled into a bun at the nape, with strands of hair that had loosened in her run to the scene catching the sunlight like a glowing halo. She was there to protect her man, and I think she said the first thing she thought of, since it didn't make much sense.

"Take the horse," she said, "and when you get another one, you can send this one back to us."

I guess the bandit wanted to avoid a shooting if he could because he immediately responded to Mother's statement. "Yes, I'll do that. I'll get another horse at the next village and then I'll send this one back to you."

Father knew this was nonsense, but when he tried to speak again, Mother whirled around to face him. "Let's go home," she said.

"Wait a minute!" Father started again. "I want. . ."

"Let's go home!" said Mother again, and for the only time in my life I saw her put a hand on him in anger. She grabbed his arm and started forcefully leading him through the crowd. Father turned his head and tried again to say something to the man who was stealing his horse, but my mom only pulled him away harder, whispering fiercely, "Shut up and go home!" I don't know which was more shocking to me, seeing my dad lose Charro or hearing my mom talk to Father that way.

So the man kept the horse and my dad kept his life, although I don't think Father ever recovered from losing Charro. He was dispirited for days afterward, and several months later, when we had lost all our savings because of the Revolution and he and Mother decided to leave Mexico and emigrate to the United States, I know the loss of his horse was one of the main reasons he decided to leave his homeland. How could he stay when the friend whose life he had saved, his special, beloved friend, had been ripped away from him forever?

More Than the Sum of His Spots

JO-ANN MAPSON

I came to horses later than most people. At thirty-two, I got talked into riding lessons with my fearless younger sister. Most lesson horses are barn-sour, and the nasty Appaloosa who clearly recognized a rube was no exception. He charged the arena, broke into a full gallop, and I managed to hang on, but the damage was done. Shortly after, I found myself in the position of accepting that I would be scared of horses for life, or facing up to the fear and working through it. That was when I met the ugly old "Appy" who would later become my horse, or more accurately, my horse teacher, allowing me to witness the world—and beyond—from his four-legged point of view.

The Appaloosa has a rich and tragic history. Its name comes from the Palouse River that runs through Washington and Idaho's Nez Perce Indian territory. "Palouse," "cayuse," and "horse" somehow transformed into Appaloosa, the name the breed carries today. It is commonly accepted that the Spanish introduced these "Ghostwind" horses to America when they came to California to conquer, Christianize, and find gold. In 1804 Meriwether Lewis wrote in his journal, "Some of these horses are pied with large spots of white irregularity . . ." And then went on to admire their conformation and spirit. On October 5th, 1877, the U.S. Cavalry captured Joseph, chief of the Nez Perce, and whatever horses weren't sold were exterminated. In

1937, the Appy caught the public eye, and the Appaloosa Horse Club was founded. Today the breed is held in high esteem, and their numbers exceed a million registered horses.

My nineteen-year-old Leopard Appaloosa came to me already named: Tonto. It was just about as politically incorrect as a name could be.

Though technically a "Few Spot Leopard Appaloosa," one of six known patterns, he was not handsome. True Leopard Appys are covered entirely with dazzling spots, and sometimes referred to as "Tiger Horses." Tonto had missed out on spot day. His gray coat looked like he'd been splattered with mud here and there. His butt in particular sported spots the size of Oreo cookies. He was of an age when most other horses retire, or die. All the other horses in the stable had dishy Arab faces, elegant necks, or flowing tails that swept the ground. Tonto was Roman-nosed and outfitted with only the essentials. His thin, gray mane and tail looked as if they belonged on an eighty-year-old man.

For decades he'd been a lesson horse. Three times a day, a beginning rider would slide into the saddle, walk, trot, and maybe canter a minute or two. Then my horse walked in circles, and waited for the next student. I'd ridden him before I bought him. He'd stop dead in his tracks when I gave him the wrong cue, and though a horse's peripheral vision allows him to see without turning his head, Tonto turned his head around and looked at me accusingly. I figured if he was willing to drive the point home I had better learn to trust him.

A specific trait of Appaloosas is "people eyes." Their sclera is white, like ours. When they look at you, there's an eerie feeling of intelligence and emotion. Tonto was pony-sized, only fourteen hands high. Appys are affectionate, gentle, and darn smart. They not only remember, they learn. They have a special gait, the "Indian Shuffle," which is a slow and economical trot. So comfortable is this gait that the Appaloosa became the cowboy's horse of choice. A rider could spend all day in the saddle without chafing his spine. The only thing Tonto liked more than eating was this gait. When I asked for a trot, he gave me half a lap of the real thing, then dropped back into his gentleman's jog. Try as I might, I could not talk him out of it. When asked for a canter, most horses will happily bolt into a full gallop; Tonto cantered in front while trotting in back, a most uncomfortable and unsightly combination.

If a horse could snicker, he surely must have as I sat atop him in my riding habit, getting frustrated and eventually giving up.

He'd done it all, Grand Prix trials, Equitation classes, jumping fences and pole bending. Entered in any class of a horse show, he'd take a ribbon. On Gymkhana days, all the tiny tots begged to ride him. Once in the ring he quickly figured out what was expected and did it without any cues from the rider. My horse trainer called him "bomb proof," meaning that you could have set a bomb off and he would have kept his lead and switched gaits the moment the judge asked for it over the microphone.

His transition from lesson horse to family horse must have come as a wonderful surprise. What a relief that he no longer had to endure amateurs yanking on the reins, or endless kicking when any fool could see there was a rattlesnake on the trail and no way he was going to step forward until it departed. I was a doting horse owner, feeding him vitamins and Senior Diet, bringing apples and watermelon. I groomed him simply for the joy of watching his coat shine. I had him wormed and shod every six weeks. If he had a bump or a bruise, I called the vet. When his neck was stiff, I called out a horse chiropractor. After the adjustment, Tonto groaned so deep and in such relief the vet laughed and said, "You've been waiting for that for a long time, haven't you?" The equivalent of a horse orgasm, I thought.

He boarded in a small pasture and for a while, ruled the herd with my husband's horse—a clubfoot Morgan/Arab—as his second in command. During one torrential California rainstorm, we brought them warm bran mash, and I swear those horses nickered for fifteen minutes solid. Tonto was gentle, but restrained from displays of affection. As his significant human, I was good for treats and for rubbing his heavy head against when he had an itch, especially satisfying when he could knock me over. He could open a plastic bag, filch the carrots, and leave the bag intact.

We took solitary trail rides into the same hills where this past year a bicyclist was killed and a woman disfigured by a mountain lion. The cactus bloomed with swollen red fruit, which Francisco, the stable manager, harvested to make a kind of potent Mexican wine. Deep in what's left of the Cleveland National Forest we encountered deer. Occasionally we'd come across a migratory giant, a Sandhill crane off course setting down for a rest before catching up with the others. Tonto studied his surroundings, but never spooked. When the regrettable idea of using peacocks as stable watchdogs was en vogue, the noise they produced was jaw shattering. Out of nowhere came heart-stopping shrieks that sounded like a scalded baby. Tonto didn't flick an ear. Yet if I approached him while in a bad mood, he'd shake all over—my animal barometer. To calm him down, I'd give him a hug, and of course, the apple slices he knew were in my jacket pocket, and the bad mood floated away.

We had over a decade together before he died, just short of his thirty-fifth birthday. Two nights previous he'd colicked. "I call because only I never before to see Tonto lay down like this," Francisco told me from the barn pay-phone. "You should I think come."

Our regular vet let me know I had interrupted him from what he alluded was a very critical point in a romantic encounter. He gave Tonto a bolus of mineral oil and an enema containing the same, and drove off in his truck saying he'd bill me. My job was to walk Tonto until he passed fecal matter. Oh, the joys of horse ownership! We circled inside the arena where we'd once jumped fences and bent poles against the clock, all seven hundred pounds of him turned to heart in pursuit of the task. When an hour ticked by and he hadn't passed anything, I kept walking. Another hour passed. Periodically he'd lie down. It was a struggle to get him up, but I knew he had to. We stumbled along at whatever pace he could manage. Toward two o'clock in the morning he stopped and would budge no further. I whispered that if he needed to die, then he should do it. My face buried in his neck, I told him I loved him, thanked him for all he'd taught me, and said how much I would miss him, that losing him would be the close of a powerful chapter in my life, but that I understood everybody has to leave someday, and above all, I didn't want him to suffer.

I wept.

He rallied.

He looked so much better that I put him in his stall and drove home to change clothes for work.

Two days later, when nobody was looking, he lay down in his stall and left behind a world that must have seemed to him utterly ridiculous. Here at the stable, horses existed to be groomed and penned, exchanged for vast amounts of money all in the effort of a tiny piece of satin ribbon. Here, horses were forced to channel all their energy into complicated moves and brief jaunts of athleticism. No blasting out the cobwebs, no running for the sheer joy of it, or to prove that an animal so poorly designed could accomplish such grace. Not even a mare nearby to flirt with. No finding shelter under a tree when it rained. Crazy food offered twice a day when any horse with half a brain knew it was smarter to graze. Living amid your own droppings. Timing your day by the whistles of the stable manager, as he mucked stalls and delivered hay flakes and pellets. His lamenting Spanish love songs fueled by cactus wine indicating dinner was again going to be late.

Oh, I didn't want to leave my house, twenty-five miles away that night. I was getting a cold. Work had piled up. That past year I'd hired a trainer to exercise Tonto while I worked under deadlines and traveled around the country on book tours. But I drove there because I just knew it was time. Soon, I'd have to adjust my heart filled with horse to having that portion cut from it. Our too brief time together would become a silhouette. Negative space.

Yet the truth is it's easy to move on after such a loss. Work is distracting. I'd find myself grieving in the dark of movie theaters, while stuck in the eternal California traffic. I had never experienced such sorrow, not even when my father died unexpectedly. This howling crouched down in my gut, waiting to level me. It wasn't until I moved to Alaska and lost a beloved dog that I realized the extent of the gap an animal's death leaves behind. Worse, that I had no idea how to deal with it, or if there was really any lesson to be learned other than that loving somebody or something that hard eventually hurts.

Therapists will tell you that it's common for children damaged in youth to identify more closely with animals than humans. They feel the animals' pain as deeply as their own, because both are at the mercy of adults, who can be cruel. For a time, the stable employed a manager who regularly whipped his horse, clearly because he was disturbed, not because the horse had acted incorrectly. When he flew into one of his rages, I'd walk right up and yell at him that he was a coward and an asshole and that I was going to call the police if he didn't stop. I've been like this all my life, unable to bear cruelty against animals, and willing endanger myself if I have a chance to stop it. Who will speak for the animals? Though answers come in the form of animal rights organizations, there is the matter of the scars that remain. How to fold them into memory, how to live with the dishonorable parts of ourselves, the shame?

After my horse died, I felt useless. I banged around my universe lopsided. The sight of any gray horse with spots made my heart leap up as if given a second chance. But none of them was Tonto. From his striped hooves to his bumpy backbone he was unique. His scent was a reassuring tang that I've never smelled on any other horse. He knew when I drove up and called out in his grandpa whinny. When I had a bad day, I'd ride him bareback and pretty much give him full rein. Never once did he let me down, lead me astray, or think of himself first.

I was stunned to find him again in—of all places—a day spa in Anchorage, Alaska. I had a gift certificate, so I decided to try a hot stone massage.

The room was dimly lit, instrumental music played on a continuous loop, and the air smelled faintly of ocean. From a bath of warm salt water, the masseuse removed smooth black rocks, oval and flat, rocks about the size of an Oreo cookie. Onto my oiled back she rubbed each stone into muscle beds, the way I once watched a chiropractic vet rub Tonto's crazily spotted neck. As she finished with each stone, she drew it down my back and left it to rest at the coccyx. When she was finished, my spine was a ladder made of stones. Then she gave me some time alone.

Deeply relaxed, the mind wanders similar to that dream state that precedes sleep, and I felt myself traveling. But unlike falling-asleep dreaming, which is dim and symbolic, something different came to me. One minute I was thinking I need to get up and let her get to her next appointment, and the split second after, I saw in clear detail, in vivid color, our two horses standing on the bank of a river.

It was autumn. The cottonwood leaves were gold. The sun was out, the sky blue, and both horses looked up at the same time, surprised, but also as if they had expected me. Then the curtain went down and I was back in a world without horses.

"Do you believe in an afterlife?" friends ask me from time to time. At one time I would have said don't be silly. But my once-callow view of the world as a hard place where we are given only a brief time to succeed has been forever altered. In my heart, I know this: My animals are waiting for me. When I die, we will be reunited. The thinly spotted horse will nudge me with his heavy head; I'll fall down, laughing. We'll stay that way "forever," whatever that means. There will be hot bran mash, and apples for all.

A Fool about a Horse

ROSS SANTEE

There's no tellin' when you'll meet up with a cow-puncher. They're such a driftin' lot. You'll work with one for months sometimes, sleepin' in the same bed. Then some mornin' he'll pull out. Mebbe you'll see him again and mebbe you won't.

Steve always was a queer cuss, an' a fool about a horse. When I first met up with Steve he was breakin' horses for the Cross S outfit in Arizona. Most peelers is pretty rough on a horse, but Steve was different. He could teach a young horse most anything without half killin' him. Most of the horses in Steve's string was rank poison. But there was one little gray bronc in the bunch he called Three T.

Three T was gentle as a kitten, an' Steve taught him to do most everything 'cept talk. Three T wouldn't run with the rest of the horses. He hung around camp just like a dog. He nearly run Slim, the horse-wrangler, crazy at first tryin' to herd him. After the ponies quieted down in the mornin', Slim always went back to camp to auger the cook. But he wouldn't any more'n get off his horse an' there 'd be Three T trailin' along after him. Slim would take him back out to the remuda, an' as long as he was in sight the little gray would graze quiet. But the minute Slim pulled out for camp there 'd be Three T right at his heels.

All this was n't settin' well with Slim, for he liked his coffee between meals. He decides to run the little gray off, but it 's no use. In an hour Three T 's back at camp hangin' around just like a dog. Slim quit botherin' him

274

after that, and, since none of the rest of the horses was any trouble to speak
of, Slim spends most of his time in camp augerin' old Sour Dough, the cook,
and fillin' his paunch full of coffee and cold steak. An' when the outfit 's in
camp, Steve 's always a-foolin' with that little gray bronc, teachin' him to
shake hands an' other such foolishness, an' a-feedin' him biscuits and sich
until the little gray got to be a plumb nuisance.

We were eatin' supper one night when the blow-off comes. The punchers
is all settin' around on their heels stowin' away the grub. Three T 's standin'
just outside the circle waitin' for a biscuit, an' old Sour Dough 's leanin' on the
gonch hook airin' his paunch about the war. Nobody else is sayin' much, for
it 's a tender subject in this outfit. Most of the punchers is expectin' their call
'most any time, an' the idea of crossin' all that water ain't settin' well with none
of them. Unless it 's Steve, an' he 's so quiet an' easy-goin' not even water
makes much difference to him.

Old Sour Dough 's right in the middle of tellin' what he 'd do if he was
n't too old to be drafted, when the little gray bronc eases up behind him and
takes a biscuit out of one of the Dutch ovens. Old Sour Dough 's so interested in his own game he don't even know what 's goin' on. Finally Dogie
Si snickered and old Sour Dough turns round in time to see Three T standin'
over the empty oven, with his nose out beggin' for more. Everybody
laughed—everybody except the cook. He swings on the little gray with the
gonch hook catchin' him just back of the ear. Three T's legs sort of buckled
under him, an' down he goes to his knees.

I looked at Steve. His face had gone a chalky white, an' he was makin' a
queer noise in his throat. Old Sour Dough swung the gonch hook again—but
it never landed. . . . It was n't much of a fight. Old Sour Dough 's unconscious
an' Steve 's still makin' that queer noise in his throat when we finally pulled
him off. Me an' the horse-wrangler washed the dishes an' sort of straightened
up the camp. We 're just finishin' up when Dogie Si come back from the
cook's bunk an' said old Sour Dough had finally come to. I looked around for
Steve, figurin' maybe he 's dragged it. But there he was foolin' with that little
bronc again, just as if nothin 'd ever happened. We 're eatin' supper not more
'n a week later when an Indian rides into camp. He 's come from headquarters with a note from the boss and Steve's notice to report in town.

It was sundown when Steve pulled out. At the top of the ridge he set
the little gray up an' looked back for a minute. Then he waved his hand an'
was gone.

The saloon is plumb full of people when I goes in. There 's a few Mexicans an' punchers scattered through the crowd, but most of the mob is tourists, an' they 're swarmin' around the bar like a bunch of magpies. Down near the end of the bar I finally get close enough to get a foot on the rail. I got a forty-dollar thirst, but when the Mexican barkeep slides me a drink I sort of hesi-tate. I 'm studyin' whether to take it out back some place an' drink it, when somebody pokes me in the ribs. I never did feel comfortable in Juarez with-out a gun, so I whirls around expectin' most anything. An' if there ain't Steve!

"Bill Jones," says he, with a grin!

The first thing Steve asks about is that little gray bronc. I 'd plumb for-got the little gray, for the outfit shipped some horses to Texas not more 'n a month after Steve left, Three T goin' along with the bunch. But when I tells Steve he don't say nothin'.

"Here 's how!" says I when the Mexican barkeep fills 'em up again.

"How!" says Steve.

It 's awful good to see Steve. I don't know what makes it, but you get to know a man better in a week out on the range than you will in a year's time in town.

"Heard you was killed in France."

"No," says Steve, "it was in the laig."

"How 'd you like the army, anyway?"

Steve shakes his head.

"I done everything they told me, but did n't do nothin' else. I finally got hit in the laig. I was in the hospital when the armistice was signed. Breakin' horses since I got out—New Mexico—come to Juarez to get drunk."

Coming from Steve, this is a heap of talk. Everybody 's leavin' the sa-loon, an' from a tourist I finally gathers there 's a bull-fight that afternoon; so me an' Steve has a few more drinks an' throws in with the crowd.

The place was pretty crowded, but we finally found a couple of seats on the shady side of the ring. Outside the entrance the band 's playin'. About half the crowd 's American tourists, I 'd say from the looks of their clothes. There 's one settin' 'longside of me an' Steve that said he was from New York. He wasn't a bad sort at that, in spite of the white suit he 's wearin'. Steve bought some bottled beer, an' the tourist give me a program. It 's printed in Spanish though, an' don't mean nothin' to me. We 're startin' on our second bottle when some *hombre* blew a bugle. There 's a hullabaloo at the entrance an' a bunch of soldiers marched in. I thought for a minute there 's another revolution, for they 're all carrying long rifles, and none of 'em 's wearin' much except cartridges. The crowd don't pay 'em any mind though, so I eases back into my seat.

The *hombre* blew his bugle again, an' the bull-fighters entered the ring.

A bunch on foot come first, carryin' red capes. Just behin' 'em comes a bunch that 's mounted. "Picadors," the tourist calls 'em. They 're wearin' different clothes an' the horses they 're ridin' look like they 'd been dead for a week. Next comes a team of horses. The *hombre* cut down on his bugle again. The team was driven out, the bull-fighters took their places about the ring.

Another gate swung open an' the bull busts into the ring. He 's pretty snuffy, an' the sight of them red capes soon gets him on the prod. They teased him around a while, when all of a sudden he sees one of the horses. I think it 's queer the horse don't dodge, an' then see he's blindfolded. I ain't finicky, but it makes me kind of sick when the horse goes down. The rider ain't hurt, but there 's blood a-pourin' from the horse's neck an' shoulders. The pony 's tryin' to get his feet when the bull charges again. The Mexicans is all on their feet, screaming. Steve 's a-makin' that queer noise in his throat, an' the tourist is cryin' like a baby. An *hombre* just below me threw his hat in the ring. I 'm for kickin' him into the ring after it, when Steve an' the tourist pull me down.

They finally killed the bull. The matador, Formalito they called him, did about as poor a piece of butcherin' as I 've ever seen. The bull don't even notice the red capes now.

He 's standin' in the center of the ring, blood pouring from his mouth. As the matador approached him the bull turned slowly away. A dozen times the matador faced him, but the bull is too weak to charge. Finally he runs his sword in the bull's neck. Stumblin' blindly to the edge of the ring, the bull sank slowly to his knees, blood pourin' from his mouth.

Steve and the tourist is for leavin', but there 's three bulls to be killed, an' I ain't given up hope of seein' a Mexican killed. We finally compromise. An' I promise to go with 'em after the next bull 's killed if they don't kill a Mexican in the meantime.

We 'd opened some more beer when the Mexicans took their places again. I ain't payin' much attention to anything except the beer, when I notice one of the horses.

He's nothin' but skin an' bones, but there 's somethin' awful familiar to me in the way he moves around. I looked at Steve; his face had gone a chalky white, an' he 's makin' that queer noise in his throat. Then I knew. I don't remember much that happened after that. Steve 's down in the bull-ring an' has the picador by the throat before anyone knew what happened. Then all hell broke loose. There 's a dozen Mexicans a-tryin' to drag Steve off that picador when I got to him. I broke a bottle over an *hombre's* head that had Steve by the hair, and then the whole remuda run over me an' I went to sleep. . . .

My head 's a-splittin' when I woke up, but it don't take me long to figure out where I am. There 's bars across the windows an' a bullet-headed *hombre* with a long rifle, standin' just outside the door. Steve ain't here. Must 'a' killed him, I figure, but my head 's a-spinnin', so I go to sleep again.

Sounds like the tourist's voice, but I 'm afraid to look at first, for fear I 'm hearin' things. But sure enough, it is.

"How 's Steve?"

"All right," he says, an' sorta smiles an' introduces me to some lawyer friend of his.

We stopped an' had a drink, an' then he heads the car for home. I can't get no information out of either of 'em. They both looks wise an' sorta smiles at everything I says. It 's an awful relief to me when we gets back across the bridge. El Paso never looked so good before. The lawyer finally stopped the car.

"My place," he says, an' asks me if I 'll have a look around.

"What about Steve?"

"Oh, he 's all right," he says, an' heads me for the barn.

Steve sorta grinned when we come in, an' then went on a-foolin' with the little gray.

He always was a queer cuss, an' a fool about a horse.

Firecracker

DAVID ROMTVEDT

The longer I work at Four Mile Ranch, the more I get to know horses—not horses in the abstract but particular horses—Trouble, Harold, Ms. P, Bobo. And the better I know these horses, the more I find myself speaking of them as if they were people or at least as important as people. Perhaps it is self-indulgent in these days of human hunger and disease, wars all over the planet, the pain and death we read about in the Congo, Rwanda, the Middle East, in our own rich country. Still, I care for the horses deeply and it's not as if I imagine them to be metaphors for universal human values. The simple truth is that maybe I do believe they are as important as we are.

Sharing our lives, horses come to share our ailments and deaths as well. They get cancer, for example. It's not even rare. The most common form is malignant melanoma. It occurs in all horses, though mostly in grays. Appaloosas and white horses suffer squamous cell carcinoma, a skin cancer.

All these words. Soon there will be horse oncologists. I don't know if that's frivolous or merely depressing. Oncologists with their words—sonogram, nuclear scanner, gamma scanner, hard radiation machine, lymphoma and lymphocyte. Then there are their diagnoses that are equal parts biochemistry, voodoo, and intuition. Right now I'm wound up on this subject and I lead myself to this story the way I lead a horse toward a trailer inside which he'll ride to the vet's.

It was seventy-five-year-old Jean Irigaray's racer Firecracker, who was twenty-six himself and hadn't been on a track in years. Firecracker's cancer was the melanoma. Jean, like most of the Basques in our Wyoming community, had come to the United States as a young man and spent his life ranching, first as a hired sheepherder, then as the owner of a small ranch. He'd never gone to school and his English was rough. He knew nothing of what was going on inside his horse's body.

Our vet, Dr. Tom, explained that most likely the bad cells filled Firecracker, that they had entered the lymphatic system, maybe the kidney and liver. Little could be done though Dr. Tom explained that he could destroy lumps along the skin—cut them out or burn them or freeze them with nitrogen.

Jean was heartbroken—a true breaking of his heart. Human or horse. Jean didn't ask that question. He asked Dr. Tom, "Is nothing more can be done?"

Dr. Tom said that he'd call the CSU vet school in Fort Collins and get back to Jean in a few days. I drove Jean home and, though it was cold, we walked in the pasture. The wind was wailing so that the dried leaves spun and danced around us, hitting our bodies as if they might find refuge under our coats.

"Twenty-six years," Jean said, and I think he meant everything—the pasture, the irrigation ditch and dams, the battered fence posts and worn barbed wire, the way the clouds boil, thick layers that shift and fly, opening and closing windows onto the blue. I looked at Jean and realized that these feelings were not some easy sentimentalization—loving an animal because it requires less than loving another person. Instead, I saw that Jean's love of the horses—and mine, too—was a way to have union with another world.

On Wednesday I drove Jean back to the vet's. Dr. Tom felt all over Firecracker's body. He ran both hands together along the horse's neck, hard questioning fingers, cool from antiseptic. Dr. Tom told Jean there were small bumps everywhere, cancer rampant under the skin. I kept quiet, picturing Firecracker's insides as a garden of foul flowers all blossoming at once, inky bloody blooms, poisonous pollen, barbs and ash.

Dr. Tom used an electric knife to cut a walnut sized lump from the base of Firecracker's neck. Though the horse was anaesthetized, he could smell the sizzle of hair and flesh, and in terror he bashed against the padded walls of the squeeze chute.

Exposed, the lump was a dull rubbery blob, somnolent and benign. Quick-frozen, sliced and dyed, it was analyzed. Later there were core samples of bone marrow—hollow needles drilled into Firecracker's pelvis—then blood and urine analyses. Dyes were injected into the loose skin between his front legs. All this went on at the university, down in Colorado.

"Treatment just like for a human," they told Jean. "We can do radiation, chemotherapy, treatment just like for a human . . ."

But you can talk to a human being, I thought. And nowadays, on humans even, the plug is pulled and people go home to die in their living rooms, the busy world at the window, friends and family passing in and out. And wouldn't a horse rather stand in the shade of a cottonwood or lean against the south wall of a shed in a winter wind than die in a building smelling of antiseptic and soap and human?

We're not so good at letting go.

As part of an experiment, CSU paid for most of the work that was done. Still, Jean spent three thousand dollars. He told me, "Money don't matter."

For a horse, I thought, but kept my mouth shut. For fifty years Jean had been one of the stingiest of the carefully stingy Basque ranchers. But when Firecracker was being treated, Jean went down to Fort Collins and stayed in a motel. He asked if I'd drive him and I did and stayed two nights. The motel room was characterless. There was a copy of a western landscape above the bed, two plastic drinking cups sealed in a cellophane bag by the sink, and a TV with cable and HBO.

After I left to come home, I pictured Jean there, rising alone each day, dressing carefully to go check on his horse. I wanted to go back and stay with him. But I didn't ask, thinking it was just ghoulish. I remembered Jean's wife, dead three years, and wondered if this attention was connected to that death, another way Jean mourned that loss. It was a cheap thought, for what mattered to Jean was the horse, the integrity of its life.

"That horse done a lot for me." Jean said. It struck me that what a horse can do for a person—for Jean, for me, for anyone—is exactly what my life in Wyoming has been teaching me all along. What a horse can do, a dog, a sheep, a coyote or mountain lion, the snow falling out of the sky. I had somehow never before seen that Jean knew this. How stupid of me. Now I had a glimpse and I knew that I'd never forget.

In Praise of Horses

MARK SPRAGG

Every fall in mid-October we packed out our hunting camp on Mountain Creek. It was a thirty-mile ride over Eagle Pass, over the lesser Dike Creek Divide. I would leave school for a week to help. There were usually six or seven of us and at least thirty-five packhorses. The packhorses ran loose. They wore muzzles of wire mesh to keep them from grazing. A single man led, and the others spaced themselves back through the packstring to keep the horses in line and moving at the same speed, to watch for a slipped pack; to be ready for accident. We ran half a dozen four-year-olds unpacked for extra mounts in case a young horse played out.

The fall I was fourteen I rode a blue roan colt on the trip out of Mountain Creek. His name was Sky. I knew he was sick when I got on him. His nose ran, and he had the shits. He felt hot and stumbled in the creek when I gathered the horses out of the meadow by camp. I meant to say something to my father about the horse, but the weather was threatening, and I was trying to be more help than problem. I knew I should have roped out one of the other young horses to ride, but we'd gotten a late start. The tents were frozen and had to be beaten with lengths of stovewood to fold them into squares small enough to toppack. It had begun to snow. I thought that Sky was normally a clumsy horse. I convinced myself that that was all it was.

I rode at the end of the packstring and kept his head up. My father was six horses ahead of me, and then Gordon and John and Phil spaced farther up the line, with Claude in the lead. The horses knew they were going home. They shouldered one another in the timber, and fanned off the trail in the meadows trying to get around the men ahead of them.

Sky lagged back on the Dike Creek Divide. I spurred him harder. In the big meadows on the Mountain Creek trail he wheezed and coughed. When he farted he sprayed his hindquarters with shit. I whipped him with my bridle reins to keep up with the others. The clouds lifted, and Pinnacle Mountain and Eagle Peak to the north, both more than eleven thousand feet, came clear and bristling with new snowcover.

On the backside of Eagle Pass, Sky tried to lie down twice. He ducked his head back toward his left shoulder and buckled at the knees. Both times I spurred him into a staggering walk. I felt him grow unsteady between my legs, strain in his solid work.

At the top of the pass I stepped off and tied him to the limb of a stunted pine. His eyes were glazed and out of focus. He did not turn to look as the packstring moved away from us. I walked to the downwind side of the pine, as though I had to piss, and stood with my back to him. My father looked back. I waved, and watched them descend. Sky labored to catch his breath. I walked to him and he nickered softly, and I stroked his nose and knew I might be killing a horse to hide my bad judgment.

I hung two switchbacks behind the others. I walked slowly and led Sky. He skidded and pulled back against the reins. When I was nearly to the bottom of the pass I heard the men shouting, horses screaming and neighing, the pounding of hooves. Two packhorses came up the trail toward me. They were running and kicking into the air. I waved my arms and turned them straight down the slope, dropping from the middle of one switchback to the trail below it. They squatted on their haunches and slid and furrowed the ground and disappeared into the trees below me. I looped Sky's reins around the limb of a deadfall and slid on my ass until my heels bit into the hard-packed level of the trail, and then released and skidded down to a lower switchback. I met my father coming back up the trail. His horse bobbed its head and double-stepped, and worked against the bit, fighting to run.

"Where's Sky?" he asked.

"Up the trail."

"Keep him there." He stepped off his horse, a lean, gaited bay we called Secret, and handed me his reins.

"What happened?"

"We rode into a hornet's nest." He turned and started back down the trail at a jog. The wings of his chaps flared and slapped at his calves. I tied Secret's reins to the limb of a pine and fell in behind my father.

We stopped on the last switchback over the creek that ran against the bottom of the pass. Three horses were staggering on its apron of stone. One trailed his packcover and lashrope and a broken box pannier. A fourth horse was turned on his back in the water, the weight of his pack holding him down. John and Gordon had their knives out. They ducked between the flail of his hooves and cut him out of his cinches and breastcollar and breeching. They kept his leadrope taut, his head above the water. They rolled him onto his side, and pulled on the leadrope, and slapped his ass and got him out of the creek. We watched as John led him into the timber and tied him. We watched him stand, and stomp, and shake, and cough.

We skidded down the cutbank and into the creek. Gordon stayed in front of the horse trailing his pack. He waved and cussed and kept the horse pinned against the creek. My father waded out of the water and caught up his lead. The horse's right rear pastern was rope burned, and his knee was skinned to its cap, and he bled from the back of his hock. Gordon lifted off the unbroken pannier, and my father knelt down at the damaged leg. The horse was a dull blond palomino we called Poco. The blood came away bright from his yellow-haired leg.

I dragged the panniers, and the packcover, and pack saddle out of the creek, one at a time, each water soaked and heavy.

"How's his leg?" Gordon asked.

"Nothing's broken." My father was binding the shag of torn flesh back up over the horse's kneecap with his kerchief. "You got any duct tape?" he asked.

"By God I do." Gordon ran to his horse and dug the tape out of his saddlebags. He knelt down by my father and they taped the kerchief in place. "That might get him home," he said.

"It will if we get out of here before he knows how bad he's hurt."

John led the other two packhorses out of the trees and tied them by his saddle horse.

"How are they?" my father asked.

"Just shook up." John stepped up onto the bay he was riding. "I'm going to see if I can catch something," he said, and turned the bay into the trees. We could hear the horse snapping through the downfall.

"Where's the rest of them?" I asked.

"They got by us," Gordon said. "Phil and Claude stayed with 'em."

"Where's the hornet's nest?"

"There," my father said and pointed into the limbs of a Douglas fir at the elbow of the switchback above us. He dumped the wet tack out of the unbroken pannier and sorted through it. He held up a cinch and a tobacco tin of nails and a shoeing hammer. "Good to know our medicine bag's not completely filled with shit," he said, but his voice didn't sound like he thought we were lucky.

Gordon went to work on the broken pannier with the nails and duct tape. I shook out the wet packcover and spread it over the rocks. I replaced the pack saddle's front cinch with the spare one, and opened my jackknife and started to splice the cut breastcollar and back rigging.

We looked up at the clatter of stones. John had one of the loose colts roped and dallied and was dragging him right to us. He stepped off his horse and walked the rope back to the colt and made a halter out of the slack in his lariat and tied the colt to a tree.

"Is that all we have left?" My father asked. He tried to make it sound like a joke.

"Claude got ahead of most of them. He's holding them against the bog at the far end of the meadows. Nothing's hurt, but some of the packs have worked loose."

"How many got past the bog?" my father asked.

"Seven," Gordon said. "Phil's gone after 'em. He thinks their packs held."

"You better get down there and help Claude." My father looked to where Poco was tied. The yellow horse bowed his head back against the lead-rope and stepped his torn hindleg toward his head and snorted. "When you get everything squared away start for home. The boy and I'll pack this colt and come along behind with him and Poco. We'll come about as fast as that palomino can walk."

John nodded and Gordon did too, and they turned the two undamaged packhorses down the trail and stepped on their saddle horses and were gone.

The colt just stood with his legs splayed, braced against us as we got him packed. He whistled and rolled his eyes but that was all.

"That's a miracle," my father said. I told him I thought so too. "Lead him away," he said. I walked the colt to where the trail came out of the creek and tied him. He walked stiffly, hunched, turning his head to stare at the pack, but he didn't buck.

I followed my father straight up the mountain, the way the packhorses had slid down. When we cut the switchback above the hornet's nest we followed the trail to where Secret was tied and led him further up the pass to Sky. Sky was down. He had fallen uphill. His feet were notched into the trail. He didn't lift his head as we walked up to him.

"This surprise you?" my father asked.

"He's sick," I said.

"How long's he been sick?"

"Since this morning."

My father looked away at the horizon. The sun was already low in the sky. When he looked back at me his face was red. He looked at me longer than I expected. He lit a cigarette, and exhaled, and held the cigarette between his lips. "Let's see if he'll get up," he said.

I pulled on the reins, and my father took his lariat off his saddle and got behind Sky and slapped his ass hard, and then again, and shouted. The roan groaned and struggled to his front feet and stood, but kept folding his head back, trying to lie back down. My father untied my slicker and denim jacket from behind my saddle and shook out the jacket and hung it over Sky's head. He handed me the slicker. "Put this on," he said, and went to his own horse and untied his jacket and slicker. He put on his slicker and turned up the collar, and eased the denim jacket over Secret's head. The horse balked and snorted and stood quiet.

"You ready?" he asked. He seated his hat tighter on his head.

"I guess I am."

We ran down the trail leading to the horses, and across the creek. The hornets were busy above us and to the sides, but they did not land or sting. We stopped in the dark timber where I had tied the colt. He whinnied and pulled back against the lariat. We pulled our jackets away from our horses' heads and Sky folded his legs and laid down. My father looked at me and then knelt by Sky's head. "You're going to have to stay with him," he said.

"I'm not afraid to," I told him.

He undid my saddle's latigo and breastcollar and pulled it away from the downed horse. He stood the saddle under a tree and laid the hairpad and blanket over its upturned skirt.

"Get that bridle off him," he said, and looked down the creek to where Poco stood. He went to his saddlebags and came back with a flashlight and hatchet and the lunch that he hadn't eaten. He handed me his slicker. "Do you have matches?" he asked. I nodded.

"How far is it to the lodge?" I asked.

"Twelve miles."

I nodded again.

"If you can get him up in the morning try to walk him out. I'll start back for you. I'll bring a spare horse in case we need one." He lit another cigarette and looked straight up from where we stood. "It doesn't look like the weather's going to change."

"It doesn't feel like it," I said.

My father led Poco up the creek, took off his wire muzzle, and half-hitched the halterrope to the horn of his saddle. He slipped John's lariat over the colt's head and put the muzzle on the colt. He stood for a moment re-coiling the lariat and then stepped onto his horse and measured his reins and held Secret on the trail. The packed colt stood in front of him.

"You nervous about this?" he asked.

"No, sir."

"You should be," he said. He stuck his chin out toward Sky. "That's a good little horse you rode down. I'll see you tomorrow."

He started into the trees leading Poco, pushing the colt ahead of them. Poco walked badly, slowly, his light hair gathering the light and holding it against the black and green of the pines. The shadows stood thick and dark as a second growth of trees. When I could not see them any longer, when the echo of their hoofstrikes was gone, I sat on the ground in my wet clothes and cried. I tried to cry because of what I had done to Sky, but I was crying for myself, and because I was afraid that careless boys grow into careless men.

In the last light of the day I broke away armloads of dead branches and stacked them and gathered dry cones and dug up the sap-loaded roots from the rotted stump of an old fir. I used the hatchet to scrape away the pine duff and chopped a firepit into the earth and built a small, hot fire. I stood my saddle on its fork by the fire and used the hairpad for a ground cover and sat and leaned back into the fleece that lined the saddle and stared into the fire. I had spread my saddle blanket over Sky's neck and front shoulder. He watched me, but did not lift his head. I thought he had come to the bedrock of himself. I felt him fall out from under me; I felt myself fall with him.

I put on my jacket and pulled my father's and my slicker up to my chin and my head nodded and I fell asleep. When I woke the night was black and cold and the slice of sky I could see directly above me, busy with stars. The fire had died into a circle of embers, and I stacked on the fir roots. They sizzled and flared and burned hot as coal. I sat cross-legged on the hairpad with my saddle cupped around my back and ate my father's lunch. There were two elk steak sandwiches and an apple and a Snickers bar. When I was done I wadded the paper sack and put it on the fire and walked to the creek and laid the flash-light on the rocks and stretched out and held my chest off the ground on my palms and drank until I was full. My ass was still wet and stung in the night air, but my legs were dry. I stomped my feet to warm them and took up the light and walked to Sky. He nickered when I played the light across his head.

I knelt by his ears and lifted his head and scooted my knees under it and laid the broad thick bone of his skull against my thighs. He did not struggle. I closed my eyes and prayed for the strength to lift him and carry him to safety, and felt no stronger, and began to cry again. I bent my mouth to the soft, furred cup of his ear and whispered that I was sorry. I knew it did not matter to him. I knew that it only mattered to me. I said that I was sorry again.

I stood away from him and straightened the blanket on his neck and shoulder and walked back to the fire and squatted with my back to the flames until my ass warmed. The black night pressed down like water. My chest felt heavy. I had to stand to get a breath.

I sat back against the saddle and pulled the slickers over me and slept. There was only the sound of the fire, and in my sleep I dreamed that I lived on the back of a horse. In the dream I was fully grown. I was a naked, gaunt, and happy man, and I never stood down upon the earth. When I was tired I lay along the horse's back to sleep. When I was thirsty the rains came and I opened my mouth and drank. I was filled with rainwater and ozone. I draped forward on the horse's neck to rest. My arms hung to the sides of his neck. My hands clenched and relaxed. I breathed into his coarse, dark mane. My lungs filled with the salted, sweetmeat taste of the horse on which I lived.

In my dream I stood on the horse's rump and pissed a yellow arc into the air and my head fell back and I screamed into the vault of the black night sky, and turned and walked to his withers and sat.

He was a pinto horse, dark eyed, dark nostriled, dark stockinged with one white hoof, front left, slightly softer than the darker three. Each foot stuck out a single note as he stepped to graze. He made music as he ran. The lighter hoof slapping the earth in a tone shallower than the other three.

I sat upright on that horse and held my arms high like the armatures of long, slim wings and leaned slightly forward, and he broke into a run. I could feel the cool air tighten my flesh. I could feel the horse grow hot and lathered, and I knew that when a horse is running flat-out toward the curve of the earth that all four feet, regardless of color, leave the ground at once. I closed my eyes. I heard us skip into the air and touch the earth again, and I knew that it was in those suspended moments, relaxed from effort, that the rider and the ridden are afforded, in that instant, and in the next, and the next after that, the sight of God. I saw God looking at me in the dream and knew it was a horse I had to thank.

I woke in the early light. A gray jay stepped through the gray ash of the fire, and when I kicked off the slickers he rose into a pine and chattered. The slickers were stiff with frost. I took off my hat and beat the frost from its crown and stomped and shook. I expected to be alone. I felt alone. I expected to find a dead horse, to shoulder my saddle and start down the trail. I didn't look up until I was close to Sky. I almost jumped back when he lifted his head. He focused hard on me and tucked his legs and rolled onto them and stood. He swayed and caught himself.

I bridled him and led him to the creek, and he sucked at the water for a long time. I took a step upstream and knelt and cupped water on my face and drank. The ground and trees were dirty white with frost. It looked as though we stood inside the skeleton of a cloud. I felt better than the boy who had gone to sleep. I felt older than the boy who'd nearly killed his horse.

I saddled Sky and rolled the slickers behind the cantle and put the hatchet and flashlight in a saddlebag. I led him and he came along. I did not try to ride. I walked as fast as his strength allowed. When he grew tired we stopped.

I hoped to meet my father more than halfway between the bottom of the pass and home. I knew I deserved what punishment he thought ought to come my way. I knew I would not tell him of my dream.

Notes on Contributors

Pennsylvania-born **Edward Abbey** (1927–1989) worked as a seasonal ranger in Utah's Arches National Monument. On his days off he rode range and helped local ranchers gathering their cattle. The author of a novel of eco-sabotage, *The Monkey Wrench Gang*, and of the seminal essay collection *Desert Solitaire* dressed western and preferred ranching as an alternative over mining, dam building, and subdividing the West. His ironic neo-Western *The Brave Cowboy* was adapted for the screen as *Lonely Are the Brave*, with Kirk Douglas in the title role. Abbey lies buried in the Sonoran desert, in a grave whose location is only known to a few.

Laura Bell migrated to northern Wyoming in 1977, drawn by the prospect of living her life on horseback. For three years, she herded sheep on the open ranges for the Lewis Ranch of Cowley, Wyoming. Since then, she has ridden for the Diamond Tail Ranch, worked as range staff on the Bighorn National Forest, led horse-pack trips into the Absaroka backcountry, and conserved wildlife habitat for The Nature Conservancy. She now lives in Cody, Wyoming and is at work on a collection of essays entitled, *Claiming Ground*.

Virginia Bennett is a regularly featured performer at the National Cowboy Poetry Gathering. She has recited at the Smithsonian Institution and been featured on PBS and NPR specials. Her work has appeared in numerous anthologies. The author of *Legacy of the Land, Canyon of the Forgotten*, and *In the Company of Horses*, Virginia is also the editor of *Cowgirl Poetry: 100 Years of Ridin' and Rhymin'* and *Cowboy Poetry: The Reunion*. Virginia has worked on western ranches since 1971, alongside her husband, Pete. She's trained horses for the public, shown hunter/jumpers, driven draft teams and drawn cowboy wages.

Buck Brannaman was a child prodigy trick roper who performed at rodeos and special events. He now makes a living as a horse "gentler," and—with trainers like Tom Brokaw and Tom Dorrance—advocates less traumatizing techniques than more traditional horse "breakers." His story of personal healing and growth into a true horseman can be found in *The Faraway Horses*. Buck Brannaman has started thousands of young horses and taught clinics throughout the West and in Australia. He was technical advisor for *The Horse Whisperer* and lives with his wife and three daughters in Sheridan, Wyoming.

As told in *The Prairie in Her Eyes*, **Ann Daum** breeds sport horses on the 13,000-acre spread in the White River Valley in South Dakota that originally was her father's. She also feels compassionately about the wild creatures with which she shares the land. This freelance writer and independent rancher travels frequently and enjoys spending the winter in Budapest, Hungary. Her first literary output was a short story about a wild horse, which she wrote at age five.

Carolyn Dufurrena teaches in a two-room school in northwest Nevada. She is the author of *Sharing Fencelines* and of *Fifty Miles from Home*, which won the Silver Pen Award from the University of Nevada Library in 2002. She also contributed poetry and prose to several anthologies including *Woven on the Wind, Crazy Woman Creek: Women Rewrite the West, The Romance and Reality of Ranching*, and *Portrait of the West*. Carolyn ranches and writes on the Quinn River Ranch with her husband, Tim, her most demanding editor.

The passions of **Gretel Ehrlich** have shifted from horses, sheepherding, and Wyoming to *really* cold places. The former filmmaker and author of *The Solace of Open Spaces* and *A Match to the Heart* survived lightning strike—twice. She recently published two travelogues of high latitudes *This Cold Heaven* and *The Future of Ice*. Her writing also appears regularly in the *New York Times, The Atlantic, Time, Life, Audubon, Harpers*, and *Outside*. Ehrlich finds respite from severe climes and a busy writing life in southern California.

Part-Choctaw **Max Evans** was given his first horse at four. He is one of the few western writers and artists who successfully combined a ranching background with working in Hollywood. *The Rounders* was adapted for the screen (starring Glen Ford and Henry Fonda), as was his book *The Hi-Lo Country*. Max won a Spur Award for his story *Super Bull* and has been honored by the National Cowboy Hall of Fame. In his 80th year, he is still going strong, working on *For the Love of a Horse*, a collection of personal horse stories.

One of the nation's foremost scholars in the ethnology of Plains Indians, **John C. Ewers** (1909–1997) was educated at Dartmouth and Yale. He served in the Navy in WWII then worked as a museum director for the Smithsonian Institution. His ethnography *The Horse in Blackfoot Indian Culture* is still the best book on this topic.

Many variants of horse origin myths circulate among the Blackfeet, attesting to the role of this animal in nomadic plains societies. Cecil Cree Medicine, who heard it from her father, Running Crane, chief of the Lone Eater's band of the Piegan, told this version in 1947.

A Native of Uvalde, Texas, **Florence Fenley** (1898–1971) was orphaned at age fourteen, when her father was shot in town. Florence had a paint pony she rode to school; raised on a ranch, she could ride before she walked. Living with her grandfather, she gained an appreciation of old-timers and their stories, which resulted in two books. She collected pioneer stories throughout the state and wrote for *The Cattleman*, *True West*, *Frontier Times*, and the Uvalde paper. In 1942 Fenley was elected state representative (one of the first women in Texas to have done so) and served for two terms.

Ralph M. Flores has taught for many years at Albuquerque's Technical Vocational Institute. He lives in a small, rural community in New Mexico, with his wife Geri, a dog, a cat, and nine chickens. *The Horse in the Kitchen* is from *Una Vida*, a collection of scenes based on his father's boyhood experiences in northern Sonora, Mexico, during the Mexican Revolution. The loss of their life savings in the course of this social upheaval eventually forced the author's parents to leave for Arizona, where they eked out a living as workers on Depression-era farms. This is Ralph Flores's first book.

Born in Chicago and raised in northern Colorado, **James Galvin** now ranches part of the year near Laramie, Wyoming. He is also permanent faculty member of the University of Iowa Writers' Workshop and the recipient of fellowships from the Guggenheim Foundation and the National Endowments for the Arts. He has written a book of nonfiction, *The Meadow*; a novel, *Fencing the Sky*; and several books of poetry, of which *Resurrection Update* was a finalist for the *L.A. Times* Book Award. Galvin is currently breaking some new colts.

The 2002 Pulitzer Prize nominee **Ray Gonzalez** was born in El Paso. Inspired by the American Southwest, he has mastered several literary genres: he is a prolific poet, long-time poetry editor of the *Bloomsbury Review* and publisher of several anthologies. A teacher of creative writing at the University of Minnesota, Gonzalez has stayed close to his Latino heritage. Topics like border politics and bilingualism inform his essay collection *The Underground Heart* and his compilation of short stories, *The Ghost of John Wayne*.

Many consider **Zane Grey** (1872–1939) the greatest storyteller of the American West. With sixty titles (ninety books overall), he is definitely the bestselling Western author of all times. The semiprofessional baseball player and half-hearted dentist from

Ohio found his calling as a self-taught and disciplined writer. His breakthrough with *Heritage of the Desert* (1910) allowed Grey to buy a home in California, as well as a hunting lodge on the Mogollon Rim near Payson, Arizona. *Riders of the Purple Sage* is a classic among adventure-romances. His selection in this anthology is from *Whirlwind*, the fictional story of a captured mustang.

A poet, novelist, short story writer, and essayist, **Jana Harris**'s award-winning books of poems include *Manhattan as a Second Language*, and *Oh How Can I Keep On Singing?: Voices of Pioneer Women*, both Pulitzer Prize nominees. The latter was also a Washington State Governor's Writers Award winner, a PEN West Center Award finalist, and has been adapted for educational television as well as for the stage. Her novel *Alaska* was a Book-of-the-Month Club alternate selection. Born in San Francisco and raised in the Pacific Northwest, she now lives with her husband in the foothills of the Cascade Mountains, where they raise horses.

The first woman to win a Western American Writers Award, **Linda Hasselstrom** grew up on a family farm in western South Dakota. She is foremost known as an essayist and working ranch woman, a poet and environmentalist. Her work has been featured in the anthology *American Nature Writing* and she is the co-editor of several volumes of western women's writings. Her own books include *Land Circle*, *Feels Like Far*, and *A Road of Her Own*. Linda Hasselstrom divides her time between Cheyenne, Wyoming, and Hermosa, South Dakota.

Linda Hussa, writer and rancher in the Great Basin, has three poetry collections and three books of nonfiction. The themes of her work are drawn from the isolated nature of ranching and her commitment to the health of the rural communities of the West. Hussa is the recipient of Nevada's Silver Pen Award. Her latest collection of poetry *Blood Sister, I Am to these Fields*, was the winner of three awards in 2002: The WRANGLER, given by National Cowboy and Western Heritage Museum, The SPUR, given by the Western Writers of America, The WILLA, given by Women Writing the West.

Born Joseph Ernest Nephtali Dufault in Quebec in 1892, **Will James** left home as a teenager to follow his dream of being a cowboy in the American West. While serving time in a Nevada prison in 1915 for his involvement in rustling, James turned to art, swaying the parole board in his favor. Afterwards, he wrote and illustrated twenty-four books, and his articles about cowboys and horses appeared in *Scribner's* and other magazines. Nearly all of his books went out of print after his death in 1942, but in recent years have been reprinted, and biographies and film documentaries about him have appeared.

Alfred A. Kroeber (1876–1960) was educated at Columbia under Franz Boas, the father of American anthropology. He conducted fieldwork among the Zuni of New Mexico and Wyoming's Arapaho. He later taught at the University of California, Berkeley, where he stressed the importance of archeology for the understanding of human societies. During the winter and spring of 1901 Kroeber collected many Gros Ventre tales on the Fort Belknap Indian Reservation in northern Montana. His informant for the tale in this anthology was "**Assiniboine**," a middle-aged man. More can be found in Kroeber's *Gros Ventre Myths and Tales*.

Sylvester Clark Long—the "glorious impostor"—was born in North Carolina in 1890, the son of ex-slaves. As a boy he joined a Wild West Show, where he became fascinated with Native Americans. After being wounded in France in WWI, he worked as a reporter and wrote articles about the Blackfoot, eagerly absorbing the elders' knowledge. Eventually, the Blood tribe adopted him and gave him his nom de plume, **Buffalo Child Long Lance**. Clark later tried to pass for Blackfoot, starred in a film, became a New York celebrity and bodyguard, and ended an alcoholic and suicide.

Grant MacEwan (1902–2000) was born in Brandon, Manitoba. He was a professor of animal husbandry at the University of Saskatchewan and Dean of Agriculture at the University of Manitoba. His political career culminated in his election as mayor of Calgary and lieutenant governor of Alberta. MacEwan published several agricultural texts and over fifty books on historical subjects, close to one book per year between 1970 and 1990. His *Blazing the Old Cattle Trail* is a prime source of anecdotes of the early Canadian cattle industry.

Jo-Ann Mapson is the author of nine novels, including bestsellers *Hank & Chloe*, *The Wilder Sisters*, and *Bad Girl Creek*. Her writing has been included in several anthologies, and her novel *Blue Rodeo* was made into a CBS movie. There are horses in every single one of her novels. For fifteen years she was owned by a Leopard Appaloosa named Tonto, during which time she studied equitation and hunt seat. She lives in Anchorage with her husband, artist Stewart Allison, and their four dogs, and teaches fiction in the University of Alaska's MFA program.

The Michigan-bred graduate of Yale University **Thomas McGuane** lives on a ranch in Sweet Grass County, Montana, where he dedicates much of his time to training cutting horses. His no-nonsense equestrian approach and humor illuminate the essay collection *Some Horses*. His ten books have been translated into as many languages. They include the highly acclaimed novels *The Sporting Club*, *The Bushwhacked Piano*, and *Ninety-two in the Shade*, which was a finalist for the National Book Award. Characteristic for a new

breed of western ranchers, McGuane is an ardent conservationist and former director
of American Rivers.

Jovita González de Mireles (1903–1983) was one of the first Texas-Mexicans with
an M.A. and a professorship. She was born on a Texas rancho, then moved to San
Antonio in 1910. Her father prohibited English being spoken at home, which did not
prevent Jovita from later excelling at it. As a teacher, she promoted Spanish in public schools. She became a pioneer collector of folklore of the Borderlands, and was influenced and inspired by the great Frank Dobie. In her book *Folklore of the
Texas-Mexican Vaquero*, she assembled narratives, proverbs, and songs. Mireles died
in Corpus Christi widely respected for her engagement and accomplishments.

Jennifer Olds was born and raised in Southern California. Her mother is a mare
midwife, her aunt is a horse trainer, and her uncle is a stuntman. She began showing
horses at the age of two. To date, Jennifer's equine education includes western and
English pleasure, dressage, gymkhana, showmanship in hand, and polo. She has had
three books of poetry published in the United States and England. Her novel *Good
Night, Henry* has just been published. An English professor, she has two sons, two
corgis, and a very indulgent husband and still lives in Southern California.

Originally from San Antonio, Texas, writer **George Patullo** had several novels and
short stories published from 1911 to 1959. For a time he was a reporter for the *Saturday Evening Post*. One of his stories was made into a silent film in 1921, but is now
missing. He traveled and worked with photographer Erwin Smith, who documented
ranch life and cowboys in west Texas and New Mexico during the early twentieth
century. His story of *Corázon* first appeared in *The Untamed*, a collection of animal
short stories.

After his father's death, **Charles Elliott Perkins** (1881–1943) took over and ex-
panded several land and cattle companies and railroad lines. His passion, however,
was raising thoroughbred hunters and jumpers and purebred Texas Hereford steers.
In 1927 he bought a 10,000-acre ranch near Santa Barbara. Perkins was a born
raconteur, and his wife suggested that he collect and publish his stories as a "family
book." *The Pinto Horse*—the fictional life story of a Montana half-mustang—became
much more: it impressed Owen Wister as an unsentimental and authentic animal bi-
ography, and Frank Dobie called it "a rarely beautiful book."

Frederic Remington (1861–1909) already drew pictures of fire horses at age
eleven. Varsity football and heavyweight boxing did not challenge this New Yorker
enough—so he lit out for Arizona and the Territory of Oklahoma after the death of
his father in 1880. He failed as a rancher in Kansas, then roamed through Mexico on

Geronimo's trail. As a journalist/illustrator for *Harper's Weekly*, *Scribner's* and *Outing*, he went to Russia, Europe and Africa. He was at Wounded Knee and followed Roosevelt's Rough Riders to Cuba, always in search of men "with the bark on"—and their horses—capturing both in sculpture, image, and word.

David Romtvedt moved to Wyoming in 1984, met and fell in love with Margo Brown and started working on her family's ranch Four Mile. A sprawling chunk of dry ground between the Bighorn Mountains and Powder River, Four Mile is where he began to know something about horses. He learned to ride and work with horses. David has written two books that are directly inspired by his ranch work, a collection of poems called *How Many Horses* and a prose book called *Windmill: Essays From Four Mile Ranch*. He admits to love hanging around horses while remaining a little wary of them.

The youngest U.S. president ever, **Theodore Roosevelt** (1856–1919) was more comfortable than any other on horseback. Conservationist, respected naturalist, and historian, he was also known for his hunting expeditions and support of the flooding of Hetch-Hetchy Valley in California. After the death of his first wife, "Teedie" set off for the Frontier and became a deputy sheriff in the Dakota Territory and badlands rancher. *Ranch Life and the Hunting Trail* contains the autobiographic writings of this period. Before age 42, Roosevelt took turns as Colonel of the Rough Riders, Assistant Secretary of the Navy, and Police Commissioner of New York City.

Ross Santee (1889–1965) was originally from Iowa. During the 1920s he worked as a cartoonist for various New York magazines. Like so many before and since, he fell under the spell of wide-open spaces, relocating to southern Arizona. He became an illustrator and writer for *Arizona Highways* and retired in Tucson, where he dedicated his time to landscape painting. His literary reminiscences of range life were published as *Cowboy* and *Men and Horses*.

Another eastern transplant who re-invented himself out West, **James Willard Schultz** (1859–1947) left New York for the Montana Territory in 1876. Initially a trader at Fort Conrad, he soon became fluent in the Blackfoot language, married a Native woman, was inducted into the Piegan tribe, and given the name "Apikuni." "Far-off White Robe" even accompanied his hosts on raids and spoke sign language. He guided naturalist George Bird Grinnell through Glacier National Park, where the Piegan later buried Schultz. His experiences of over a decade among the Blackfoot found expression in several books, most notably in *My Life as an Indian*.

The advocate of a non-agrarian lifestyle and promoter of Native American values **Ernest Thompson Seton** (1860–1946) hailed from an industrial town in England.

One of eleven children, he showed an early interest in nature. His family immigrated to Ontario in 1866, to homestead. He became a renowned wildlife illustrator and naturalist and well known for his animal stories. Seton went on to study art in Paris in the 1890s. From there he moved to a ranch in New Mexico and eventually to retirement in a castle he built near Santa Fe. The father of the Woodcraft Indian Youth Movement influenced Baden Powell and befriended Theodore Roosevelt.

Mark Spragg grew up on the oldest dude ranch in Wyoming, without TV or radio. The recollections of his youth, *Where Rivers Change Directions* won the Mountains and Plains Booksellers Award. This book and his novel *Fruit of Stone* have been translated into seven languages. He is also the editor of a pictorial/essay collection about mustangs. His saga of family strife and redemption *An Unfinished Life* is being made into a movie directed by Lasse Halström, and Spragg wrote the screenplay, together with his wife Virginia. They both live in Cody, Wyoming.

Deanne Stillman's contribution is an excerpt from her new book *Horse Latitudes: Last Stand for the Wild Horse in the American West.* The *L.A. Times* called her critically acclaimed bestseller *Twentynine Palms* "one of the best books of 2001," and it is under option to Lions Gate Films. Deanne also contributes to *Rolling Stone*, the *Los Angeles Times*, *Slate*, and other periodicals. She learned to ride in Ohio, where her mother was one of the first women in the country to race professionally. For the past twenty years, she has been exploring trails of the desert West, on foot and atop horses.

The seventy-seven-year-old western painter and sculptor **J. N. "Jack" Swanson** is best known for his portrayal of California vaqueros and high desert buckaroos. He worked in the Tehachapis in the early '40s, and after WWII broke and sold wild horses in Oregon, working among top hands of the northwestern cow country. He and his wife Sally reside on the ranch in the Carmel Valley they built forty-four years ago, still raising and training fine stock horses. Jack's work is represented in the Cowboy Hall of Fame, and he is a regular contributor to *Western Horseman*.

N. Howard "Jack" Thorp (1867–1940) was a tenderfoot to begin with. When his father's New York fortune crashed, he learned about cattle at his brother's ranch in Nebraska. The 6-foot-2 mandolin-picking cowboy and composer of ballads gradually drifted west, finding work with outfits in New Mexico. One day in 1889 he mounted his horse and set out on a 1,500 hundred-mile trip through the Southwest, to collect the legends and songs of the cattle culture. His *Songs of the Cowboys* (1908) is the first published collection of cowboy songs, and in *Pardner of the Wind* he recalls being wounded in a shootout with horse thieves.

Better known as **Mark Twain**, Samuel L. Clemens (1835–1910) led a colorful life, including stints as a printer, a steamboat pilot, gold prospector, journalist in Nevada and San Francisco during the Gold Rush, and a lecturer with a flair for humor, storytelling and stage performances. His memoir *Roughing It*, a boisterous adventure tale, sprang from Twain's roaming the country between 1861 and 1866. After crossing the Plains from Missouri to Nevada Territory, he continued on to Utah, California, and Hawaii. With over thirty works of satire, historical fiction, short stories, and nonfiction, Twain is considered one of the greats of world literature.

A lover of horses since she was a city girl, poet **Laurie Wagner Buyer** came into her own true-life fantasy when she moved West at age twenty to live and work on ranches in the Rocky Mountain region. Horses are the inspiring subjects of many of her poems in *Glass-eyed Paint in the Rain* and *Red Colt Canyon*. When she is not backpacking in the high country or on the road performing, speaking, and presenting workshops, Laurie lives in Woodland Park, Colorado, where she also devotes time to mentoring other writers and to her editing business.

Permissions

Grateful acknowledgment is made to the following for permission to reprint or adapt from previously published or unpublished material. In the case of adaptation, the author may have retitled excerpts. All other selections reprinted herein are in the public domain.

Edward Abbey: *The Moon-Eyed Horse*, excerpt from *Desert Solitaire*. Copyright 1968 by Edward Abbey, renewed 1996 by Clarke Abbey. Reprinted by permission of Don Congdon Associates, Inc.

Laura Bell: *Feral Heart*, excerpt from *Thunder of the Mustangs* (Mark Spragg, ed.). Copyright 1997 by Laura Bell. Published by Tehabi Books. Reprinted by permission of the author.

Virginia Bennett: *My Heroes Have Always Been Horses*. Copyright 2004 by Virginia Bennett. Previously unpublished. Printed by permission of the author.

Buck Brannaman: *Dancing from a Distance*, excerpt from *The Faraway Horses*. Copyright 2001 by Buck Brannaman. Published by The Lyons Press. Reprinted by permission of the publisher.

Ann Daum: *Mares*, excerpt from *The Prairie in Her Eyes*. Copyright 2001 by Ann Daum. Published by Milkweed Editions, Minneapolis. Reprinted by permission of the publisher.

Carolyn Dufurrena: *A Colt with Some Heart*, adapted from *Fifty Miles from Home*. Copyright 2005 by Carolyn Dufurrena. Published by the University of Nevada Press. Reprinted by permission of the author.

Gretel Ehrlich: *The Bluebird of Happiness*, excerpt from *Horse People* (Michael Rosen, ed.). Copyright 1998 by Gretel Ehrlich. Published by Artisan. Reprinted with permission of the author.

Max Evans: *A Horse to Brag About*. Copyright 1972 by Max Evans. Published in *Horse Tales Annual*. Reprinted by permission of the author.